What readers are saying about *Rails for Java Developers*

Every Java developer should be exposed to ideas from different languages, and Ruby/Rails is a wellspring of good ideas. Read this book—it will help you learn Ruby and Rails, and give you new ideas transferable to Java.

► **David Bock**
  Technical Director, Federal and Commercial Division, FGM Inc.

Stuart and Justin have pulled off what I once thought was an impossible feat: consolidating all the knowledge that a Java developer needs to understand Ruby on Rails. Until this book, you would have to read at least three books (and thousands of pages) to get the same understanding encapsulated in this excellent text. They clearly understand both sides of the equation (RoR and Java), which allows them to cut through irrelevancies and hone in on the important topics. This book should be required reading for more than just the people learning Rails: every Java developer will benefit from learning the important lessons that Rails teaches.

► **Neal Ford**
  Application Architect/Developer, Thoughtworks

If you are a Java developer and you want to explore Ruby on Rails, this is *the* book to get. Justin and Stu do a masterful job of revealing the intricacies of Ruby and Ruby on Rails from a Java developer's perspective. Not only that, this book is extremely well written, and is a pleasure to read.

► **David Geary**
  Author of *Graphic Java Swing* and co-author of *Core JavaServer Faces*

Stu and Justin offer the Java developer the unique opportunity to "get" Rails by presenting the Rails stack from a perspective that's familiar and comfortable. In doing so, they prove that Rails and Java don't have to be mutually exclusive.

▶ **Ted Neward**
Author of *Effective Enterprise Java*

If you are a Java developer trying to learn Rails, this book is the place to start. There is no better resource for quickly coming up to speed with Rails, Ruby, Rake, and ActiveRecord.

▶ **Mark Richards**
Senior IT Architect, IBM

To hear some tell it, there's tension and rivalry between the Java and Rails web development camps, but that's hard to see from where I stand. Most of the happy Rails developers I know have a long history as Java programmers, and while we love Java for what it does well, web development in Java leaves a lot to be desired. Rails is a delightful breath of fresh air, and I'm confident this book will open the eyes of a lot of other Java developers who are looking for a nicer way to build web applications.

▶ **Glenn Vanderburg**
Independent Ruby and Java consultant

Rails for Java Developers

Rails for Java Developers

Stuart Halloway

Justin Gehtland

The Pragmatic Bookshelf
Raleigh, North Carolina   Dallas, Texas

Our Pragmatic courses, workshops, and other products can help you and your team create better software and have more fun. For more information, as well as the latest Pragmatic titles, please visit us at

> http://www.pragmaticprogrammer.com

Printed in the United States of America.

ISBN-10: 0-9776166-9-X

ISBN-13: 978-0-9776166-9-5

Printed on acid-free paper with 85% recycled, 30% post-consumer content.

First printing, February, 2007

Version: 2007-1-15

Contents

Foreword

The first time I met Stuart, several years ago at this point, he was giving a presentation about the internals of the Java classloader. At the time, I had recently completed my work at Sun with the Java Servlet specification and Tomcat. In that work, I'd become very familiar with the subject of class loading and learned that it is full of subtle interactions. These interactions are quite complex and sometimes lead to surprising results. Even most Java experts don't have a deep grasp of some of the issues that are at the heart of the classloader. In fact, up until the point I was watching Stu present, I hadn't heard anyone outside of the core Java team get all of the interactions right. Stu, however, nailed it and filled his presentation with realistic examples that communicated the depths of the subject in a clear and easy-to-grasp manner.

After that presentation, I went up and congratulated Stu on nailing his subject. And ever since then, I've made sure to go to any presentation that he gives. Every one has been insightful and entertaining at the same time. Justin, who I met much later, is the same way. He brings passion and knowledge to the subjects he touches, and then brings his explanations to life in a way that is sometimes spontaneous and always humorous.

One hundred years ago, Justin and Stuart would have been the guys tinkering with the latest internal combustion engines, trying to eke more performance out of them while making them simpler. They'd have figured out the best way to flow air into and out of the engine, and probably have invented fuel injection in the process. At the same time, they'd be featured in *Popular Mechanics* with articles titled "Optimizing the Fuel-Air Mixture to Increase Your Horsepower." In today's world, they spend their time delving into the hot-rod technology of today: software. They dive in, rip it apart, see what makes it tick, and then show you how it works with a sparkle in their eye.

Five years ago, these two were shoulder-deep in Java, figuring out how it ticked and then making sure that they knew how it all worked so that they could explain their findings to others, as well as build solutions on top of it. They've brought that same approach to Rails. They've gone deep into the code to figure out what makes Rails tick. When asked a tough question, they know just where to look in the codebase to find the answer and then present a prototypical solution.

I have to say that every time I watch Justin and Stuart talk about either Rails and Java, it always makes me laugh—sometimes with a cringe—as they've been on the same path from Java to Rails as I have been. Everything that I've experienced along my journey from Java to Ruby and Rails, they've run into as well.

I can't think of anyone better to be your guide to bridge the gap between Java and Rails. Even better, they've got the ability to help you make the jump yourself, and they'll do so in a way that really lives up to the name of Chapter 3: *Ruby Eye for the Java Guy*. It's a silly title for a chapter, but it embodies just the way in which they work. They'll give you the essence of what you need to be a competent Rails programmer without changing who you are. In other words, you're in good hands.

James Duncan Davidson
December 2006
Creator of Apache Ant and Apache Tomcat

Preface

Ruby on Rails is a full-stack framework for developing web applications. Rails embraces many good ideas that are familiar in the Java world: the Model-View-Controller (MVC) pattern, unit testing, agile development, the ActiveRecord pattern, and many others. At the same time, Rails challenges many standard practices: Instead of miles of XML configuration files, Rails relies on conventions where possible. Rails is built with Ruby, a dynamic language, and is deployed as source code.

But forget the technical points for a moment. The reason that any of this matters is that Rails programmers are *getting things done*, and fast. Rails programmers have made (and substantiated) some amazing claims about developer productivity. They are having a lot of fun, too.

Should Java programmers be alarmed by this upstart? Absolutely not. Java programmers are uniquely positioned to take advantage of Ruby on Rails. This book will explain how to get started.

Who Should Read This Book?

This book is for all Java programmers. OK, let us narrow that down a little. This book is for two subsets of Java programmers:

- Those who want to program in Ruby and Rails
- Those who do not

To the first group: We wrote this book because we love Java, and we love Rails. We believe that Java programmers are uniquely qualified to take advantage of Rails, because Java programmers have lived through a lot of the struggles behind the good (and sometimes controversial) ideas in Rails.

To the second group: Rails is not for everything, just like any other tool isn't. However, Rails is such an interesting tool, and Ruby is different from Java in so many fascinating ways, that we think it is the single best complement you can learn to round out your skill set.

To both groups: We have had a great time writing this book, because we share a common language with you, our readers. By assuming a common vocabulary of the Java language and patterns, we are able to move quickly to the meat of topics. We believe that, page for page, this is a much better book for Java developers than a general-purpose book can ever be. Yes, that's bragging, and we are boasting about you, our fellow Java developers. Thanks for all the work you have put in to build a baseline of industry knowledge on which we hope to build.

Why *This* Rails Book?

A lot of Rails books exist. One aspect that sets this book apart is our Java background. We focus on the parts of Rails that will be different, new, and interesting to a Java developer.

The second aspect that sets this book apart is our emphasis on Rails as an ecosystem, not just as a framework. As a Java developer, you are accustomed to having an enormous ecosystem around your programming language. You have great IDEs, monitoring tools, and widgets for every situation. Rails has an ecosystem too—not as big as Java's but important nevertheless. In this book, we spend less time hashing through every random API detail in Rails. Instead, we demonstrate the key points and then move into the ecosystem to show how those key points are used, extended, and sometimes even replaced.

Who Should Read Some Other Book?

This book is a reference for experienced Java programmers who want to learn Ruby and Rails. This is not a tutorial where each chapter walks you through building some sample application. For a tutorial, plus a general introduction to the Ruby language, we recommend *Programming Ruby* [TFH05]. For a tutorial and introduction to Rails, we recommend *Agile Web Development with Rails* [TH06].

This book is not a comparison of Java and Ruby for managers considering a Ruby project. For that, we recommend *From Java to Ruby: Things Every Manager Should Know* [Tat06].

This book is not an introduction for nonprogrammers; for that we recommend *Learn to Program* [Pin06].

Why Ruby on Rails?

Rails is making programmers productive and happy. Plus, we are finding that using Ruby exercises our minds more than any other mainstream language. If you want to start a watercooler conversation about the merits of Ruby and Rails, here are a few talking points:

- *Full-stack web framework.* Rails includes everything you need: Model-View-Controller, O/RM, unit testing, and build and deployment automation. Because everything is tightly integrated, it is ridiculously easy to get started.
- *Opinionated software.* Rails is not designed to let you do anything. It is designed to help you do *the right things.*
- *Convention over configuration.* The danger of both the previous points is that you might not be able to customize the framework to meet your needs. Rails avoids this with convention over configuration. All of Rails' moving parts are held together by convention, but you can override those conventions whenever you need to do so. You get to pay as you go, relying on conventions where necessary and overriding only exactly what you need.
- *One language for application and configuration.* Rails uses Ruby for configuration as well as for application code. Ruby is easier to manage than XML and much more powerful when configuration becomes complex.
- *The secret sauce is Ruby.* Ruby is powerful and elegant, and it has become the language we think in most of the time. Ruby includes good ideas from mainstream programming languages. As a Java programmer, you will have a head start in understanding Ruby's approach to classes, objects, inheritance, and polymorphism. Ruby also includes many features of Smalltalk and Lisp that are missing from mainstream languages. As a Java programmer, you will be delighted to discover how blocks, closures, duck typing, metaprogramming, and functional programming can make your code more expressive and maintainable. Rails is the gateway drug; Ruby is the addiction.

How to Read This Book

All readers should read the entirety of Chapter 1, *Getting Started with Rails*, on page 1. The chapter includes instructions for quickly setting up your environment so you can follow along with all the example code.

Next you have a choice: Ruby first or Rails first? If you are a bottom-up learner who cannot pass by a line of code without understanding it completely, start with the Ruby chapters (Chapter 2, *Programming Ruby*, on page 19 and Chapter 3, *Ruby Eye for the Java Guy*, on page 53). Ruby is radically different from Java, even more than the syntax suggests. Your investment will pay for itself quickly.

If you are the "getting things done" type, jump straight into Rails, which begins with Chapter 4, *Accessing Data with ActiveRecord*, on page 77 and continues through the rest of the book. When you see Ruby idioms that interest you, you can always return to the chapters about the Ruby language. (If you don't know the Ruby name for something, just use Appendix A, on page 289. The dictionary is organized by Java terminology and includes pointers to relevant sections in the book.)

Other than that, feel free to skip around. The book is extensively cross-referenced throughout, so you cannot get too lost.

Make sure you follow the instructions in the next section for downloading the sample code. Ruby and Rails enable an interactive development experience, and you will learn much more if you follow along with the examples.

How to Get Sample Code

The sample code for the book uses Rails version 1.1.6 or newer[1] and Ruby version 1.8.4 or newer. All the sample code for the book is available as a single zip file online.[2]

The sample code includes two Rails applications, named People and Rails XT. The People application is extremely simple and demonstrates how to use Rails to create a front end for a single database table. We build the entire People application from scratch as we go through the book. Section 1.2, *Rails App in Fifteen Minutes*, on page 2 has instructions to set up the People application.

Rails XT stands for "Rails Exploration Testing." The Rails XT application doesn't have a unified feature set that addresses some problem domain. Instead, Rails XT is a holding tank for dozens of fragments that

---

1. A few examples rely on features in Rails 1.2, which is still under development as of this writing. These examples are noted in the text as they occur.
2. See http://pragmaticprogrammer.com/titles/fr_rails4java/code.html

demonstrate Rails' capabilities. Because of its heterogeneous nature, Rails XT requires a bit more setup. You don't need to set up Rails XT to get started. When you need to do so, you can find instructions in the sidebar on page 79. Here is a quick overview of the sample directory structure:

rails_xt
> This contains the Rails exploration tests (see Section 1.6, *Running the Unit Tests*, on page 13) and the Quips sample application. Throughout the book, Ruby examples should be executed from this directory unless otherwise noted.

java_xt
> You will use the Java exploration tests throughout the book.

appfuse_people
> You will use the Java People application throughout the book.

junit4
> You will find any tests that require JUnit4 here.

Rake
> This includes Rake and Ant examples from Chapter 8, *Automating the Development Process*, on page 217.

hibernate_examples
> This includes Hibernate examples from Chapter 4, *Accessing Data with ActiveRecord*, on page 77.

The Java examples are split into several directories to simplify classpath management. That way, you can install just the libraries you need. For example, you don't need to install Struts, Hibernate, and so on, to run the language examples in java_xt.

How We Developed the Java Examples

This is a book about two worlds: the world of Java programming and the world of Rails programming. Whenever worlds collide, you can expect to hear statements like "Java sucks, and Rails rocks..." (or the reverse).

You won't hear that tone here. To us, that is like a carpenter saying "Hammers suck, and saws rock." Carpenters use many tools, and programmers should too. More important, the confrontational approach limits an important opportunity. When you have multiple ways to solve a problem, you can learn a lot by comparing them.

Our goal in visiting this new world (Rails) is to learn by comparison with our shared history (Java). But what exactly is our shared history? Ruby on Rails is a web framework, which means you could compare it to about a gazillion things in the Java world. Should we look at Java? Plain servlets? Servlets plus JSP? Aged MVC frameworks such as Struts? Rich component frameworks such as Tapestry? Java EE standard architectures such as JSF? Or all of these?

(We asked a lot of people.)

When we needed a Java baseline to compare with Rails, we chose Struts, Hibernate, and Axis. We picked these because our careful statistical research indicated these were best-known among Java developers. Moreover, we limit our Java usage to techniques that are typical in applications we have seen in the field. As a result, the Java code in this book should look familiar to most Java web developers.

The downside of this approach is that "typical" and "familiar" Java code is not necessarily best practice. So although this approach is useful for teaching Rails, it does not provide a comprehensive review of Java best practices. (That's a whole 'nother book.) Where we have skipped interesting Java approaches for reasons of space, we have included margin notes and references at the ends of the chapters.

Many of the Java examples are built starting with Matt Raible's excellent AppFuse (http://www.appfuse.org). AppFuse is a metaframework that allows you to quickly jump-start a web application using the frameworks of your choice. If you want to compare Rails to Java frameworks not covered in this book, AppFuse is a great place to start.

Acknowledgments

We would like to thank our wives. Joey and Lisa, none of this would have happened, or would have meant as much, without you. We would also like to thank our extended families. Without your love and support, this book would have been stalled until at least 2025.

Thanks to our reviewers: David Bock, Ed Burns, Scott Davis, Mark Richards, Ian Roughley, Brian Sletten, Venkat Subramaniam, Bruce Tate, and Glenn Vanderburg. We would never have believed that such a talented, busy group of people could devote so much time and attention to this project. Thank you; this book is immeasurably better for it.

To the Pragmatic Programmers: Thank you for building the kind of publishing company that can produce a book like this, on this timeline. You are consummate professionals.

To the Relevance Gang: We are in for an exciting ride. Thanks for your smarts, thanks for your excellent work, but thanks most for the fun environment.

To the Pragmatic Studio: Thanks for leading the way in getting Ruby and Rails people together, all over the country. We can't wait for the first Rails Edge.

To the No Fluff, Just Stuff Gang: Thanks for sharing our secret lives. Our ideas about Java (and Ruby) are sharpened every weekend at our semiclandestine encounters.

To Jay Zimmerman: Thanks for building a community around excellent people and around excellence in software development.

To James Duncan Davidson: Thanks for spreading the Mac meme.

To Neal Ford: Thanks for the cross-the-board expertise, from agility and DSLs all the way to food and fashion. Who says we have to specialize?

To Bruce Tate: Thanks for helping kick-start our Rails consulting business and for being a companion in our professional journey. You were country when country wasn't cool.

To Dave Thomas: You make everything around you better, and you have fun doing it. Thanks for your inestimable contributions to Ruby, to Rails, and to our work.

To Jim Weirich: Thanks for the just-in-time technical support on Flex-Mock questions.

To Al von Ruff: Thanks for your work on the Internet Speculative Fiction Database.[3] We have enjoyed it as readers, and we particularly appreciate you making the schema and data available for some of the examples in this book.

To Matt Raible: Thanks for AppFuse. Without it we'd still be in a bottomless pit of XML configuration files.

To the folks at Coke, Pepsi, Red Bull, Macallan, and Lagavulin: Thank you for the beverages that fueled this book. Bet you can't guess which drinks go with which chapters!

Yes, we drink both Coke and Pepsi. And we like both Java and Ruby.

---

3. http://www.isfdb.org

## Chapter 1

Getting Started with Rails

In this chapter, we show how to install Rails and quickly build a small web application. Rails is famous for being simple and easy, so pay attention to what you *don't* have to do in this chapter. There is no XML configuration to write (and very little configuration of any kind). For simple database applications, you don't have to write much code, either.

At the same time, "easy" does not mean "not serious" or "compromising on quality." Take note of the quality orientation that every Rails project has from the start. You will see that even the simplest Rails application begins life with automated testing, documentation, and other product automation already in place. When your Rails application starts to get complicated, you will already have the tools you need.

1.1 Setting Up Ruby and Rails

Setting up Ruby and Rails is straightforward on all the major operating systems. If you like building your software tools from scratch, you can certainly do that with Ruby and Rails. But you do not have to do so. Rails enthusiasts have created prepackaged solutions that install everything you need to get started.

On Windows

On Windows, Instant Rails[1] provides a self-contained Rails environment. Instant Rails includes Ruby, Rails, Apache, and MySQL, all in a sandbox separate from anything else installed on your machine. Instant

---

1. http://instantrails.rubyforge.org

Rails is a perfect, no-risk environment for trying out the code in this book. Thanks to Curt Hibbs and everyone else involved in making Instant Rails.

On the Mac

On the Mac, Locomotive[2] is a self-contained Rails environment. Like Instant Rails on Windows, Locomotive includes everything you need to run the code in this book and keep it isolated from everything else on your box. Thanks very much to Ryan Raaum for this tool.

Rails depends on Ruby, and the current version of Mac OS X includes a slightly dated version of Ruby, version 1.8.2. Sooner or later most developers install a more recent version. When you decide to upgrade your Ruby install, MacPorts[3] provides an easy way to build more recent versions of Ruby.

The next version of Mac OS X, 10.5 (Leopard), will have Rails already installed. W00t!

On Linux

If you are running Linux, you know how to suck bits off the Web. Start with the Rails Wiki,[4] and find instructions for your flavor of Linux.

All the examples in the book will assume MySQL as a database. Both Locomotive and Instant Rails install an isolated MySQL instance for you. If you are on Linux, the instructions listed at the Rails Wiki show how to set up the database.

1.2 Rails App in Fifteen Minutes

With Rails you can build an simple web application nearly instantly, using the scaffold code generator. This section will walk you through creating a functioning web app in about fifteen minutes. You'll create a simple, form-based application for creating, reading, updating, and deleting people. We won't explain the steps in detail here—that's what the rest of this book is for—but you can find pointers at the end of this section to the chapters that discuss each aspect of the following code example in more detail.

---

2. http://locomotive.raaum.org
3. http://www.macports.org/
4. http://wiki.rubyonrails.com/rails/pages/GettingStartedWithRails

Start in some temporary directory and create a Rails application named people:

```
$ cd ~/temp
$ rails people
    create
    create  app/controllers
    create  app/helpers
    (...dozens more create lines...)
    create  log/development.log
    create  log/test.log
```

Change to the people directory. All the Rails support scripts assume you are at the top-level directory of your Rails project, so you should stay in the people directory for all subsequent steps:

```
$ cd people
```

Create two databases, named people_development and people_test.[5]

```
$ mysql -u root
Welcome to the MySQL monitor.  Commands end with ; or \g.
Your MySQL connection id is 1 to server version: 4.1.12-standard

Type 'help;' or '\h' for help. Type '\c' to clear the buffer.

mysql> create database people_development;
Query OK, 1 row affected (0.30 sec)
mysql> create database people_test;
Query OK, 1 row affected (0.30 sec)
mysql> exit
Bye
```

Create an ActiveRecord model object. (Note that on Windows you will need to explicitly name the Ruby interpreter, such as ruby script/generate instead of simply script/generate.)

```
$ script/generate model Person
     exists  app/models/
     exists  test/unit/
     exists  test/fixtures/
     create  app/models/person.rb
     create  test/unit/person_test.rb
     create  test/fixtures/people.yml
     create  db/migrate
     create  db/migrate/001_create_people.rb
```

---

5. Warning: The following instructions assume MySQL, with no password on the root account. You could translate these instructions to some other database/account/password combo, but please don't! Setting up a database can be harder than starting with Rails, so this will be easier if you follow the script exactly.

Notice how the model file is named person but the fixture file (which may contain more than one person) is named people. Rails works hard to sound like the way people talk and automatically uses the singular or plural form of words where appropriate.

Edit the db/migrate/001_create_people.rb file so the setup section looks like this:

```ruby
def self.up
  create_table :people do |t|
    t.column :first_name, :string
    t.column :last_name, :string
  end
end
```

Back at the console, update the database by running the rake db:migrate task. Rake is an automation tool similar to Java's Ant:

```
$ rake db:migrate
(in /Users/stuart/temp/people)
== CreatePeople: migrating ============================
-- create_table(:people)
   -> 0.1449s
== CreatePeople: migrated (0.1462s) ==================
```

Generate a scaffold:

```
$ script/generate scaffold Person
      exists  app/controllers/
      (...lots of output snipped...)
      create  public/stylesheets/scaffold.css
```

Run your application:

```
$ script/server
=> Booting lighttpd (use 'script/server webrick' to force WEBrick)
=> Rails application started on http://0.0.0.0:3000
=> Call with -d to detach
=> Ctrl-C to shutdown server (see config/lighttpd.conf for options)
```

Now browse to http://localhost:3000/people. You should see a simple, form-based application for creating, reading, updating, and deleting people, as in Figure 1.1, on the facing page.

Try it for a few minutes, and make sure everything is working. The scaffold isn't pretty, but it provides a lot of functionality for little work. If you review the steps you just went through, there were only two lines of code, and those were to create the model object. If you already had a database schema, those two lines would go away, and you would have a web application up and running with zero lines of handwritten code.

Listing people

First name Last name

Stuart	Halloway	Show Edit Destroy
Justin	Gehtland	Show Edit Destroy

New person

Figure 1.1: THE RAILS SCAFFOLD

Now, let's run the automated tests for your application:

```
$ rake
(in /Users/stuart/temp/people)
/bin/ruby -Ilib:test [snip] "test/unit/person_test.rb"
Loaded suite [snip]
Started
.
Finished in 0.093734 seconds.

1 tests, 1 assertions, 0 failures, 0 errors
/bin/ruby -Ilib:test [snip] "test/functional/people_controller_test.rb"
Loaded suite [snip]
Started
........
Finished in 0.337262 seconds.

8 tests, 28 assertions, 0 failures, 0 errors
```

That is interesting, since we didn't write any tests yet. When you ran script/generate scaffold, Rails generated some tests for you. Earlier, when you first ran rails people, Rails created a build script (rakefile) that would automatically run the tests under rake. Rails helps you test your project by putting testing in place on day one.

We do not want to oversell the scaffold, because it is only a small part of Rails. But the icing on the cake is the part you taste first. The rest of this book is about the cake itself: the elegant Model-View-Controller design, the tasteful use of convention over configuration, and a series of design choices and approaches that make Rails incredibly productive.

> ### Joe Asks...
> #### Is Rails Yet Another Code Generator?
>
> If you have seen any brief demonstrations of Rails, you have probably seen somebody generate the Rails scaffolding before. Because scaffolding makes good demoware, it would be easy to assume that Rails is primarily about generating code. Nothing could be further from the truth. Although scaffolding can help you get the skeleton of your app up and running quickly, it will most likely be gone by the time your application is complete. In fact, many experienced Rails developers do not use the scaffolding at all.

If any of the steps we just zipped through particularly intrigued you, here is a guide to where they are covered in more detail:

rails people
> Section 1.1, *Setting Up Ruby and Rails*, on page 1

create database people_development
> Section 1.7, *Rails Environments*, on page 13

script/generate model Person
> Chapter 4, *Accessing Data with ActiveRecord*, on page 77

editing db/migrate/001_create_people.rb
> Section 4.2, *Managing Schema Versions with Migrations* on page 81

rake db:migrate
> Section 4.2, *Managing Schema Versions with Migrations* on page 81

script/server
> Section 1.9, *Rails Support Scripts*, on page 17

rake Chapter 8, *Automating the Development Process*, on page 217

1.3 The Rails Development Cycle

In Rails, the development cycle is carefully designed to minimize interruption. You change your code and refresh your browser to see the changes. That's all. There is no compile, deploy, or server bounce necessary. This simple cycle has two huge impacts on productivity. First, work goes faster. Since you do not have to wait to see the results of a change, you do more changing and less waiting. Second, and more subtly, *you learn more as you go*. In Rails it is easy to just "try things" and do little experiments as you go. In environments with a more complicated development cycle, these little experiments simply do not happen.

To see this in action, let's make a few improvements to the People application. If you do not still have the application running, start it again with script/server. We will leave the application running continuously as we make a series of changes.

Our People application does no data validation. If you create a person with an empty first name and last name, it will happily store a bogus record in the database. Validation is critical to web applications, and Rails makes validation simple. To add validation, open the file app/models/person.rb. Edit the file to look like this:

code/people/app/models/person.rb

```
class Person < ActiveRecord::Base
  validates_presence_of :first_name, :last_name
end
```

The validates_presence_of part requires that both the first name and the last name be present; that is, they should not be nil. Now, take your browser to http://localhost:3000/people/new, and try to create a man with no name. When you click Create, you will see an error message like the one in Figure 1.2, on the following page.

When you add validations to a model, their effects automatically propagate to the view, with no additional work necessary. Validations are covered in detail in Section 4.5, *Validating Data Values*, on page 94.

Next, let us make a change to the people list view. If you browse to http://localhost:3000/people/list, you should see a list of people. We could make the list more useful by adding a search box. Open the file app/views/people/list.rhtml, and insert the following code right after <h1>Listing people</h1>:

code/people/app/views/people/list.rhtml

```
<%= start_form_tag('', :method=>'get') %>
  People named:
  <%= text_field_tag 'search', @search %>
  <%= submit_tag 'Find'%>
<%= end_form_tag %>
```

New person

2 errors prohibited this person from being saved

There were problems with the following fields:

- First name can't be blank
- Last name can't be blank

First name

Last name

Create

Figure 1.2: FORM VALIDATION

The code inside the <%= %> is embedded Ruby, which we will cover in Chapter 6, *Rendering Output with ActionView*, on page 149. For now, if you refresh your browser to http://localhost:3000/people/list, you should see a search form like the one shown in Figure 1.3, on the next page. Of course, the search form doesn't change the behavior of the application. No matter what you search for, the list will show all people (or the first ten, anyway). To change the behavior of the application, you will need to modify an action method in the controller. Open the file app/controllers/people_controller.rb, and find the list method:

```
def list
  @person_pages, @people = paginate :people, :per_page => 10
end
```

If the user specifies no search term, the method should continue to work as is. If there is a search term, we'll be nice and compare against both first and last names. Replace list with this expanded version:

code/people/app/controllers/people_controller.rb

```
def list
  @search = params[:search]
  if @search.blank?
    @person_pages, @people = paginate :people, :per_page => 10
  else
    query = ['first_name = :search or last_name = :search',
            {:search=>@search}]
    @person_pages, @people = paginate :people,
                              :per_page => 10, :conditions=>query
  end
end
```

Listing people

People named: [   ] Find

First name Last name

John   Doe   <u>Show</u> <u>Edit</u> <u>Destroy</u>

Jane   Doe   <u>Show</u> <u>Edit</u> <u>Destroy</u>

<u>New person</u>

Figure 1.3: SEARCH FORM

Now, refresh your view of http://localhost:3000/people/list, and add a few people if you haven't already. Then try some search terms. The list should automatically contract to show only the matching names. Controllers are covered in detail in Chapter 5, *Coordinating Activities with ActionController*, on page 115.

As is so often the case with Rails, the important aspect is what *isn't* here. We didn't have to do anything to test our changes, other than refresh the browser. Our changes themselves were minimal and to the point. We didn't have to tell Rails how to convert URLs into controller methods, how to connect models to views, or how to find the right view for a controller action. Almost everything in Rails has a default, and you need configuration only when you want to override the defaults.

1.4   Finding Information in Online Documentation

All Rails developers should bookmark these documentation sites:

http://api.rubyonrails.org
> Up-to-date documentation for the entire Rails API.

http://www.ruby-doc.org/
> Ruby documentation metasite. Pointers to library docs, books, training, and more.

http://www.ruby-doc.org/core
> Ruby Core documentation (roughly analogous to java.lang, java.io, and java.util).

http://www.ruby-doc.org/stdlib/
> Ruby Standard Library documentation. It is roughly analogous to everything in the JDK not in the packages listed previously.

Ruby API documentation is usually presented in RDoc format. RDoc is similar to Javadoc; both tools build documentation by reading the source code and embedded comments.

Rails includes Rake tasks to build documentation files on your local machine. From any Rails project, you can build the documentation by running rake doc:app. This will create a top-level documentation file at doc/app/index.html within your project. We cover Rake in detail in Chapter 8, *Automating the Development Process*, on page 217.

1.5 Editors and IDEs

In 1997, Java IDEs were primitive compared to their C++ counterparts.

GUI tools (such as IDEs) for Ruby and Rails are primitive compared to their Java counterparts. But they are better than Notepad. Here are a few pointers:

TextMate (Mac only)
> If you are willing to spend money, get TextMate.[6] It has most of the power and customizability of Emacs, plus the GUI savvy of a native Mac application.

Radrails (cross-platform, open source)
> Radrails (http://www.radrails.org/) is built on top of Eclipse,[7] so it runs almost everywhere. It is a perfect choice if Eclipse is already your IDE of choice for Java.

IntelliJ IDEA (cross-platform)
> IntelliJ IDEA[8] is expected to have Rails support via an IDEA 6.0 plugin. We haven't used it yet, but we have high hopes. IDEA is our preferred IDE for Java development.

Old school...
> There is a good Rails plugin for vim.[9] There is also a Rails minor mode for Emacs.[10]

---

6. http://macromates.com/
7. http://www.eclipse.org
8. http://www.jetbrains.com/idea/
9. http://www.vim.org/scripts/script.php?script_id=1567
10. http://rubyforge.org/projects/emacs-rails/

1.6   Running the Samples

Instructions for downloading the sample code are on page xvi. The sample code in this book appears in three forms:

- Very small examples that can be run directly in *irb*, the Ruby interactive shell   *irb*
- Stand-alone Ruby programs that can be run using the *ruby* command   *ruby*
- Rails applications and support scripts that can be launched using the various *script/** commands, which are automatically included in every Rails project   *script/**

Detailed instructions for running each type of sample appear in the following sections. We strongly encourage you read this book with a working environment close at hand. One of Ruby's greatest strengths is the ease of trying it yourself.

Running irb Samples

irb is the interactive Ruby shell. Given a working Ruby installation (see Section 1.1, *Setting Up Ruby and Rails*, on page 1), you can start the interactive shell by typing irb. You will be greeted with a prompt where you can enter Ruby code. This prompt is configurable, but the default on your system will probably look like this:

```
$ irb
irb(main):001:0>
```

From the irb prompt, you can enter Ruby code, such as puts("hello"):

```
code/rails_xt/sample_output/hello.irb
```

```
irb(main):001:0> puts("hello")
hello
=> nil
```

The previous shell is displaying the following:

- Ruby code as you type it (line 1)
- Console interaction (line 2)
- The return value from the last statement (line 3)

Unless otherwise noted, the irb examples in the book are all self-contained and show all the Ruby code you need to type. For the sake of brevity, we frequently omit console output and return values where they are irrelevant to the point being made.

It is possible to type longer blocks, such as this three-line if...end block:

```
irb(main):002:0> if true
irb(main):003:1>   puts "tautology"
irb(main):004:1> end
tautology
=> nil
```

If you make as many typing mistakes as we do, you can also paste multiple lines of code into irb. When code starts to be long enough that it is unwieldy to enter into irb, you will want to switch to full Ruby programs.

Running Ruby Samples

All the Ruby samples for the book are from the rails_xt/samples directory, unless otherwise noted in the text. So, if you see the following command:

```
$ ruby foo.rb
```

you can execute the same command within the rails_xt/samples directory after you unzip the sample code.

Running Rails Samples

The samples include a Rails application in the rails_xt directory. All Rails commands should be run from this directory, unless otherwise noted. When you see a command that begins with script, such as script/console or script/server, run that command from the rails_xt directory.

The script/console command is particularly important. It gives you an interactive Ruby shell with Rails and your application's environment already loaded. Try running script/console from the rails_xt directory in the sample code.

```
$ script/console
Loading development environment.
>> puts "Hello"
Hello
```

This is just like irb, except you can also now call Rails API methods. For example, you could ask what database Rails is using:

```
>> ActiveRecord::Base.connection.current_database
=> "rails4java_development"
```

The default prompt in script/console is >>. When you see this prompt in the book, you should be able to run the same code using script/console in the rails_xt directory.

Running the Unit Tests

We wrote much of the code in this book as *exploration tests*. Exploration *exploration tests*
tests are unit tests written for the purpose of learning, teaching, and
exploring. Sample code should be tested for the same reason people
unit test anything else: It is easy for us (and you!) to quickly verify that
the code works correctly.

You don't need to run the unit tests to follow along in the book (except
in the testing chapter!), and we typically do not clutter the prose by
including them. For example, here is the code from Section 4.8, *Preventing the N+1 Problem*, on page 111, demonstrating a solution to the
N+1 problem in Hibernate:

```
code/hibernate_examples/src/TransactionTest.java
Criteria c = sess.createCriteria(Person.class)
              .setFetchMode("quips", FetchMode.JOIN);
Set people = new HashSet(c.list());
```

That's the code you will see in the book, which demonstrates the point
being made. Notice that the listing begins with the filename. If you go
to that file in the sample code, you will find the code is followed immediately by assertions that prove the code works as intended:

```
assertEquals(2, people.size());
sess.close();
for (Iterator iterator = people.iterator(); iterator.hasNext();) {
  Person p = (Person) iterator.next();
  assertEquals(25, p.getQuips().size());
}
```

For more about exploration testing, also known as *learning tests*, see *learning tests*
"How I Learned Ruby"[11] and "Test Driven Learning."[12]

1.7   Rails Environments

Web applications run in three distinct environments:

- In a development environment, there is a developer present. Code
  and even data schemas tend to change rapidly and interactively.
  Data is often crufted up by the developer, such as John Smith at
  Foo Street.

---

11. http://www.clarkware.com/cgi/blosxom/2005/03/18#RLT1
12. http://weblogs.java.net/blog/davidrupp/archive/2005/03/test_driven_lea.html

- In a test environment, automated tests run against prepackaged sample data. A developer may or may not be present. Data schemas are regularly trashed and rebuilt to guarantee a consistent starting state for the tests.

- In a production environment, code and schemas change much more rarely. The database data is real and valuable, and developers are rarely present.

In Java web frameworks, environments have historically been ad hoc: Each team evolves its own, using a collection of scripts and Ant tasks to manage environments and move code and data between them.

In Rails, environments are a first-class concept. Each application starts life with the three environments in place. Rails environments are used to select databases, log file destinations, policies for loading code, and more. Here are some of Rails' environmental defaults:

Development:

- The log file is log/development.log.
- The database is {appname}_development.
- The breakpoint server is enabled.
- Web pages show error stack traces.
- Classes reload for each page.

Test:

- The log file is log/test.log.
- The database is {appname}_test.
- The breakpoint server is disabled.
- Web pages show generic error messages.
- Classes load once at start-up.

Production:

- The log file is log/production.log.
- The database is {appname}_production.
- The breakpoint server is disabled.
- Web pages show generic error messages.
- Classes load once at start-up.

You can change environmental defaults by editing the appropriate environment file. Environment files are named for the environment they control, such as config/environments/development.rb for the development environment. (You can even create new environments simply by adding files to the config/environments directory.) There is a top-level environment file named config/environment.rb that contains settings common to all environments.

It is worth reading through the environment files to get a sense of the automation that Rails provides. Here is a snippet:

code/people/config/environments/development.rb

```
# Log error messages when you accidentally call methods on nil.
config.whiny_nils = true

# Enable the breakpoint server that script/breakpointer connects to
config.breakpoint_server = true

# Show full error reports and disable caching
config.action_controller.consider_all_requests_local = true
config.action_controller.perform_caching              = false
```

The most noticeable aspect is that the configuration is just Ruby. In a Java web application, code is one language (Java), and configuration is in another (XML). In Rails applications, Ruby is often used for both code and configuration.[13]

Let's try modifying the Rails environment. Although Rails' knowledge of English grammar is pretty good, you might decide it is not good enough. To experiment with Rails, you can run script/console from any Rails project, such as the People application at code/people in the sample code.

```
$ script/console
Loading development environment.
>> "emphasis".pluralize
=> "emphases"
>> "focus".pluralize
=> "focus"
```

The Rails environment includes a pluralization rule smart enough for emphasis but not for focus. We can add our own pluralization rules to the environment. We'll edit config/environment.rb (that way our rule will be available in all environments):

code/people/config/environment.rb

```
Inflector.inflections do |inflect|
  inflect.irregular 'focus', 'foci'
end
```

---

13. Other parts of Rails configuration use YAML (YAML Ain't Markup Language), which is intended to be easier to read than XML. We cover YAML in Section 9.3, *YAML and XML Compared*, on page 245.

Now you should be able to pluralize() your focus:

```
$ script/console
Loading development environment.
>> "focus".pluralize
=> "foci"
```

Rails support scripts and Rake tasks automatically select the environment most likely to be right. For example, script/console defaults to development, and rake test defaults to test. Many scripts report the environment they are working in so you don't forget:

```
$ script/console
Loading development environment.
```

It is easy to override the environment for a command. Simply prepend RAILS_ENV=envname. For example, you might need to open a console against a production server to troubleshoot a problem there:

```
$ RAILS_ENV=production script/console
Loading production environment.
```

1.8   How Rails Connects to Databases

Rails programs access relational data through the ActiveRecord library (see Chapter 4, *Accessing Data with ActiveRecord*, on page 77). Underneath ActiveRecord, there is a driver layer. You will rarely call down into the driver layer yourself, but you may need to configure the driver for your application.

The database driver configuration is in the file config/database.yml. This file is in YAML format.[14] The top-level names in database.yml are Rails environments—by default, they are the three environments discussed in Section 1.7, *Rails Environments*, on page 13. Each top-level name introduces a collection of indented, name/value pairs to configure the driver for a particular environment.

Rails chooses database names based on your application name plus the environment name. For an application named Whizbang, the initial config/database.yml would look like this:

```
development:
  adapter: mysql
  database: whizbang_development
  # ...more driver settings ...
```

---

14. See Section 9.3, *YAML and XML Compared*, on page 245 for more about YAML.

```
test:
  adapter: mysql
  database: whizbang_test
  # ...more driver settings ...
production:
  adapter: mysql
  database: whizbang_production
  # ...more driver settings ...
```

You can override the database names as you see fit by editing the configuration file. One common override is to strip the _production part from the production database name.

Don't put anything too important in the test database, since Rails blows this database away as part of running unit and functional tests.

In this book, we are connecting to MySQL as the root user with no password, because that is the exact setting that a new Rails application generates by default.

1.9 Rails Support Scripts

Every new Rails application includes a script directory, with a set of supporting Ruby scripts. script is similar to the bin directory in many Java projects. These scripts are run from the top directory of a Rails project, like this:

```
stuthulhu:~/myproj stuart$ script/server
```

Do not navigate into the script directory and run scripts from there. Relative paths in Rails are always considered from the top project directory, available within Rails as RAILS_ROOT.

You have already seen several scripts in this chapter: script/console, script/server, and script/generate. All the scripts are summarized here:

script/about
> Describes the Rails environment: Rails library versions, RAILS_ROOT, and RAILS_ENV

script/breakpointer
> Is an interactive Ruby shell that will take control of a Rails application when a breakpoint statement is encountered

script/console
> Is an interactive Ruby shell with access to your Rails app

script/destroy
> Destroys code created by script/generate (be careful!)

script/generate

> *generator*

Creates starter code from a template called a *generator*

script/performance/benchmarker

Runs a line of Ruby code *n* times and reports execution time

script/performance/profiler

Runs a line of Ruby code *n* times and reports relative time spent in various methods

script/plugin

Installs and manages plugins (third-party extensions)

script/runner

Runs a line of code in your application's environment

script/server

Launches the web server and Rails application

You now know the basic structure of a Rails application, plus some of the tools you can use to manage the development process. You will not use all this information at once, though. Instead, use this chapter as a road map as you move through the book.

In the next chapter, we will take you on an extended tour of Ruby. Take the time now to learn a bit of Ruby, and the rest of the book will be a snap.

Chapter 2

Programming Ruby

Ruby syntax looks pretty foreign to a Java programmer. The mission of this chapter is to explain Ruby syntax and the underlying concepts this syntax supports. You will be happy to find that many of the underlying concepts are shared with Java: Ruby's strings, objects, classes, identity, exceptions, and access specifiers are easily mapped to their corresponding numbers in the Java world.

2.1 Primitive Types

Java divides the world into primitive types and objects. The primitive types represent numeric values of various ranges and precision (sometimes interpreted in non-numeric ways, for example as text characters or **true/false**). Objects represent anything they want to and are composed of behaviors (methods) and state (other objects and/or primitives). This section introduces the primitive types and their Ruby counterparts.

Consider the Java primitive type **int**:

code/java_xt/src/TestPrimitives.java

```
public void testIntOverflow() {
  int TWO_BILLION = 2000000000;
  assertEquals(2, 1+1);
  //Zoinks -- Not four billion!
  assertEquals(-294967296 , TWO_BILLION + TWO_BILLION);
}
```

Three factors are immediately evident in this simple example:

- Java variables are statically typed. On line 2, the keyword **int** indicates that TWO_BILLION must be an int. The compiler will enforce this.
- Java takes advantage of a syntax we all know: infix math. To evaluate one plus one, you can say the obvious 1+1 (line 3), rather than something annoying such as 1.plus(1).
- On line 5, two billion plus two billion does not equal four billion. This is because Java's primitives are confined to a specific number of bits in memory, and four billion would need too many bits.

To represent arbitrarily large integers, Java uses the BigInteger class:

`code/java_xt/src/TestPrimitives.java`

```java
public void testBigInteger() {
  BigInteger twobil = new BigInteger("2000000000");
  BigInteger doubled = twobil.multiply(new BigInteger("2"));
  assertEquals(new BigInteger("4000000000"), doubled);
}
```

In this example, BigInteger differs from **int** in three ways:

- You cannot create a BigInteger instance with literal syntax. Instead of BigInteger b = 10;, you say BigInteger b = new BigInteger("10") (line 2).
- You cannot use infix mathematical notation. On line 3, you have to say a.multiply(b) instead of a*b.
- On line 4, two billion multiply two *does* equal four billion.

Ruby also knows how to manipulate integers. Like Java, Ruby needs to do the following:

- Enforce type safety
- Provide a convenient syntax
- Deal smoothly with the human notion of integers (which is infinite) inside a computer (which is finite)

Ruby takes a radically different approach to achieving these goals:

```
irb(main):010:0> 1+1
=> 2
irb(main):001:0> TWO_BILLION = 2*10**9
=> 2000000000
irb(main):002:0> TWO_BILLION + TWO_BILLION
=> 4000000000
```

- Everything in Ruby is an object, and types are usually not declared in source code. So instead of int TWO_BILLION=..., you simply say

TWO_BILLION=.... There is no compiler to make sure TWO_BILLION is really an integer.

- Ruby allows infix math syntax (2+2) for integers and any other types that want it.
- Two billion plus two billion *does* equal four billion, as expected.

Behind the scenes, Ruby deals with integers of unusual size by managing two different types: Fixnum for small integers that have a convenient representation and Bignum for larger numbers. It is possible to find out which type is actually being used:

```
irb(main):016:0> 1.class
=> Fixnum
irb(main):017:0> TWO_BILLION.class
=> Bignum
```

Most of the time you will not care, because Ruby transparently uses the appropriate type as needed:

```
irb(main):004:0> x = 10**9
=> 1000000000
irb(main):005:0> x.class
=> Fixnum
irb(main):006:0> x *= 100
=> 100000000000
irb(main):007:0> x.class
=> Bignum
```

Notice that x smoothly shifts from Fixnum to Bignum as necessary.

We could repeat the previous comparison for the other Java primitives, but this would be a waste of space, because the underlying story would be mostly the same as for **int**. Here are a few other factors to remember when dealing with numeric types in Ruby:

- Numeric types are always objects in Ruby, even when they have a literal representation. The equivalents for methods such as Java's Float.isInfinite are instance methods on the numerics. For example:

```
irb(main):018:0> 1.0.finite?
=> true
irb(main):019:0> (1.0/0.0).finite?
=> false
```

Note that the question mark at the end of finite? is part of the method name. The trailing question mark has no special meaning to Ruby, but by convention it is used for methods that return a boolean.

- Like Java, Ruby will coerce numeric types in various reasonable ways:

```
irb(main):024:0> (1 + 1).class
=> Fixnum
irb(main):025:0> (1 + 1.0).class
=> Float
```

If you try something unreasonable, you will know soon enough because Ruby will throw an exception:

```
irb(main):027:0> (1.0/0)
=> Infinity
irb(main):028:0> (1/0)
ZeroDivisionError: divided by 0
```

For information about character types, see Section 2.2, *Strings*, below. For booleans, see Section 2.5, *Control Flow*, on page 32.

2.2 Strings

In Java, strings are commonly represented as double-quoted literals. The implementation of Java String is a class, with methods, fields, and constructors.

However, because string concatenation is so fundamental to many programming tasks, String also has some special abilities. The most important of these is concatenation with the + sign:

code/java_xt/src/DemoStrings.java

```
String name = "Reader";
print("Hello, " + name);
```

The Ruby syntax is similar:

```
irb(main):001:0> name = "Reader"
=> "Reader"
irb(main):002:0> "Hello, " + name
=> "Hello, Reader"
```

Java Strings also have a format method, which uses sprintf-like format specifiers:

```
print(String.format("Hello, %s", name.toUpperCase()));
```

string interpolation

Ruby offers a different approach for formatting, using a literal syntax called *string interpolation*. Inside a double-quoted string, text between #{ and } is *evaluated* as Ruby code.

This is similar to ${} property expansion in Java's Ant. You could write the preceding example with string interpolation:

```
code/rails_xt/sample_output/interpolation.irb
irb(main):005:0> "Hello, #{name.upcase}"
=> "Hello, READER"
```

In Java, you can use backslash escapes to represent characters:

```
print(String.format("Hello, \"%s\"\nWelcome to Java", name));
```

Ruby also uses backslash escapes:

```
irb(main):008:0> puts "Hello, \"#{name}\"\nWelcome to Ruby"
Hello, "Reader"
Welcome to Ruby
```

In both the previous Ruby and Java examples, we escaped the double-quote character inside the string (\") to avoid terminating the string. This kind of escaping can be confusing to read if you escape a lot of characters:

```
irb(main):009:0> puts "\"One\", \"two\", and \"three\" are all strings."
"One", "two", and "three" are all strings.
```

In Ruby, you can get rid of all these backslash escapes. You simply pick an alternate string delimiter such as {} by prefixing a string with %Q:

```
code/rails_xt/sample_output/quoting.irb
irb(main):011:0> puts %Q{"One", "Two", and "Three" are strings"}
"One", "Two", and "Three" are strings"
```

In Java, individual characters are represented by single quotes. You can pull individual characters from a string via the charAt method:

```
code/java_xt/src/TestStrings.java
  public void testCharAt() {
    assertEquals('H', "Hello".charAt(0));
    assertEquals('o', "Hello".charAt(4));
  }
}
```

Ruby handles individual characters differently. Character literals are prefixed with a question mark:

```
irb(main):015:0> ?A
=> 65
irb(main):016:0> ?B
=> 66
```

Ruby also handles extraction differently. For example, you could call a method named slice, but Ruby programmers would typically prefer to use the [] syntax instead:

```
irb(main):019:0> ?H == "Hello".slice(0)
=> true
irb(main):020:0> ?H == "Hello"[0]
=> true
```

The really cool part of using slice/[] is that it performs reasonable tasks with all kinds of arguments. You can count from the back of a string with negative offsets:

```
irb(main):022:0> ?o == "Hello"[-1]
=> true
```

You can take substrings by passing two arguments:

```
irb(main):025:0> "Hello"[1,4]
=> "ello"
```

Asking for a character past the end of a string returns nil:

```
irb(main):026:0> "Hello"[1000]
=> nil
```

But, attempting to set a character past the end of a string throws an exception:

```
irb(main):009:0> "Hello"[1000] = ?Z
IndexError: index 1000 out of string
```

Although interpolation is useful, you will not want it in all cases. To turn off string interpolation, use a single-quoted string instead of a double-quoted one:

```
irb(main):028:0> "Hello, #{name.upcase}"
=> "Hello, READER"
irb(main):029:0> 'Hello, #{name.upcase}'
=> "Hello, \#{name.upcase}"
```

In Java, you can create multiline strings by embedding \n characters:

```
print("one\ntwo\nthree");
```

The embedded backslashes are legal Ruby too, but there is an easier way. Ruby provides an explicit syntax for multiline strings called a here document, or *heredoc*.

heredoc

A multiline string begins with <<, followed by a string of your choice. That same string appears again at the beginning of a line to terminate the heredoc:

```
code/rails_xt/sample_output/heredoc.irb
```
```
irb(main):035:0> puts <<MY_DELIMITER
irb(main):036:0" one
irb(main):037:0" two
irb(main):038:0" three
irb(main):039:0" MY_DELIMITER
one
two
three
```

Regular expressions provide a powerful syntax for finding and modifying ranges of characters within Strings. For example, here is a Java method that uses a regular expression to bleep out any four-letter words that appear in a String:

```
code/java_xt/src/Bowdlerize.java
```
```java
  public static String bleep(String input) {
    return input.replaceAll("\\b\\w{4}\\b", "(bleep)");
  }
}
```

Ruby uses a literal syntax for regular expressions, delimiting them with //. As a result, a Ruby programmer might bleep like this:

```
code/rails_xt/sample_output/regexp.irb
```
```
irb(main):041:0> 'Are four letter words mean?'.gsub(/\b\w{4}\b/, "(bleep)")
=> "Are (bleep) letter words (bleep)?"
```

The gsub method replaces all matches of its first argument with its second argument.

Notice that the regular expression itself looks slightly different in the Ruby and Java versions. Where you see a single backslash in the Ruby version, the Java version has a double backslash. The Java regular expression is built from a Java string, and the paired backslashes translate to single backslashes after the string is parsed. The Ruby regular expression does not pass through a temporary "string phase," so the single backslashes are represented directly.

2.3 Objects and Methods

In this section, we will show how to use objects by calling their methods. In Section 2.6, *Defining Classes*, on page 38, we will show how to define your own classes of objects.

You have already seen some examples of objects and methods in Section 2.2, *Strings*, on page 22. Strings are just a kind (class) of object: A method is code that is defined by an object to manipulate the object, return a result value, or both. To invoke a method on a string, or any other object, append a dot (.), the name of the method, and parentheses, as in (). For example, to get the lowercased version of a string in Java, you use the following:

code/java_xt/src/DemoMethods.java
```
print("HELLO".toLowerCase());
```

Ruby is similar, except the parentheses are optional:

```
irb(main):047:0> "HELLO".downcase()
=> "hello"
irb(main):048:0> "HELLO".downcase
=> "hello"
```

Methods often have arguments: one or more pieces of additional information that the object uses. For example, Java has a Math object, with a cos method that takes a single argument, the angle in radians:

code/java_xt/src/DemoMethods.java
```
print(Math.cos(0));
```

In this case, the Ruby version can match exactly, since Ruby also provides a Math object.

```
irb(main):051:0> Math.cos(0)
=> 1.0
```

In Ruby, you can omit the parentheses around arguments, if the syntax is otherwise unambiguous:

```
irb(main):051:0> Math.cos 0
=> 1.0
```

type-safe

In Java, objects are *type-safe*. Objects know what they are capable of, and you cannot ask them to perform methods they do not have. The following code will fail in Java, since strings do not have a cos method:

code/java_xt/src/DemoMethods.java
```
print("hello".cos(0));
```

Ruby objects are also type-safe:

```
irb(main):057:0> "hello".cos 0
NoMethodError: undefined method 'cos' for "hello":String
        from (irb):57
```

Type Safety Does Not Ensure Correctness

Type safety is a very weak assurance that your program actually works as intended. Type safety says that your pieces fit together, not that you have chosen all the right pieces. Imagine your car's lubrication system filled with orange juice. It is "type-safe" in that the lubrication system contains the right "type" (a liquid), but we wouldn't recommend driving it.

Returning to our math example, what if you thought Math.cos expected degrees instead of radians?

```
irb(main):067:0> Math.cos 180
=> -0.598460069057858
```

There is nothing in the previous Ruby code, or its Java equivalent, to tell that your result is radically different from what you intended:

```
irb(main):069:0> Math.cos Math::PI
=> -1.0
```

In September 1999, a "little problem" similar to this one destroyed the Mars Climate Orbiter. A miscalculation based on English instead of metric units caused the orbiter to pass too close to Mars, where it was destroyed by the atmosphere.

One approach to these type-safety issues is to add even more type safety. Instead of using primitive types, you could create value types with embedded units in an enumeration. Without first-class language support, this makes code more cumbersome. A more likely approach in Ruby is to have good automated tests.

Although both Ruby and Java are type-safe, they achieve type safety in different ways. Ruby uses dynamic typing. Objects carry type information with them, and that information is used at runtime to determine the set of legal methods for the object. Java also provides static typing: Variables have types that are enforced *at compile time* by the Java compiler. Both approaches have their merits, and the difference will crop up several times throughout this book.

We believe that type safety can never be perfect. No matter how rigorously you enforce typing, type errors can still occur. See the sidebar on the current page for a few examples.

2.4 Collections and Iteration

Computer science is filled with all manner of esoteric collections (data structures). Being general-purpose languages, Java and Ruby can handle any of these, but daily use often boils down to three concerns:

- Ordered collections such as arrays accessed by numeric index
- Fast mappings from keys to values, also known as *dictionaries* or *hashes*
- Iteration, the generic traversal of any collection or stream of data

The following sections cover these most common usages of collections and iteration.

Arrays

Java deals with collections in two ways: arrays and collection classes. Arrays are a language construct, and they hold a fixed-size collection of some primitive type or object.

The collection classes work with objects, and they implement a wide variety of different data structures. Here's a simple example that loops over the array of program arguments, printing them to the console:

```
code/java_xt/src/PrintArgs.java
```

```java
public class PrintArgs {
  public static void main(String[] args) {
    for (int n=0; n<args.length; n++) {
      System.out.println(args[n]);
    }
  }
}
```

Here is the Ruby equivalent:

```
code/rails_xt/samples/print_args.rb
```

```ruby
ARGV.each {|x| puts x}
```

Running the program produces the following:

```
$ ruby samples/print_args.rb one two three
one
two
three
```

Let's start by talking about what *isn't* in the Ruby version:

- The Ruby version does not have an equivalent to the Java PrintArgs class. Ruby programs begin life with an implicit top-level object, so simple programs do not need to define any classes at all.

- The Ruby version does not have a main method. Ruby executes any code it encounters, so simple programs do not need to define any methods either.
- Ruby's puts is (roughly) equivalent to Java's System.out.println. The call to puts does not need an explicit object; it is invoked on the implicit top-level object.

Now, back to the one line of code. Here is the Ruby equivalent:

```
ARGV.each {|x| puts x}
```

Ruby populates ARGV as an array of command-line arguments. The rest of the line does the following: "Take each element from ARGV, one at a time. Assign it to *x*. Then perform the *block* of code between the curly braces (and after the |x|)." If you want to spread a block over multiple lines, you can use do...end. Here's the argument-printing program, using do...end:

block

code/rails_xt/samples/print_args_long.rb

```
ARGV.each do |x|
  puts x
end
```

Ruby arrays have a literal syntax, so they can easily be created inline:

```
irb(main):009:0> ['C', 'Java', 'Ruby'].each {|lang| puts "#{lang} is fun!"}
C is fun!
Java is fun!
Ruby is fun!
=> ["C", "Java", "Ruby"]
```

If each item in the array is a word, there is an even shorter syntax, the %w shortcut:

```
irb(main):002:0> ['C', 'Java', 'Ruby'] == %w{C Java Ruby}
=> true
```

Ruby arrays respond in a reasonable way to mathematical operators:

code/rails_xt/sample_output/array_literals.irb

```
irb(main):002:0> [1,2] + [3]
=> [1, 2, 3]
irb(main):003:0> [1,2,3] * 2
=> [1, 2, 3, 1, 2, 3]
irb(main):004:0> [1,2,1] - [2]
=> [1, 1]
irb(main):005:0> [1,2] / 2
NoMethodError: undefined method '/' for [1, 2]:Array
        from (irb):5
```

Ruby arrays are resizable and can use push and pop to act like stacks:

```
irb(main):006:0> skills = ['C', 'Java']
=> ["C", "Java"]
irb(main):007:0> skills.push 'Ruby'
=> ["C", "Java", "Ruby"]
irb(main):008:0> skills.pop
=> "Ruby"
```

Java Map and Ruby Hash

Java has several implementations of Maps, which are collections that manage key/value pairs. One such collection is the environment variables. Here, then, is a simple program that enumerates the environment variables:

`code/java_xt/src/PrintEnv.java`

```java
import java.util.*;

public class PrintEnv {
  public static void main(String[] args) {
    Map map = System.getenv();
    for (Iterator it = map.entrySet().iterator(); it.hasNext();) {
      Map.Entry e = (Map.Entry) it.next();
      System.out.println(String.format("%s: %s", e.getKey(), e.getValue()));
    }
  }
}
```

Here is the Ruby equivalent:

`code/rails_xt/sample_output/hashes.irb`

```
irb(main):032:0> ENV.each {|k,v| puts "#{k}: #{v}"}
TERM_PROGRAM: Apple_Terminal
TERM: xterm-color
SHELL: /bin/bash
ANT_HOME: /users/stuart/java/apache-ant-1.6.2
...lots more...
```

Ruby sets ENV to the environment variables. After that, iteration proceeds with each. This time, the block takes two parameters: k (key) and v (value). Blocks are a completely general mechanism and can take any number of arguments. Functions that use blocks for iteration tend pass one or two parameters to the block, as you have seen.

Most Ruby objects that manage key/value pairs are instances of Hash. Like arrays, hashes have a literal syntax:

```
irb(main):037:0> dict = {:do => "a deer", :re => "a drop of golden sun"}
=> {:do=>"a deer", :re=>"a drop of golden sun"}
```

Curly braces introduce a hash. Keys and values are separated by =>, and pairs are delimited by commas. You can get and set the values in a hash with the methods fetch and store:

```
irb(main):013:0> dict.fetch(:do)
=> "a deer"
irb(main):014:0> dict.store(:so, "a needle pulling thread")
=> "a needle pulling thread"
```

But Ruby programmers prefer to use the operators [] and []=:

```
irb(main):015:0> dict[:so]
=> "a needle pulling thread"
irb(main):016:0> dict[:dos] = "a beer"
=> "a beer"
```

The [] and []= operators are easy to remember, because they borrow from mathematical notation. They are also more compact than the named methods fetch and store.

Better Than For, and More Than Each

Java 5.0 introduced a more expressive syntax for iteration. The following example uses Java 5.0's For-Each loop to enumerate first the command-line arguments and then the environment variables:

`code/java_xt/src/ForEach.java`

```java
import java.util.Map;

public class ForEach {
  public static void main(String[] args) {
    for (String arg: args) {
      System.out.println(arg);
    }
    for (Map.Entry entry: System.getenv().entrySet()) {
      System.out.println(
          String.format("%s : %s", entry.getKey(), entry.getValue()));
    }
  }
}
```

This is nice! Notice that Java arrays and collections can now both be handled with a parallel syntax.

Also, Ruby uses each and blocks to do much more than we have shown here. For example, you can perform a transformation on each item in a collection using collect:

```
irb(main):017:0> [1,2,3,4,5].collect {|x| x**2}
=> [1, 4, 9, 16, 25]
```

Or, you can find all the items that match some criterion by passing find_all, a block that is interpreted as a boolean:

```
irb(main):021:0> [1,2,3,4,5].find_all {|x| x%2==0}
=> [2, 4]
```

We want to make two important points from these examples:

- *Languages evolve and improve over time.* Usually improvement comes not from thin air but from ideas that have already been explored elsewhere. Java's For-Each syntax was inspired by other languages that have similar features. The programmers who facilitate this kind of cross-pollination are those who become fluent in multiple programming languages.

- *Languages evolve at many levels.* Runtimes can change, language syntax can change, and libraries can change. In Java, iteration changes like the addition of For-Each are *language* changes. Similar changes in Ruby are *library* changes, since each et. al. are method calls. Library changes are easier to make than language changes. (Many developers write libraries, few developers write languages, and language evolution tends to be retarded by standards bodies, backward compatibility, and so on.) *Merely pointing out that Java and Ruby enable different approaches to change is not a value judgment.* However, it may lead to value judgments in a specific context (which you must provide). What parts of your system need to change? On what timeline, and under whose direction? Conversely, what parts need to stay rock-solid stable and be guaranteed to work in the same fashion across different projects over time?

2.5 Control Flow

Ruby's if and while are similar to Java's but have alternative forms that are shorter in some circumstances. Instead of a for loop, Ruby uses Range#each. Where Java has switch, Ruby provides a more general case. Each is described in the following sections.

if

Java's if statement, with optional else, allows programs to branch based on the truth value of an expression:

`code/java_xt/src/DemoControlFlow.java`

```
if (n > 5) {
  print("big");
} else {
  print("little");
}
```

Ruby also has an if statement. Instead of using curly braces to delimit the optional code, Ruby uses newlines and end:

`code/rails_xt/samples/control_flow.rb`

```
if n>5
  puts "big"
else
  puts "little"
end
```

Everything in Ruby has a return value, so instead of putting the puts inside both branches of the if statement, you can hoist it out:

```
puts(if (n>5)
  "big"
else
  "little"
end)
```

The if inside parentheses looks odd to us, and we wouldn't usually code Ruby this way. A more compact form exists. The ternary operator works just as it does in Java:

```
puts n>5 ? "big" : "little"
```

Java will not automatically coerce values to create booleans for a conditional. To check whether an object exists, you cannot say this:

`code/java_xt/src/DemoControlFlow.java`

```
if (o) {
  print("got o");
}
```

You must explicitly compare the object to null:

```
if (o != null) {
  print("got o");
}
```

Ruby will automatically coerce values to booleans. The following code produces false

`code/rails_xt/samples/control_flow.rb`

```
o = nil
puts o ? true : false
```

Only false/nil is false. *Even zero coerces to true.* The following code produces true.

```
o = 0
puts o ? true : false
```

Often, the body of a control statement is a single expression. Ruby can pack multiple statements on one line separated by semicolons, so you might be tempted to replace this:

```
if lines > 1
  puts "you have more than one line"
end
```

with the following:

```
if lines > 1; puts "you have more than one line"; end
```

statement modifier

Or maybe not—that's a bit ugly. Fortunately, Ruby provides a short form called a *statement modifier*. The following code is equivalent to the two preceding snippets:

```
puts "you have more than one line" if lines > 1
```

Sometimes you want to take action if a condition is *not* true. As a convenience, you can use unless, which is the opposite of if. The following statements are equivalent:

```
puts "you've got lines" if lines != 0
puts "you've got lines" unless lines == 0
```

while

Java's while loop is like if, except it repeats as long as the condition remains true. The following code prints the squares of numbers from one to five:

```
int n=1;
while (n<=5) {
  print(n*n);
  n++;
}
```

Ruby also does while:

```
i=1
while (i<5)
  puts i*i
  i+=1  # no ++ in Ruby
end
```

The opposite of while is until, which repeats as long as a condition stays false:

```
i=1
until (i>5)
  puts i*i
  i+=1
end
```

Like with if, you can use while and unless as statement modifiers. The following program runs an input loop, shouting back everything passed via stdin:

```
line = ""
puts "Shouting back #{line.upcase}" while line=gets
```

Ranges

Is it possible to use the statement modifier form of while to implement our number-squaring example in a single line of code? Yes, but it isn't pretty:

```
irb(main):026:0> i=1; puts(i*i) || i+=1 while i<=5
1
4
9
16
25
```

The ugliness here comes from using the boolean operator || to shoehorn two statements into one to conform to the requirements of the statement modifier form. We would not write code like this, and fortunately you do not have to in Ruby. The preferred one-line implementation is as follows:

```
irb(main):029:0> (1..5).each {|x| puts x*x}
1
4
9
16
25
```

The expression (1..5) is a literal for a Ruby type: the Range. Ranges make it easy to represent repetitive data, such as "the numbers one through five" in this example.

The call to each and the block syntax work exactly as they did for arrays and hashes back in Section 2.4, *Java Map and Ruby Hash*, on page 30. That is, the block is invoked once for each item in the range, with *x* assigned to the value of the item.

Ranges include their first element. The last element is included if you use (1..10) but excluded if you add another dot, as in (1...10):

```
irb(main):014:0> (1..10).max
=> 10
irb(main):015:0> (1...10).max
=> 9
irb(main):016:0>  (1..10).exclude_end?
=> false
irb(main):017:0> (1...10).exclude_end?
=> true
```

Ranges are not just for numbers:

```
("A".."C").each {|x| puts x*5}
AAAAA
BBBBB
CCCCC
```

You can conveniently step through Ranges, skipping some elements:

```
code/rails_xt/sample_output/range_step.irb
```

```
irb(main):003:0> ('A'..'I').step(2) {|x| print x}
ACEGI
```

case

Java provides a **switch** statement that can branch to different actions by testing equality with different values. Although you could implement the same logic using **if**, **switch** results in cleaner code if quite a few branches are possible.

Here is an example that calculates a number grade from a letter grade:

```
code/java_xt/src/DemoSwitch.java
```

```java
public static int numberGrade(char letter) {
  switch(letter) {
    case 'a':
      return 100;
    case 'b':
      return 90;
    case 'c':
      return 80;
    case 'd':
      return 70;
    case 'e':
    case 'f':
      return 0;
  }
  return 0;
}
```

Ruby's answer to **switch** is **case**:

code/rails_xt/samples/case.rb

```ruby
def number_grade(letter)
  case letter
    when 'A': 100
    when 'B': 90
    when 'C': 80
    when 'D': 70
    else 0
  end
end
```

Now let's turn the example around and write a function that returns a letter grade for a number or letter grade. This will demonstrate the power of **case**:

code/rails_xt/samples/case.rb

```ruby
def letter_grade(x)
  case x
    when 90..100: 'A'
    when 80..90:  'B'
    when 70..80:  'C'
    when 60..70:  'D'
    when Integer: 'F'
    when /[A-F]/:  x
    else raise "not a grade: #{x}"
  end
end
```

As this example shows, **case** does not do a standard equality comparison. It does something much more powerful. Ruby defines an operation called *case equality*. Case equality is a special comparison that is done in **case** statements. This allows different types to define their own notion of how to match in a **case** statement. The letter_grade example shows how case equality works for several different classes:

case equality

- Ranges such as 90..100 define case equality to mean "match any number in the range."

- Classes such as Integer define case equality to mean "match any object of this type."

- Regular expressions such as /[A-F]/ define case equality to mean "match this regular expression."

The case completes as soon as it encounters a true when, so you should list more specific matches first:

```
irb(main):018:0> case('John')
irb(main):019:1>   when('John'): 'a name'
irb(main):020:1>   when(String): 'a word'
irb(main):021:1> end
=> "a name"
```

You can also invoke the case equality operator directly; it is written as a triple equals (===):

```
irb(main):002:0> (90..100) === 95
=> true
irb(main):003:0> (90..100) === 95.5
=> true
irb(main):004:0> (90..100) === 0
=> false
irb(main):005:0> Integer === 95
=> true
irb(main):006:0> Integer === 95.5
=> false
```

2.6 Defining Classes

In both Java and Ruby, classes encapsulate behavior and state. Simple classes typically contain the constructs shown in Figure 2.1, on page 40. To demonstrate these constructs, we will build Java and Ruby versions of a Person class. These Persons have simple state: a first name and a last name. They also have simple behavior: They can marry another Person, resulting in both Persons sharing a hyphenated last name. The next sections build Persons one step a time; for complete listings, see Figure 2.2, on page 43, and see Figure 2.3, on page 44.

Declaring Fields

The Java Person begins with a class declaration and some fields:

`code/java_xt/src/Person.java`

```java
public class Person {
  private String firstName;
  private String lastName;
```

Fields are usually marked **private** so they can be accessed only from within the class. This way, you can change the underlying representation later. For example, you could store the entire name in a fullName field, and only other code that might change would be within the class itself.

The Ruby Person begins simply with a class declaration:

code/rails_xt/samples/person.rb

```
class Person
```

That's it. There is no need to declare instance variables (the Ruby equivalent of fields) because they come into existence automatically when they are used.

The other attributes of a declaration (types and protection modifiers) are irrelevant in Ruby. Ruby instance variables do not need a type such as String, because they accept any type. Ruby instance variables are implicitly **private**, so this designation is unneeded as well.

Defining Constructors

The Java definition continues with a constructor that sets the initial values of the fields:

```
public Person(String firstName, String lastName) {
  this.firstName = firstName;
  this.lastName = lastName;
}
```

Constructors have the same name as their class and are often marked public so that all other classes can use them. Notice that the constructor arguments share the same names as the **private** fields: firstName and lastName. To disambiguate, you explicitly prefix the instance variables with this.

The Ruby declaration also continues with a constructor that sets the initial value of instance variables:

The convention of having constructor arguments with the same names as fields is confusing but well established. Most programmers use IDEs to autogenerate constructors, reducing the potential for error.

```
def initialize(first_name, last_name)
  @first_name = first_name
  @last_name = last_name
end
```

In Ruby, the "constructor" is just a method named initialize. Method definitions begin with def and end with end (duh). In Ruby, instance variables must begin with a @, so there is no danger of a name collision with method parameters.[1]

---

1. Ruby has a different name collision problem; it's between local variables and method calls. See Section 2.6, *Defining Accessors*, on the following page.

Java name	Ruby name	Meaning
Fields	Instance variables	State that is owned/managed by an instance of the class
Methods	Methods	Functions that are called "on" an instance of the class and have access to that instance's state
Constructors	Initializers	Special creation functions that are called once per new instance to set and validate the instance's initial state

Figure 2.1: WHAT'S IN A CLASS?

Defining Accessors

accessor methods

The Java definition continues with *accessor methods*. Accessors are methods that allow callers to read and write properties of an object:

```java
public String getFirstName() {
  return firstName;
}
public void setFirstName(String firstName) {
  this.firstName = firstName;
}
public String getLastName() {
  return lastName;
}
public void setLastName(String lastName) {
  this.lastName = lastName;
}

public String getFullName() {
  return String.format("%s %s", firstName, lastName);
}
```

getters

setters

As you can see, methods divide into *getters* (methods that read a property) and *setters* (methods that write a property). Some getters, such as the ones for getFirstName and getLastName, may directly return **private** fields.

Other "computed" accessors, such as getFullName, may do more work to compute a value based on one or more fields. Setters can also be more complicated than those shown here and perform tasks such as validating their arguments.

Ruby also has accessor methods:

```
attr_accessor :first_name, :last_name

def full_name
  "#{first_name} #{last_name}"
end
```

The attr_accessor method makes getter and setter methods for a comma-delimited list of names. This greatly reduces lines of code, since you do not have to type (or use IDE magic to create) boilerplate getters and setters. Ruby also provides attr_reader and attr_writer if you want read-only or write-only properties. Accessors that actually do something must still be coded by hand, as in the case of full_name.

Ruby's naming convention for accessors does not use get and set prefixes. Given the definition of Person, you would access attributes in this way:

code/rails_xt/samples/demo_person.rb

```
p.first_name = 'Justin'
p.last_name = 'Gehtland'
puts "Hello from #{p.first_name}"
```

To a Java eye, this looks like direct access to the fields first_name and last_name, but in Ruby these are method calls. Even the punctuation (=) is part of a method name. To make this clearer, here is a hand-coded version of the accessors:

```
# don't do this--use attr_accessor!
def first_name
  @first_name
end
def first_name=(new_name)
  @first_name = new_name
end
```

Creating Behavioral Methods

We are using the name *behavioral methods* to describe methods that actually make an object do something, other than simply managing properties. Here's the Java implementation of marry:

```
public void marry(Person other) {
  String newLastName =
      String.format("%s-%s", getLastName(), other.getLastName());
  setLastName(newLastName);
  other.setLastName(newLastName);
}
```

Note that some of the accessor method calls are prefixed with an object reference (other.), and other accessor calls are not. Methods not prefixed by an explicit object reference are invoked on this, the object whose method is currently executing.

Here's the Ruby marry:

```
def marry(other)
  other.last_name = self.last_name = "#{self.last_name}-#{other.last_name}"
end
```

Since Ruby methods always return the last expression evaluated, writer (setter) methods return the new value set. This means that multiple setters can be chained together, as in other.last_name = self.last_name = ... Note that the Ruby setter methods being called in marry are prefixed by an object, either other or self. Ruby's self is the equivalent of Java's this. The explicit use of self here is important. In Ruby, last_name="X" is ambiguous. Depending on the context, this might mean "Create a local variable named last_name with value "X"" or "Call the method last_name=, passing the parameter "X." Using self makes it clear that you want the "method" interpretation.

If you forget to prefix a setter with self, you may create hard-to-find bugs. Java does not suffer from this ambiguity, so be careful.

Creating Static Methods

static methods

Sometimes methods apply to a class as a whole, instead of to any particular instance of a class. In Java these are called *static methods*:

```
public static String getSpecies() {
  return "Homo sapiens";
}
```

class methods

In Ruby, these methods are called *class methods*:

```
def self.species
  "Homo sapiens"
end
```

For purposes of this book, we can pretend that Java static methods and Ruby class methods are similar beasts.[2]

---

2. The Ruby story is actually a good bit more complex than this. Unlike Java methods, Ruby class methods are polymorphic. There are at least five alternate syntaxes that you can use to define a Ruby class method. There is a good RubyGarden discussion on class methods at http://www.rubygarden.org:3000/Ruby/page/show/ClassMethods. In addition, Ruby also has class variables, but we think you should avoid them. See http://www.relevancellc.com/archives/2006/11.

code/java_xt/src/Person.java

```java
public class Person {
  private String firstName;
  private String lastName;

  public Person(String firstName, String lastName) {
    this.firstName = firstName;
    this.lastName = lastName;
  }

  public String getFirstName() {
    return firstName;
  }
  public void setFirstName(String firstName) {
    this.firstName = firstName;
  }
  public String getLastName() {
    return lastName;
  }
  public void setLastName(String lastName) {
    this.lastName = lastName;
  }

  public String getFullName() {
    return String.format("%s %s", firstName, lastName);
  }
  public void marry(Person other) {
    String newLastName =
        String.format("%s-%s", getLastName(), other.getLastName());
    setLastName(newLastName);
    other.setLastName(newLastName);
  }

  public static String getSpecies() {
    return "Homo sapiens";
  }
}
```

java_xt/src/Person.java

Figure 2.2: A JAVA PERSON

```
code/rails_xt/samples/person.rb
class Person
  def initialize(first_name, last_name)
    @first_name = first_name
    @last_name = last_name
  end

  attr_accessor :first_name, :last_name

  def full_name
    "#{first_name} #{last_name}"
  end

  def marry(other)
    other.last_name = self.last_name = "#{self.last_name}-#{other.last_name}"
  end

  def self.species
    "Homo sapiens"
  end
end
```

rails_xt/samples/person.rb

Figure 2.3: A RUBY PERSON

2.7 Identity and Equality

Object identity

Java distinguishes object identity and object equality. *Object identity* asks the question "Are two objects at the same location in memory?" Testing object identity is the responsibility of the runtime, which manages memory. *Object equality* asks the question "Do two objects have state that is semantically equivalent?" Testing object equality is the responsibility of the implementer of a class. This short Java example illustrates the difference:

Object equality

```
code/java_xt/src/TestEquals.java
public void testEquals() {
  String s1 = "Java rocks!";
  String s2 = s1;
  String s3 = new String("Java rocks!");
  assertTrue(s1 == s2);
  assertFalse(s1 == s3);
  assertTrue(s1.equals(s3));
}
```

The == operator tests for identity. Strings s1 and s2 are == because they point to the same object. Strings3 is *not==* to the others. It contains the same characters, but it is at a different location in memory.

The equals method tests equality, which Java strings define to mean "containing the same characters." Thus, string s3.equals the others.

Ruby also distinguishes between identity and equality. Each unique object has an object_id. Two objects are identical if they have the same object_id, and the equal? method tests for this:

code/rails_xt/sample_output/identity.irb

```
irb(main):001:0> s1 = s2 = "Ruby rocks!"
=> "Ruby rocks!"
irb(main):002:0> s1.object_id
=> 190400
irb(main):003:0> s2.object_id
=> 190400
irb(main):004:0> s2.equal? s1
=> true
```

To test equality, Ruby provides two equivalent methods: == and .eql?.[3]

Like Java's equals, these methods can be overridden by class implementors to compare semantic equality. Ruby's strings define these methods to return true if two strings have the same characters, regardless of identity:

code/rails_xt/sample_output/equality.irb

```
irb(main):006:0> s3 = "Ruby rocks!"
=> "Ruby rocks!"
irb(main):007:0> s4 = "Ruby rocks!"
=> "Ruby rocks!"
irb(main):008:0> s3==s4
=> true
irb(main):009:0> s3.eql? s4
=> true
irb(main):010:0> s3.equal? s4
=> false
```

Even though the concepts are roughly the same, you need to be careful when switching between Java and Ruby in your mind. Some of the terminology gets reversed: Java's == tests for identity, while Ruby's == usually tests for equality.

---

3. Why two methods? See the sidebar on the next page.

> ### Why Does Ruby Have Two Methods for Object Equality?
>
> Ruby has two different methods for testing object equality: ==
> and eql?. In fact, Ruby often has two (or even more) methods
> that perform the same task. Ruby's approach is often called
> "There's more than one way to do it" (TMTOWDI, pronounced
> "Tim Toady"). This contrasts with Java, which falls more in line
> with Bertrand Meyer's belief that "A programming language
> should provide one good way of performing any operation of
> interest; it should avoid providing two."
>
> Martin Fowler uses the term *humane interface* to describe the
> approach taken in, for example, Ruby, Perl, and Lisp; he uses
> the term *minimal interface* for the approach in, for example,
> Java, Python, and Eiffel. You can find plenty of information to
> support both sides in Martin's Bliki:
>
> http://www.martinfowler.com/bliki/HumaneInterface.html as well as
> http://www.martinfowler.com/bliki/MinimalInterface.html.

2.8 Inheritance

single implementation inheritance

extend

Java provides *single implementation inheritance*. (See Section 3.6, *Polymorphism and Interfaces*, on page 66.) This means a class can *extend* a single other class.

`code/java_xt/src/Programmer.java`

```
public class Programmer extends Person {
```

In Ruby the keyword **extends** is replaced by <:

`code/rails_xt/samples/programmer.rb`

```
class Programmer < Person
```

In the previous two examples, the Programmer class is extending the Person, previously introduced in Figure 2.2, on page 43, as well as Figure 2.3, on page 44. The extending class Programmer is called a *subclass* or *derived class*. The class being extended (Person) is called a *base class* or *superclass*. A derived class can have its own members:

```
private String favoriteLanguage;

public String getFavoriteLanguage() {
  return favoriteLanguage;
}
```

```java
public void setFavoriteLanguage(String favoriteLanguage) {
  this.favoriteLanguage = favoriteLanguage;
}
```

The Ruby version is as follows:

```ruby
attr_accessor :favorite_language
```

Derived classes methods and constructors can call the base class member with the same name, using the super keyword. This is commonly used in constructors:

```java
public Programmer(String firstName, String lastName, String favoriteLanguage) {
  super(firstName, lastName);
  this.favoriteLanguage = favoriteLanguage;
}
```

Here it is in Ruby:

```ruby
def initialize(first_name, last_name, favorite_language)
  super(first_name, last_name)
  @favorite_language = favorite_language
end
```

The power of subclassing comes from that derived classes get to use their own members *plus the members of their base class(es)*:

code/java_xt/src/DemoProgrammer.java

```java
Programmer p = new Programmer("David", "Gosling", "Java");
//do Person things:
System.out.println(p.getFirstName());
System.out.println(p.getLastName());
//do Programmer thing:
System.out.println(p.getFavoriteLanguage());
```

Again, the Ruby version is similar:

code/rails_xt/samples/programmer.rb

```ruby
p = Programmer.new "James", "Hansson", "Ruby"
# do Person things
puts p.first_name
puts p.last_name
# do Programmer thing
puts p.favorite_language
```

Neither Ruby nor Java supports multiple implementation inheritance. For situations where you wish you had multiple inheritance, see Section 3.5, *Delegation*, on page 64 and Section 3.8, *Mixins*, on page 71.

Specifier	Access Level	Commonly Used For
private	Access only by same class	Fields
(Not specified)	Access by any class in the same package	Closely collaborating classes
protected	Access by any class in the same package or any sub-class	Base class methods
public	Everybody	Client interface

Figure 2.4: JAVA ACCESS SPECIFIERS

2.9 Controlling Access with Access Specifiers

Java has four access specifiers, shown in Figure 2.4.

package private

The "Not specified" case is called *package private* but has no corresponding keyword. Access specifiers are applied per method, field, or constructor. For example:

code/java_xt/src/AccessMe.java

```java
import java.util.*;

public class AccessMe {
  private String name;
  private List stuff;
  public AccessMe(String name) {
    this.name = name;
    stuff = new ArrayList();
  }
  public String getName() {
    return name;
  }
  protected List getStuff() {
    return stuff;
  }
  private void clear() {
    name = null;
    stuff = null;
  }
}
```

Ruby does not have any equivalent for package private but supports **public**, **protected**, and **private**:

code/rails_xt/test/examples/access_test.rb

```ruby
class AccessMe
  def initialize(name)
    @name = name
    @stuff = []
  end
  attr_accessor :name

  protected

  attr_accessor :stuff

  private

  def clear
    @name = @stuff = nil
  end
end
```

An access control method call appearing alone on a line defines the access level for subsequent methods. The initial default is public. So, AccessMe's name accessors are **public**, the stuff accessors are **protected**, and so on.

Although access control specifiers set a general rule for how you can use a class, the general rule may need to bend in some circumstances. For example, an object serializer may bypass protection modifiers to access all of an object's state. In Ruby, you can bypass access control specifiers with send:

code/rails_xt/test/examples/access_test.rb

```ruby
a = AccessMe.new("test")
a.send :stuff=, 'some stuff'
puts a.send(:stuff)
```

The first argument to send is the symbol for the method to invoke, and subsequent arguments are passed on to the method. The following two lines do the same thing:

code/rails_xt/test/examples/access_test.rb

```ruby
a.send :stuff=, 'other stuff'
a.stuff = 'better not try this'
```

Well, they would do the same thing, except the second line will fail because stuff= is protected.

Access control methods can also take arguments. When called with arguments, access control methods expect symbol parameters. These symbols look up methods and set their access levels. You can invoke the access control methods more than once for the same symbol. At first glance this may seem silly—why would a class want to have different levels of access control at different times? One possibility is temporarily setting methods **public** so that unit tests can test them:

code/rails_xt/test/examples/access_test.rb

```ruby
def test_clear
  AccessMe.send :public, :clear, :stuff
  a = AccessMe.new("test")
  a.clear
  assert_nil a.stuff
end
```

This sample uses only techniques we have covered thus far. You can use cleaner ways to set methods **public** for the duration of a test. One approach is to use the extend method, described in Section 3.8, *Mixins*, on page 71.

2.10 Raising and Handling Exceptions

checked

Java programs typically use exceptions to indicate errors. Some exceptions are *checked* exceptions. Checked exceptions must be explicitly handled, either by using a **catch** block or by adding the exception to the method signature, which passes the buck to the caller. Here's a method that may fail with a checked exception:

code/java_xt/src/DemoException.java

```java
static void methodThatOpensFile()
    throws FileNotFoundException {
  new FileInputStream("nonexistent.file");
}
```

FileNotFoundException must appear in the **throws** clause, providing an indication to potential callers of a possible failure mode. Callers can also use a **throws** keyword, but eventually some caller must take responsibility for dealing with the problem in a catch block:

```java
try {
  methodThatOpensFile();
} catch (FileNotFoundException fnfe) {
  System.out.println("File not found " + fnfe);
} catch (Exception e) {
  System.out.println("Caught " + e);
}
```

You can provide more than one catch, in which case the first matching catch is invoked.

Ruby's exception handling implements almost all of the same ideas but with different terminology:

code/rails_xt/samples/demo_exception.rb

```
Line 1   begin
   -       File.read 'nonexistent'
   -     rescue SystemCallError => e
   -       puts 'system call failed'
   5     rescue Exception => e
   -       puts 'generic failure of some kind'
   -     else
   -       puts 'nothing failed'
   -     ensure
   10      puts 'this always executes'
   -     end
```

- line 1: begin instead of try

- line 3: rescue instead of catch

- line 9: ensure instead of finally

As in Java, specific exceptions should be listed first, followed by more general exceptions such as Exception (line 5). Ruby also has a rarely used else clause (line 7), which executes if no exception occurred.

The most noticeable difference is there are no checked exceptions in Ruby, and **throws** clauses are thus not used. Ruby exceptions are more like Java's unchecked exceptions, which do not need to be declared. The following Java code throws a java.lang.ArithmeticException but doesn't declare the possibility since ArithmeticException is unchecked:

```
static void methodThatDividesByZero() {
  int z = 0;
  int ten = 10;
  int in = ten/z;
}
```

Java exceptions include an error message and the call stack at the time of the exception:

```
try {
  methodThatDividesByZero();
} catch (Exception e) {
  System.out.println(e.getMessage());
  e.printStackTrace();
}
```

> ### Checked Exceptions: Feature or Flaw?
>
> Checked exceptions are controversial. Advocates for checked exceptions see them as a distinguishing benefit of Java, and detractors believe the opposite. For further reading, check out Java expert Bruce Eckel's perspective.[*]
>
> ---
>
> [*]. http://www.mindview.net/Etc/Discussions/CheckedExceptions

Ruby provides the same:

```
begin
  1/0
rescue Exception => e
  puts "Message " + e.message
  puts "Backtrace " + e.backtrace.join("\n")
end
```

Ruby also has a **throw/catch** syntax that is intended for unwinding the stack in nonerror conditions, as a means of control flow. This feature is rarely used and has no analog in Java, so don't be confused by the terminology. For error handling, stick with **begin...end**, **rescue**, and **ensure**.

As you have seen in this chapter, Ruby and Java have much in common. Once you get past a few syntax differences, you will find that your knowledge of object-oriented programming in Java is directly relevant for programming in Ruby as well. But that is only half the story. Ruby also supports a number of idioms that are different from Java programming. These idioms are borrowed from many places, including Perl, Smalltalk, and Lisp. In the next chapter, you will learn how to use these idioms to do more work with less code, and you will learn how to write Ruby that is expressive and beautiful.

## Chapter 3

Ruby Eye for the Java Guy

After the last chapter, you can speak Ruby, but with the awkward accent of someone learning a second language by rote. In this chapter, you will improve your accent by learning idioms more particular to Ruby.

3.1 Extending Core Classes

Programmers often need to add methods to classes that are part of the language runtime itself. Subclassing is typically not an option here, since the method needs to be available to instances of the base class itself. For example, neither Java nor Ruby have a method that tells if a String is blank, in other words, null, empty, or just whitespace. A blank-testing method is useful, because many applications want to treat all blank inputs in the same way. For both Java and Ruby, the open source community has provided methods that test for blankness. Here is a Java implementation of isBlank() from Apache Commons Lang:

`code/Language/IsBlank.java`

```java
public class StringUtils {
  public static boolean isBlank(String str) {
    int strLen;
    if (str == null || (strLen = str.length()) == 0) {
      return true;
    }
    for (int i = 0; i < strLen; i++) {
      if ((Character.isWhitespace(str.charAt(i)) == false)) {
        return false;
      }
    }
    return true;
  }
}
```

Since methods cannot be added to core classes, Commons Lang uses a standard Java idiom, collecting extensions methods as static methods in another class. The implementation of isBlank() lives inside a StringUtils class.

Callers of isBlank() prefix each call with the helper class name StringUtils:

`code/java_xt/src/TestStringUtils.java`

```java
import junit.framework.TestCase;
import org.apache.commons.lang.StringUtils;

public class TestStringUtils extends TestCase {
  public void testIsBlank() {
    assertTrue(StringUtils.isBlank(" "));
    assertTrue(StringUtils.isBlank(""));
    assertTrue(StringUtils.isBlank(null));
    assertFalse(StringUtils.isBlank("x"));
  }
}
```

open

Ruby classes are *open*—you can modify them at any time. So, the Ruby approach is to add blank? to String, as Rails does:

`code/rails/activesupport/lib/active_support/core_ext/blank.rb`

```ruby
class String
  def blank?
    empty? || strip.empty?
  end
end
```

Here are some calls to blank?:

`code/rails_xt/test/examples/blank_test.rb`

```ruby
require File.dirname(__FILE__) + '/../test_helper'

class BlankTest < Test::Unit::TestCase
  def test_blank
    assert "".blank?
    assert " ".blank?
    assert nil.blank?
    assert !"x".blank?
  end
end
```

What about null?

The Java version of isBlank() uses a helper class, StringUtils, for a second reason. Even if you could hang the method isBlank() on String, in Java you would not want to do so. Calls to isBlank() need to return **false** for

null Strings. In Java, calling any method on null will cause a NullPointerException. By testing the first parameter to a static StringUtils method, you avoid the trap of trying to write a String method that (nonsensically) compares **this** to **null**. Why doesn't the Ruby approach work this way as well?

Ruby nil Is an Object

The Ruby equivalent of Java **null** is **nil**. However, **nil** is an actual object. You can call methods on **nil**, just like any other object. More important to the task at hand, you can *add* methods to **nil**, just like any other object: The following code causes nil.blank? to return **true**.

`code/rails/activesupport/lib/active_support/core_ext/blank.rb`

```
class NilClass #:nodoc:
  def blank?
    true
  end
end
```

Rails provides reasonable definitions of blank? for several other objects too: **true**, **false**, empty arrays or hashes, numeric types, and even the Object class.

3.2 Mutable and Immutable Objects

Most programmers probably think first in terms of *mutable* objects (objects whose state can change). However, *immutable* objects (objects whose state never changes after creation) have many uses. Immutable objects have many desirable properties: *mutable* *immutable*

- Immutable objects are thread-safe. Threads cannot corrupt what they cannot change.

- Immutable objects make it easier to implement encapsulation. If part of an object's state is stored in an immutable object, then accessor methods can return that object to outside callers, without fear that those callers can change the object's state.

- Immutable objects make good hash keys, since their hash codes cannot change.

Java supports immutability with the **final** keyword. A field marked **final** can never be changed. To make an entire object immutable, all of its fields would be marked **final**.

Ruby takes a very different approach. Mutability is a property of an instance, not of an entire class. Any instance can become immutable by calling freeze:

code/rails_xt/sample_output/immutable.irb

```
irb(main):005:0> a = [1,2]
=> [1, 2]
irb(main):006:0> a.push 3
=> [1, 2, 3]
irb(main):007:0> a.freeze
=> [1, 2, 3]
irb(main):008:0> a.push 4
TypeError: can't modify frozen array
        from (irb):8:in 'push'
        from (irb):8
```

Once you decide to make an object immutable, you have several other issues to consider:

- An object needs to be fully initialized before becoming immutable. In Java, this means the object must initialize all fields in every constructor. In Ruby, the implementation is up to you, since the timing of freeze is at your discretion.

- Setter methods are illegal for an immutable object. In Java, this is enforced at compile time, so immutable classes will not have setter methods. In Ruby, the implementation is up to you—but writer methods will throw an exception if called on an immutable object.

Immutable objects also make an important demand on their users: "Modifier" methods cannot change an immutable object and so must return a new object. Callers must remember to capture this return value. The following code does not behave as intended:

code/java_xt/src/DemoImmutable.java

```
String s = "Go go Java String!";
s.toUpperCase();
System.out.println("Shouting: " + s);
```

The call to toUpperCase does not modify s. It cannot—Java strings are immutable. String methods like toUpperCase return a new object, which must be captured, as in this corrected version:

code/java_xt/src/DemoImmutable.java

```
String s = "Go go Java String!";
s = s.toUpperCase();
System.out.println("Shouting: " + s);
```

Ruby strings are not automatically immutable, but the same issue can occur anyway:

```
irb(main):001:0> s = "Go Ruby String!"
=> "Go Ruby String!"
irb(main):002:0> s.upcase
=> "GO RUBY STRING!"
irb(main):003:0> p "Shouting: #{s}"
"Shouting: Go Ruby String!"
```

Ruby methods often provide a hint via the method name. In addition to upcase, there is also upcase!. By convention, method names ending with the bang are mutators, while the same name without the bang leaves the object unchanged, returning a new object. So, one possible option for fixing the preceding code is this:

code/rails_xt/sample_output/bang.irb

```
irb(main):004:0> s = "Go Ruby String!"
=> "Go Ruby String!"
irb(main):005:0> s.upcase!
=> "GO RUBY STRING!"
irb(main):006:0> p "Shouting: #{s}"
"Shouting: GO RUBY STRING!"
```

3.3 Packages and Namespaces

The number of possible class names based on human-language words is large. Nevertheless, name collisions and ambiguity are likely, particularly for common words. If we create a User class, and you do too, how will anyone tell them apart?

Java solves this problem with packages. Package names are lower-case and dot-delimited. They typically begin with your domain name in reverse and can then have other portions meaningful within your organization. Since domain names are supposed to be globally unique, name collisions are unlikely. The package name appears separately, at the top of the class definition:

code/java_xt/src/com/codecite/User.java

```
package com.codecite;

public class User {
  private String name;

  public User(String name) {
    this.name = name;
  }
}
```

This similar-looking class is totally different, because it belongs to a different package, com.relevancellc:

`code/java_xt/src/com/relevancellc/User.java`

```java
package com.relevancellc;

public class User {
  private String name;

  public User(String name) {
    this.name = name;
  }
}
```

When you use one of the two previous classes, you must specify its full name, with the package plus the class name. For example:

`code/java_xt/src/UseBoth.java`

```java
public class UseBoth {
  public static void main(String[] args) {
    com.codecite.User u1 = new com.codecite.User("Stu");
    com.relevancellc.User u2 = new com.relevancellc.User("Justin");
  }
}
```

Most of the time you will not have two names in collision. If this is the case, you can **import** a package. You can write imported packages in their short form (class name only), and Java uses the **import** statement to determine the class to which you are referring:

`code/java_xt/src/UseCodeciteUser.java`

```java
import com.codecite.User;

public class UseCodeciteUser {
  public static void main(String[] args) {
    User u = new User("Stu");
  }
}
```

modules   Ruby programs use *modules* to create namespaces. The two following User classes are in separate modules:

`code/rails_xt/samples/user.rb`

```ruby
module Relevance
  class User
    def initialize(name); @name=name; end
    attr_accessor :name
  end
end
```

Why Doesn't Ruby Specify a Naming Scheme for Modules?

Java programmers are strongly encouraged to begin package names with domain names reversed. So, for example, code in the Apache Commons Lang project begins with org.apache.commons.lang. Ruby has no such guideline, so modules tend to be named for what they do or for branding reasons. For example, the Rails MVC controller code lives in the ActionController module. Ruby programmers worry less about naming collisions for three reasons:

- Name collisions at the class or module level are easy to work around. Ruby's type safety depends on duck typing (Section 3.7, *Duck Typing*, on page 70), which has almost no reliance on class or module names.

- Duck typing does depend on method names, so you might expect name collisions to reappear at this level. However, Ruby makes it easy to rename or undefine methods, so method name collisions cause few problems in practice.

- Ruby has fewer name collisions because Ruby programs use fewer names to begin with. Dynamically typed languages tend to be more terse, both in lines of code and in number of names used, than statically typed languages.

It is also worth noting that neither Java nor Ruby is dogmatic about namespace names. Some popular Java packages did not get the memo about domain names (think junit.framework). We sometimes use Relevance as a top-level namespace in Ruby programs. It isn't exactly our domain name, but it is based on our organization name. Guess it's the Java influence. . . .

```ruby
module Codecite
  class User
    def initialize(name); @name=name; end
    attr_accessor :name
  end
end
```

As with Java, you can specify which module you are referring to with a prefix. In Ruby, the prefix is followed by the scope operator, ::, and then the class name.

> code/rails_xt/samples/user.rb

```
u1 = Relevance::User.new("Justin")
u2 = Codecite::User.new("Stu")
```

Also as with Java, you can use the short form of the name, so you do not have to keep typing module prefixes. Ruby programs will often include a module:

> code/rails_xt/samples/user.rb

```
include Relevance
u3 = User.new("Jared")
puts "u3 is a #{u3.class}"
```

Although we are using include as an analog of Java's **import**, their true natures are radically different. Java's **import** is a compile-time concept and is used to look up the "real" package-qualified name. Compiled Java bytecodes never use the short form of a name. Ruby's include changes the object model at runtime, inserting a module into the inheritance hierarchy of the current object self. You can watch the inheritance hierarchy change by calling the ancestors method before and after a call to include:

> code/rails_xt/samples/user.rb

```
puts "Before: #{self.class.ancestors.join(',')}"
include Codecite
puts "After: #{self.class.ancestors.join(',')}"
```

which prints the following:

⇒
```
Before: Object,Kernel
After: Object,Codecite,Kernel
```

Since include changes the object model, it has uses far beyond just namespacing. See Section 3.8, *Mixins*, on page 71 for more possibilities for include.

3.4 Deploying Code

classpath

In Java, you can manage deployment directly by setting the *classpath*: a local list of directories to search for compiled classes. At a higher level, you can deploy components or applications over the network using the Java Network Launch Protocol (JNLP). Ruby deployment offers rough analogs to these via the Ruby load path and RubyGems.

The Load Path

In Java, source code files are compiled into classes. These classes are usually (but not always) then aggregated into JAR files.

When a Java program runs, an object called a *class loader* automatically loads the classes the program needs from the appropriate .jar or .class files. It finds these files by searching the classpath. Consider the following simple program:

class loader

```
code/java_xt/src/ImplicitLoading.java
```
```
import com.relevancellc.User;

public class ImplicitLoading {
  public static void main(String[] args) {
    User u = new User("John");
  }
}
```

When the ImplicitLoading class prepares to call new User, the User class is not yet loaded. Java's class loader searches the *classpath* for a User. In the simplest case, the classpath is an environment variable, containing a list of JAR files and directories. The following command line sets the classpath:

classpath

```
$ java -cp helpers.jar:classes ImplicitLoading
```

Given this command, Java's class loader will execute the following steps, stopping when the User class is found:

1. Look inside helpers.jar for a file with path name com/relevancellce/User.class.

2. Look inside the classes directory for the same path name, in other words, classes/com/relevancellc/User.class.

As you can see, Java class loading relies on a couple of conventions. First, classes usually live in .class files of the same name. Second, package names are converted into directories and subdirectories; for example, a package named com.relevancellc becomes the directory named com/relevancellc.

In Ruby, code loading is almost totally different. In place of Java's classpath, Ruby has a *load path*, with a terse name a Perl programmer would love: $:.

load path

Here is a typical load path from an irb session, formatted to fit the page:

```
code/rails_xt/sample_output/classpath.irb
```

```
irb(main):001:0> $:
=> ["/opt/local/lib/ruby/site_ruby/1.8",\
    "/opt/local/lib/ruby/site_ruby/1.8/powerpc-darwin8.2.0",\
    "/opt/local/lib/ruby/site_ruby", "/opt/local/lib/ruby/vendor_ruby/1.8",\
    "/opt/local/lib/ruby/vendor_ruby/1.8/powerpc-darwin8.2.0",\
    "/opt/local/lib/ruby/vendor_ruby", "/opt/local/lib/ruby/1.8",\
    "/opt/local/lib/ruby/1.8/powerpc-darwin8.2.0", "."]
```

Unlike Java, Ruby is not class-oriented. A particular source file might contain a single class, but it might just as well contain several classes or none. So it would not make sense to make classes the unit of code loading. Instead, the source files are the units of code loading. To load a source file, you **require** it. The .rb suffix is not necessary:

```
code/rails_xt/samples/explicit_load.rb
```

```
require 'super_widget'
w = new SuperWidget("phlange")
```

The call to require 'super_widget' searches the load path for the file super_widget.rb. In this case, super_widget.rb does contain the code for the class SuperWidget:

```
code/rails_xt/samples/super_widget.rb
```

```
class SuperWidget
  attr_accessor :name
  def initialize(name); @name=name; end
end
```

The naming convention implied by the preceding example is common: class names LikeThis and associated source files like_this.rb. But don't assume this will always hold; it is not required by the Ruby language.

RubyGems

Loading individual files with **require** is fine for small Ruby programs (much as .class files are fine for small Java programs). Large programs will want to work with larger chunks. In Ruby these chunks are called RubyGems. RubyGems provide mechanisms to do the following:

- Group related Ruby files into a gem

- Build documentation files

- Serve gems over the Web

- Manage multiple versions of the same gem over time

Building and serving gems is usually not necessary in a Rails application and is beyond the scope of this book. Our focus will be on acquiring and using gems. To see what gems you have on your system, use the following arguments to the gem command:

```
$ gem list --local
*** LOCAL GEMS ***
(lots of gems omitted to save a dead tree or two...)

pdf-writer (1.1.3)
    A pure Ruby PDF document creation library.

(more gems omitted)
```

One of the gems on our system is pdf-writer. That sounds pretty useful; many web applications may want to offer PDF as one possible download format. Let's load this gem and write a PDF. If you don't already have pdf-writer on your system, no problem—just run the following command. If you are on *nix, you may need to prefix the gem command with sudo.

```
$ gem install pdf-writer
Attempting local installation of 'pdf-writer'
Local gem file not found: pdf-writer*.gem
Attempting remote installation of 'pdf-writer'
Updating Gem source index for: http://gems.rubyforge.org
Successfully installed pdf-writer-1.1.3
Installing RDoc documentation for pdf-writer-1.1.3...
```

Now you can use the gem mechanism to load pdf-writer and create a PDF document:

```
code/rails_xt/samples/write_pdf.rb
```

```ruby
require 'rubygems'
require_gem 'pdf-writer'

pdf = PDF::Writer.new
pdf.select_font "Times-Roman"
pdf.text "Hello, Ruby.", :font_size => 72, :justification => :center
pdf.save_as("hello.pdf")
```

The call to require 'rubygems' loads the gem mechanism, and then the call require_gem 'pdf-writer' loads the pdf-writer gem.[1]

---

1. As of RubyGems 0.9.0.8, require_gem is deprecated in favor of the more accurate name gem. Since most code, including Rails, still uses the require_gem form, that is what we show in the main text.

One of the most tedious aspects of software development is coping with multiple versions of the same library. On Windows this is known as *DLL Hell*, and in Java it is sometimes called *JAR Hell*. RubyGems provides some help with this problem. If you need a particular version of a gem, you can ask for it by name:

> `code/rails_xt/samples/write_pdf_future.rb`

```
require 'rubygems'
require_gem 'pdf-writer', '= 2.0.0'
```

If the particular version your code needs is not available, RubyGems will raise an exception:

```
$ ruby write_pdf_frozen.rb
/lib/ruby/site_ruby/1.8/rubygems.rb:204:in 'report_activate_error':\
RubyGem version error: pdf-writer(1.1.3 not = 2.0.0) (Gem::LoadError)
```

You can even install Rails using gems, so it's easy to guarantee your application gets the specific version of Rails it needs. You can request your Rails applications to use a specific version of their gems or even a specific checkout from the Rails source repository. Binding your application to a specific version of Rails is called *freezing*. Rails includes Rake tasks to freeze and unfreeze your application; see Section 8.4, *Controlling Which Version of Rails You Use*, on page 225 for details.

freezing

3.5 Delegation

Inheritance is not the only mechanism for reuse in Java. Objects often delegate work to other objects. For example, the following Manager delegates all interesting method calls to instances of Programmer or Tester:

> `code/java_xt/src/del/Manager.java`

```java
public class Manager {
  private Programmer programmer;
  private Tester tester;

  public void debug(int hours) {
    programmer.debug(hours);
  }

  public void code(int hours) {
    programmer.code(hours);
  }

  public void writeTestPlan(int hours) {
    tester.writeTestPlan(hours);
  }
```

> ### How Does require_gem Work?
>
> When you call **require_gem**, new modules and classes become available. Behind the scenes, gems accomplish this by modifying the load path and by using **require** to load Ruby source files. A little reflection in irb will catch **require_gem** in the act. Here's the world before a call to require_gem 'pdf-writer':
>
> ```
> irb(main):001:0> require 'rubygems'
> => true
> irb(main):002:0> $:.size
> => 9
> irb(main):003:0> ObjectSpace.each_object(Class) {}
> => 429
> ```
>
> And now, after requiring the gem, here's the code:
>
> ```
> irb(main):004:0> require_gem 'pdf-writer'
> => true
> irb(main):005:0> $:.size
> => 15
> irb(main):006:0> ObjectSpace.each_object(Class) {}
> => 539
> ```
>
> If you compare the size of $: before and after, you will see that loading the pdf-writer gem adds six directories to the load path. Likewise, the calls to ObjectSpace show that loading the gem brought in 110 new classes.
>
> Incidentally, this little example demonstrates how easy it is to explore Ruby interactively. The combination of irb and reflective objects such as ObjectSpace is powerful, and it encourages a "try it and see" approach to learning Ruby.

```java
public void runTests(int hours) {
  tester.runTests(hours);
}
//getters and setters follow...
```

Callers do not have to know that a programmer or tester is behind the scenes. They can simply talk to the manager:

`code/java_xt/src/del/DemoManager.java`

```java
Manager m = getManager();
m.writeTestPlan(5);
m.code(3);
m.runTests(6);
m.debug(2);
```

Ruby objects can also delegate. Here is an equivalent Manager:

`code/rails_xt/samples/delegate.rb`

```ruby
require_gem 'rails'
class Manager
  attr_accessor :programmer, :tester
  delegate :code, :debug, :to=>:programmer
  delegate :write_test_plans, :run_tests, :to=>:tester
end
```

Note that delegate is not part of Ruby proper; it is added by Rails. The call to require loads Rails, which extends Ruby's object model to include delegation[2]. As with Java, callers need to talk only to the manager:

`code/rails_xt/samples/delegate.rb`

```ruby
m.write_test_plans 5
m.code 3
m.run_tests 6
m.debug 2
```

3.6 Polymorphism and Interfaces

When you write a program, you specify by name some method that you want to invoke. At runtime, the actual method chosen depends not just on the name but also on the specific object through which *dynamically dispatched* the invocation occurs. Method calls are *dynamically dispatched* to a specific implementation, based on the type the object used to call the method. Here is a Java example:

`code/java_xt/src/poly/Demo.java`

```java
Employer e1 = new Company("Hal");
Employer e2 = new BusinessPerson("Steve", "Startup");
Person stu = new BusinessPerson("Stu", "Halloway");
Employee stillStu = (Employee) stu;
e1.addEmployee(stillStu);
e2.addEmployee(stillStu);
```

In this example, e1 and e2 are of the same type, Employer. However, they have different implementations of addEmployee(). When you call addEmployee(), Java selects the correct implementation at runtime based on the actual type of the variable, in this case either a Company or a BusinessPerson.

---

2. The Ruby Standard Library also includes a Delegator class. It does not matter much which library provides delegation support. The important thing is that the Ruby language is open enough that delegation can be a *library* feature, not a *language* feature.

This little bit of indirection enables many good features. You (or any other programmer) can use an Employer class without knowing any specific details about how it works.

You can create new implementations of Employer in the future, and well-crafted programs can take advantage of these new implementations *without recompilation*. You can assemble new applications out of parts (classes) that have never met before, and they "just work." When objects have different types, allowing them to respond to the same methods in different ways, it is called *polymorphism*.

polymorphism

Polymorphism works with implementation inheritance, which is covered in Section 2.8, *Inheritance*, on page 46. But it is more interesting, and more powerful, with interfaces. In the previous example, Employer is an interface:

`code/java_xt/src/poly/Employer.java`

```java
package poly;

public interface Employer {
  int employeeCount();
  Employee[] getEmployees();
  void addEmployee(Employee e);
  void removeEmployee(Employee e);
}
```

An interface lists methods without implementations, and classes then *implement* the interface by providing bodies for each method:

implement

`code/java_xt/src/poly/EmployerImpl.java`

```java
package poly;

import java.util.ArrayList;

public class EmployerImpl implements Employer {
  private ArrayList employees;
  public EmployerImpl() {
    employees = new ArrayList();
  }

  public int employeeCount() {
    return employees.size();
  }

  public Employee[] getEmployees() {
    return (Employee []) employees.toArray(new Employee[employees.size()]);
  }
```

```java
public void addEmployee(Employee e) {
  Employer previous = e.getEmployer();
  if (previous != null) {
    previous.removeEmployee(e);
  }
  employees.add(e);
  e.setEmployer(this);
}

public void removeEmployee(Employee e) {
  employees.remove(e);
  e.setEmployer(null);
}
}
```

The power of interfaces comes from being able to implement more than one. Where classes can extend only one other class, they can implement any number of interfaces.

The BusinessPerson class from the previous example actually implements three interfaces:

code/java_xt/src/poly/BusinessPerson.java

```java
public class BusinessPerson
    implements Person, Employee, Employer {
```

Here are all three interfaces in use:

code/java_xt/src/poly/Demo.java

```java
Employer e1 = new Company("Hal");
Employer e2 = new BusinessPerson("Steve", "Startup");
Person stu = new BusinessPerson("Stu", "Halloway");
Employee stillStu = (Employee) stu;
e1.addEmployee(stillStu);
e2.addEmployee(stillStu);
((Employer)stu).addEmployee(stillStu);
```

In the last line, you cannot call addEmployee() via the stu variable. Instead, you must cast stu to a Employer first. This line represents a two-step process.

First, you see a cast to Employer, which does a runtime check to make sure stu actually is an Employer. Then, you see a call to the addEmployee() method, which is *guaranteed to exist at compile time*.

If stu cannot addEmployee(), then the failure will occur at runtime during the first step, the cast to Employee.

Since Ruby does not have a compile time, you can bet that Ruby's approach to polymorphism will look different:

```
code/rails_xt/samples/poly_demo.rb
```

```ruby
e1 = Company.new("Hal")
e2 = BusinessPerson.new("Steve", "Startup")
me = BusinessPerson.new("Stu", "Halloway")
e1.add_employee(me)
e2.add_employee(me)
me.add_employee(me)
```

In the Ruby version, BusinessPerson is again a Person, an Employee, and an Employer. However, Ruby does not have any interface keyword, and no cast is necessary. *Ruby is type-safe at method granularity, not interface granularity.* In the Ruby version, an object can either add_employee or cannot. If you try to add_employee to an object that does not implement an add_employee method, Ruby will throw a NoMethodError.[3] For example, the following similar program uses a nonemployer Person instead of a BusinessPerson:

```
code/rails_xt/samples/non_employer.rb
```

```ruby
require 'poly_demo'
e1 = Company.new("Hal")
me = Person.new("Stu", "Halloway")
me.add_employee(e1)
```

Executing this code results in the following:

```
$ ruby non_employee.rb
non_employee.rb:4: undefined method 'add_employee' ... (NoMethodError)
```

Both Java and Ruby are polymorphic and type-safe, but they differ in priorities and implementation. Since Java programs enforce type safety by casting to some interface or class, Java programmers tend to talk about type safety at the coarse granularity of *who you are*: "Jim cannot hire people because Jim *is not an employer*." Ruby programs enforce type safety at the finer granularity of *what you can do*: "Jim cannot hire people because Jim *has no add_employee method*."

Both languages can simulate the approach of the other. Java programmers regularly create interfaces with one method only to approximate

---

3. We have simplified a bit here. Individual objects can add, change, or remove method implementations at runtime. Objects can also implement method_missing and choose to handle arbitrary methods. See the *Joe Asks...* on page 91 for an example of method_missing.

method granularity (think Runnable). Ruby programmers could do more up-front type checking by calling kind_of?. For example:

```
code/rails_xt/samples/poly_demo.rb
class Object
  def must_be(*types)
    types.each {|type| raise "Must be #{type}" unless self.kind_of?(type)}
  end
end
```

Programs can call must_be with any number of types (classes or modules) that an object must support:

```
code/rails_xt/samples/poly_demo.rb
me = BusinessPerson.new("Stu", "Halloway")
me.must_be(Person, Employer, Employee)
```

Although Ruby programmers *could* develop idioms such as must_be, they rarely do. Instead, they embrace duck typing.

3.7 Duck Typing

Duck typing

Duck typing means an object type is defined by what it can do, not by what it is. "If it walks like a duck and talks like a duck, then to the interpreter, it is a duck." Duck typing allows you to plug in new implementations without a lot of busywork. Simply write an object that implements the methods you need, and then drop it into your system in place of some other object. In practice, this saves time (and code) in three major ways:

- It is easy to write stub objects for unit tests. If you need a dummy version of some object in a unit test, duck typing makes this trivial—implement only exactly the methods needed by the test.
- Duck typing knocks down artificial boundaries that lead to repetitive code.
- Duck typing makes it easier to refactor from specific relationships to more general ones.

Duck typing also has one notable disadvantage: It is more difficult (although not impossible) for automated tools to guess the possible methods associated with a variable. Because of this (and the lack of investment to date), Ruby IDEs do not offer nearly the level of code completion and refactoring that the best Java IDEs do.

3.8 Mixins

In Section 3.6, *Polymorphism and Interfaces*, on page 66, you learned how polymorphic methods are called in Java. Often, multiple polymorphic implementations are similar, and they delegate to the same underlying code.

For the Employer implementations, we chose to have both Company and BusinessPerson delegate to a helper class EmployerImpl. Here's the code from Company, and we'll spare you the nearly identical code in BusinessPerson:

`code/java_xt/src/poly/Company.java`

```java
package poly;

public class Company implements Employer {
  private String name;
  private EmployerImpl employerImpl;
  public Company(String name) {
    this.name = name;
    this.employerImpl = new EmployerImpl();
  }
  public int employeeCount() {
    return employerImpl.getEmployees().length;
  }
  public Employee[] getEmployees() {
    return employerImpl.getEmployees();
  }
  public void addEmployee(Employee e) {
    employerImpl.addEmployee(e);
  }
  public void removeEmployee(Employee e) {
    employerImpl.removeEmployee(e);
  }
}
```

This could be translated directly into Ruby, or it could be improved as shown in Section 3.5, *Delegation*, on page 64.

Ruby *mixins* provide still another approach: Code is written once and can be mixed into any number of classes or modules as needed. Here is Employer as a module intended for mixin use:

mixins

`code/rails_xt/samples/employer.rb`

```ruby
module Employer
  def employees
    @employees ||= []
  end
```

```ruby
  def add_employee(employee)
    employee.employer.remove_employee(employee) if employee.employer
    self.employees << employee
    employee.employer = self
  end
  def remove_employee(employee)
    self.employees.delete employee
    employee.employer = nil
  end
end
```

Classes such as BusinessPerson can then pick up Employer functionality
by calling include Employer:

code/rails_xt/samples/business_person.rb

```ruby
class BusinessPerson < Person
  include Employer, Employee
end
```

Now the BusinessPerson class can call any Employer methods:

```
irb(main):001:0> require 'business_person'
=> true
irb(main):002:0> boss = BusinessPerson.new("Justin", "Gehtland")
=> #<BusinessPerson:0x54394 @first_name="Justin", @last_name="Gehtland">
irb(main):003:0> drone = BusinessPerson.new("Stu", "Halloway")
=> #<BusinessPerson:0x4f9d4 @first_name="Stu", @last_name="Halloway">
irb(main):004:0> boss.add_employee(drone)
=> etc.
```

The fact that include is a method call has interesting implications. The
object model is not static, and you could choose to have BusinessPerson
include Employer under some circumstances and not others. In fact,
you can make object model decisions *per instance* instead of per class.
The extend method works like include but on a specific instance. So, a
specific person could become an Employer at runtime:

```
irb(main):001:0> require 'business_person'
=> true
irb(main):002:0> p = Person.new("Stu", "Halloway")
=> #<Person:0x5490c @first_name="Stu", @last_name="Halloway">
irb(main):003:0> class <<p; ancestors; end
=> [Person, Object, Kernel]
irb(main):004:0> p.extend Employer
=> #<Person:0x5490c @first_name="Stu", @last_name="Halloway">
irb(main):005:0> class <<p; ancestors; end
=> [Employer, Person, Object, Kernel]
```

The variable p starts life as a "plain old Person" with class ancestors
[Person, Object, Kernel]. The extend Employer call turns p into an Employer
as well, and the ancestor list changes appropriately. The odd-looking

statement `class <<p` accesses the *singleton class* of p. A singleton class *singleton class* might better be known as an instance-specific class. You have modified the inheritance hierarchy of p, so it is not "just a Person." It now has its own instance-specific class, which tracks its unique ancestors list.

3.9 Functions

Strictly speaking, neither Java nor Ruby has functions. Nevertheless, it is reasonable to talk about functions: Sometimes a function can be handy, and both Java and Ruby have important idioms for these situations. Consider this simple example, a program that reads a bunch of lines from stdin and then prints them back sorted:

code/java_xt/src/SortWords.java

```java
import java.io.*;
import java.util.*;

public class SortWords {
  public static void main(String[] args)
      throws IOException {
    BufferedReader br = new BufferedReader(new InputStreamReader(System.in));
    List al = new ArrayList();
    String line = null;
    while (null != (line = br.readLine())) {
      al.add(line);
    }
    Collections.sort(al);
    System.out.println("sorted:");
    for (Iterator it = al.iterator(); it.hasNext();) {
      System.out.println(it.next());
    }
  }
}
```

Here is an equivalent program in Ruby:

code/rails_xt/samples/sort_words.rb

```ruby
puts readlines.sort.unshift("sorted:\n").join
```

Both programs produce output like this:

```
$ ruby samples/sort_words.rb
quick
brown
fox      (close stdin here with Ctrl-D or equivalent...)
sorted:
brown
fox
quick
```

Fine so far. But what if you wanted to sort by some other criteria, such as word length or preponderance of vowels? If you can imagine lots of different criteria, or if new criteria might turn up at runtime, you will quickly want a general solution that might look like this:

```
Collections.sort(al, sortByWordLength);
```

In English, this might read as "Sort the collection al using the function sortByWordLength() to compare words." And, in fact, Java works exactly like this—except without the f-word.[4] Instead of using a function, you can build a function-like object out of pieces you do have: interfaces and inheritance. Java's collections API provides a Comparator interface:

```
public interface Comparator {
  int compare(Object o, Object o1);
}
```

You can write your own class that implements Comparator and compares strings by some criteria you care about. Return a negative number if the first object is lesser, 0 if the objects are equal, and a positive number if the second object is the lesser of the two. Creating an entirely new class just to specify a sort order is often a big diversion, so Java provides a shortcut called the *anonymous inner class*. Using an anonymous inner class, you can specify the sort "function" directly inside the call to sort:

code/java_xt/src/SortWords2.java

```
Collections.sort(al, new Comparator() {
  public int compare(Object o, Object o1) {
    return ((String)o).length() - ((String)o1).length();
  }
});
```

Java's anonymous inner classes, when used in this way, are functions in everything but name. Having an ordering function return negative, 0, or positive is common to Java and Ruby (and many other languages). In Ruby, you can use a block to implement the sort "function":

code/rails_xt/samples/sort_words_2.rb

```
sorted = readlines.sort {|x,y| x.length-y.length}
puts "sorted:\n#{sorted.join}"
```

The block syntax (curly braces or do...end) is the same syntax you examined in Section 2.4, *Collections and Iteration*, on page 28. In Ruby, you will typically use a block whenever you want to "pass a function to a

---

4. The seven-letter f-word. Shame on you.

method." Function passing turns out to be a very common idiom, both in Java and in Ruby. Other obvious examples in Java include event handling in Swing, scheduling Callables using the concurrency API, and enforcing security constraints on a PrivilegedAction. In Ruby and Rails, this idiom is even more common.

Blocks are useful to implement wrappers for tasks. For example, suppose you wanted to call a function that you *expect* to raise an exception. You could write a wrapper like this:

code/rails_xt/samples/expect_exception.rb

```ruby
def expect_exception(type)
  begin
    yield
  rescue type => e
    return
  end
  raise "Expected exception: #{type}"
end
```

Ruby's **yield** statement executes the code in a block, if one was passed   *yield*
to the function. The expect_exception works as follows: "Call the block that was passed in, and return if an exception of type is raised. Otherwise, raise an exception." Given this definition for expect_exception, the following code returns untroubled:

code/rails_xt/samples/expect_exception.rb

```ruby
expect_exception(ZeroDivisionError) {10/0}
```

The code in the block (10/0) is executed when expect_exception hits **yield**. The following call fails with an Expected exception: ZeroDivisionError:

code/rails_xt/samples/expect_exception.rb

```ruby
expect_exception(ZeroDivisionError) {}
```

There is a second syntax for calling blocks. Instead of using **yield**, you can capture a block, if there is one, with an explicit parameter. The block parameter must be listed last and be prefixed with an ampersand:

code/rails_xt/samples/expect_exception_2.rb

```ruby
def expect_exception(type, &blk)
  begin
    blk.call if block_given?
  rescue type => e
    return
  end
  raise "Expected exception: #{type}"
end
```

Regardless of which syntax you choose, you can call block_given? to determine whether a block was actually passed to the method. (In the case of expect_exception, passing no block would represent extreme paranoia—presumably *doing nothing* will not raise an exception!)

Blocks are incredibly common in Ruby programming and are one of the biggest syntactic stumbling blocks for Java programmers. Remember, blocks provide a terse syntax for performing the same actions you would use an interface+anonymous inner class to accomplish in Java.

The Ruby idioms in this chapter, plus some more advanced techniques, can greatly reduce the burden that repetitive code places on an application. One of the most repetitive tasks in web development is converting between objects and the database rows that (often) stand behind them. In the next chapter, you will see how ActiveRecord puts Ruby idioms to use to create a data access API that is lean and elegant.

## Chapter 4

Accessing Data with ActiveRecord

Martin Fowler, during his keynote at RailsConf 2006, described Rails' ActiveRecord as the best and most complete implementation of the "Active Record" pattern that he had ever seen. The pattern and the library expose persistence-related behavior on the objects that model the data directly. Other technologies choose to offload this knowledge of the data store to other layers (DAOs and data facades and the containers themselves). By embedding this knowledge in the domain objects, ActiveRecord creates a tight coupling between the models and the database beneath them. This tight coupling is made transparent through a series of assumptions about how models map to data schemas. When people talk about Rails as being "opinionated software," they are often talking about ActiveRecord and its particular ideas about the mapping between domain objects and data tables.

Although ActiveRecord is part of Rails, you can also install it as a free-standing gem:

```
gem install activerecord
```

We will compare ActiveRecord to Hibernate (http://www.hibernate.org), a high-quality O/RM framework that is probably the most popular choice in the Java world. As you will see throughout this chapter, ActiveRecord and Hibernate differ in one deep, fundamental way: Hibernate supports caching, where ActiveRecord does not. As a result, Hibernate has better performance characteristics for some common usage patterns, but ActiveRecord is easier to use.

Of course, O/RM caching is possible in Ruby, and lighter-weight solutions are possible in Java. We have selected the most popular framework because that's the one you are most likely to know.

For much of this chapter, we will use the ActiveRecord gem directly. This is useful for comparison with Hibernate, which is also a freestanding library. Also, you may find Ruby to be a good language for automating database tasks and choose to use ActiveRecord outside of Rails web applications. Of course, we'll also show how ActiveRecord fits into Rails.

Most of the example code in this chapter (and for the remainder of the book) refers to the Rails XT sample application. Make sure you read the sidebar on the next page, called "Configuring the Rails XT App"; perform the steps in the sidebar so you can follow along with the examples.

4.1 Getting Connected

Most Java applications interact with relational databases, almost always via JDBC. Each RDBMS has a different API; JDBC hides these distinctions by providing a standardized API. JDBC providers act as the bridge between JDBC and the specific RDBMS you are targeting. Your job, as a Java developer, is to install the appropriate driver, instantiate it, and feed it to the JDBC library for use during your application.

adapters

ActiveRecord likewise uses a provider model, but refers to the providers as *adapters*. An adapter can be a pure Ruby implementation or a hybrid Ruby/C extension. From your application code, you need to specify only the name of the adapter you want to use; ActiveRecord will provide the Ruby bridge code and worry about loading the native extension (if necessary). If the adapter is not provided, or cannot be loaded, ActiveRecord will raise an exception detailing the problem.

You can either configure ActiveRecord programmatically or configure Ruby via a configuration file. To configure the connection programmatically, call the establish_connection method on ActiveRecord::Base:

`code/rails_xt/samples/activerecord/connecting.rb`

```
require 'rubygems'
require_gem 'activerecord'

ActiveRecord::Base.establish_connection(
  :adapter=>:mysql,
  :database=>:rails4java_development
)
```

In addition to specifying an adapter and a database, you will also specify connection settings such as username and password. However,

Configuring the Rails XT App

The Rails XT application has some initial setup requirements, because it demonstrates several third-party extensions to the Rails platform. The setup steps are listed next, and we explain them in more detail as they come up in the course of the book.

1. Install the third-party gems that Rails XT requires:

```
gem install mocha
gem install flexmock
gem install selenium
gem install markaby
```

2. The Rails XT application demonstrates features of Rails 1.2. At the time of this writing, Rails 1.2 has not been released. Until the official release, you can follow the instructions on the Rails website* and install the most recent Release Candidate.

3. Create the application databases. If you are using the MySQL console, use this:

```
$ mysql -u root
Welcome to the MySQL monitor.  Commands end with ; or \g.
Your MySQL connection id is 1 to server version:
4.1.12-standard

Type 'help;' or '\h' for help. Type '\c' to clear the buffer.

mysql> create database rails4java_development;
Query OK, 1 row affected (0.30 sec)
mysql> create database rails4java_test;
Query OK, 1 row affected (0.30 sec)
mysql> exit
Bye
```

4. After you have downloaded the code, you can run a Rake task to create the database tables:

```
cd rails_xt
rake migrate
```

If this command fails, verify that you have a working MySQL install with no password for the root user. (This is the default setup for MySQL.)

---

*. Follow the link to Rails 1.2 at http://www.rubyonrails.org/

ActiveRecord will default arguments wherever possible, so the previous connection will use root/no password, which is MySQL's standard initial setup. In a Rails application, you do not have to establish the connection yourself. Rails automatically reads the connection settings from config/database.yml. By default, database.yml contains settings for the development, test, and production environments:

```
development:
  adapter: mysql
  database: rails4java_development
  username: root
  password:
  host: localhost

test:
  adapter: mysql
  database: rails4java_test
  username: root
  password:
  host: localhost

# production looks similar
```

This file is in YAML (YAML Ain't Markup Language). As you can see, the configuration is repetitive. If you want, you can DRY[1] this out by using YAML's *aliases* and *anchors*. The ampersand introduces an alias, and then an asterisk creates an anchor that refers to the alias.

aliases

anchors

```
irb(main):004:0> YAML.load "[&foo 1, *foo, *foo]"
=> [1, 1, 1]
```

Applying an alias to the common portion of a Rails database configuration yields the following:

code/rails_xt/config/database.yml

```
common: &shared
  adapter: mysql
  username: root
  password:
  host: localhost

development:
  database: rails4java_development
  <<: *shared
```

---

1. DRY stands for Don't Repeat Yourself. We use DRY as both a noun and a verb, so to "DRY your code" is to eliminate repetition. See *The Pragmatic Programmer* [HT00] for an in-depth discussion of why DRY is so important.

> **What about Multiple Databases?**
>
> By default, Rails assumes that all models come from the same database. If you need to pull different models from different databases, you can override establish_connection() on a specific model class. In addition, ActiveRecord respects these settings in a hierarchy of types. Every model class uses the connections settings applied most proximally to it in the hierarchy; thus, if the model itself has custom settings, they will be used. Next, its direct parent class's settings will be used, and so on, until it gets back to ActiveRecord::Base.

```
test:
  database: rails4java_test
  <<: *shared
production:
  database: rails4java_production
  <<: *shared
```

The '<<' is called a *merge key*, and it inserts one mapping into another.   *merge key*
So, all three database configurations share all the values in common.

4.2   Managing Schema Versions with Migrations

What makes code agile, that is, able to change? Most developers would answer "automated testing and version control." Unfortunately, data schemas do not get the same love that code does. Even development teams that are agile in adapting their code struggle with frozen, unchanging schemas.

Enter migrations. Migrations are Rails' way of creating, modifying, and versioning your data schema. With migrations, your schema can be (almost) as agile as your code base.

An individual migration associates a schema change with a particular point in time, and Rails provides scripts to run the clock forward and backward over your schema. We are not going to compare migrations to any specific Java approach, because there isn't anything approaching a standard convention in Java.

A migration is a piece of Ruby code that can perform two tasks: change a database schema in some way and reverse that change (if possible). We will now show how we used migrations to create the data schema for the sample application. Our first model object is a Quip, which is some witty saying in the blogosphere. To create the quip, we ran this:

```
> script/generate migration create_quips
```

This creates a new migration named db/migrate/001_create_quips.rb. We then edited the migration file to look like this:

code/rails_xt/db/migrate/001_create_quips.rb

```ruby
class CreateQuips < ActiveRecord::Migration
  def self.up
    create_table :quips do |t|
      t.column :text, :text
      t.column :author_id, :int
    end
  end

  def self.down
    drop_table :quips
  end
end
```

The self.up() method tells how to create the quips table, and self.down() tells how to reverse that process. Notice that the table creation is done with Ruby, not raw SQL. This allows migrations to be portable across different databases. It is also possible to use raw SQL, if you need to access a database-specific capability or do something not currently supported in the Migrations API.

You can execute migrations by running rake migrate:

```
$ rake migrate
(in /Users/stuart/FR_RAILS4JAVA/Book/code/rails_xt)
== CreateQuips: migrating ===========================
-- create_table(:quips)
   -> 0.3117s
== CreateQuips: migrated (0.3133s) ==================
```

Now your database has a quips table. You can also run migrations with a specific version number. All migrations include a filename prefix that is a version number, such as 001_create_quips.rb. When you migrate to a specific version, Rails will check the current version of the schema. If you ask for a more recent (higher-numbered) version, Rails will call the appropriate up() methods. If you ask for an older (lower-numbered) version, Rails will works its way backward, calling down() methods.

Schema Versioning in Java

For many Java applications, data schema maintenance is overlooked. In our experience, it is rare to find data schemas managed by a source control system, let alone in such a way that versions of the schema can be easily tracked. Some libraries provide solutions for this; Hibernate and Kodo, for example, provide tools for generating schema from metadata, or vice versa, and this leads to an automated strategy for keeping track of the changes to the database over time.

With Hibernate, if you have made changes to your business objects and want to manage the schema update, you could specify the new properties in the .hbm.xml files and then run the SchemaUpdate tool provided by Hibernate. This will attempt to retrieve the current schema and diff it against the values in the latest .hbm files. Any differences that can be handled by the current JDBC driver will be written to the database. This is convenient but has two major drawbacks: First, if the driver can't handle the change, the change won't be made. Second, there is no automated way to reverse the process. Likewise, Kodo provides the Mapping Tool to ensure that the data schema is up-to-date with the current object model but does not provide an automated strategy for managing the schema independently and focuses only on one-way transitions.

Since CreateQuips is our first migration, the only number we can go down to is 0, or back to the beginning:

```
$ rake migrate VERSION=0
(in /Users/stuart/FR_RAILS4JAVA/Book/code/rails_xt)
== CreateQuips: reverting ============================
-- drop_table(:quips)
   -> 0.2387s
== CreateQuips: reverted (0.2401s) ===================
```

Rails uses an extra table in the database to track the migration version. If you look at a Rails application, you will see a table called schema_info. This table has one column, called version, and one row, which contains the current version number of the schema.

Rolling forward and backward through a single migration as we have done here is hardly worth the trouble. Where migrations become powerful is in situations where you have a series of database modifications over time. For example, imagine that you need to change the schema of an app that is already in production. You can build and test your migrations in the development and test environment and then run them in production once you are confident that everything works properly. If you make a mistake, you can always run a down migration to get your schema back to its last known good state.

Because these migrations are written in Ruby, not SQL, they rely on the database adapter to generate the appropriate SQL statements to make the desired modifications. As long as you stick to the pure Ruby API, you could run this migration against MySQL as easily as against Oracle. One of the interesting features of migrations that enables this is the autogeneration of the primary key field. Notice that we never specified an id column when creating the quips table. For the users and roles tables, ActiveRecord creates a column called id automatically and uses the current database's default method for managing the value of the column.

Migrations can be used outside of Rails. In fact, the migration approach to schema versioning is so useful that we use it for all of our Java projects as well. If you live in a multilanguage environment like we do, migrations can provide a good way to get some practice with Ruby by using it to support an existing Java project.

We have built the sample application in an agile fashion, extending the schema incrementally as necessary. Take a look through the migrations in db/migrate to get a feel for what migrations have to offer.

4.3 Mapping Data to Classes

In Hibernate, JDO, EJB, and other Java persistence libraries, mapping has historically been done in a separate XML or properties file. For Hibernate, there's hibernate-configuration.xml plus the assortment of .hbm.xml files. In Kodo, there's the persistence.xml file. With EJBs, there are all the descriptor files. Lately, with the release of Java 5.0 annotations, the Jakarta Commons Annotations project, and Spring's metadata support, inline configuration is becoming more and more the norm.

ActiveRecord relies on convention over configuration. Wherever possible, ActiveRecord guesses the correct configuration by reflecting against the data schema. When you do need a specific override, you specify the override directly in your model class.

Conventions

Given a schema, here is the process for creating a Hibernate model class. First, create a Plain Old Java Object (POJO) with reasonably named fields:

code/hibernate_examples/src/Person.java

```java
private long id;
private String firstName;
private String lastName;
private String middleName;
private String bio;
private String url;
```

Create JavaBean accessors for those fields:

```java
public String getFirstName() {
  return firstName;
}

public void setFirstName(String firstName) {
  this.firstName = firstName;
}
// repeat for each field
```

Then create a mapping that tells Hibernate how to associate database columns with object properties:

code/hibernate_examples/config/person.hbm.xml

```xml
<?xml version="1.0"?>
<!DOCTYPE hibernate-mapping PUBLIC "-//Hibernate/Hibernate Mapping DTD 3.0//EN"
 "http://hibernate.sourceforge.net/hibernate-mapping-3.0.dtd">
<hibernate-mapping>
  <class name="Person" table="people">
    <id name="id" type="java.lang.Long">
      <generator class="native"/>
    </id>
    <version name="version" column='lock_version'/>
    <property name="firstName" type="string" column="first_name"/>
    <property name="lastName" type="string" column="last_name"/>
    <property name="middleName" type="string" column="middle_name"/>
    <property name="bio" type="string" column="bio"/>
    <property name="url" type="string" column="url"/>
    <set name="quips" inverse="true" cascade="all">
      <key column="author_id"/>
      <one-to-many class="Quip"/>
    </set>
  </class>
</hibernate-mapping>
```

The ActiveRecord approach requires exactly one line of Ruby code and no YAML or XML. *Simply create a class with the right name:*

```
class Person < ActiveRecord::Base; end
```

That's it. ActiveRecord scans the database metadata, looking for a table named people (the plural of the class name Person). It then automatically generates all the necessary constructors, fields, accessor methods, and even finder methods.

Overriding Defaults

Convention over configuration looks great when it guesses everything right. The true test is what happens when you need to customize a bit. Let's assume you have class names and table names that don't follow the Rails convention. For your people table, you want to have a Peeps class. No problem:

```
$ script/console
>> class Peeps < ActiveRecord::Base
>>   set_table_name :people
>> ended<
```

The set_table_name() class method overrides Rails' regular naming rules. Other conventions have their own override methods, so you are never stuck with "the Rails way." Note also that this configuration is Ruby code, inside the class definition. This differs markedly from most Java configuration, which is usually XML living in a separate file.

We executed the previous Peeps example inside a script/console session. We do not usually write model code in an interactive session like this, but it is a satisfying demonstration of how simple and dynamic Rails is in responding to your intention. With just the previous three lines, you now have full-functioning access to the people table:

```
>> Peeps.create :first_name=>'Dave', :last_name=>'Thomas'
=> #<Peeps:0x2459e0c ...>
>> Peeps.count
=> 3
>> Peeps.find(:all, :order=>'first_name asc').map(&:first_name)
=> ["Dave", "Justin", "Stuart"]
```

We'll see how these and other CRUD (Create, Read, Update, and Delete) methods work in the next section.

4.4 Create, Read, Update, and Delete: Access Patterns

Once you have a database schema and some object mappings, you are ready to access data. Since ActiveRecord is an Object/Relational Mapping (O/RM) framework, you generally access the data via object-oriented APIs.

However, as is the case with any O/RM framework, these methods are not always suitable for the task at hand. When necessary, you can dip beneath the object-oriented veneer and directly utilize SQL statements to do what you need with the database.

Loading Data

In Hibernate, the sole mechanism for loading data is through the Session object. To load individual objects from the database, you use session.load, and to load collections of objects, you use session.find or session.criteria_query. Let's take the simplest form, which is loading a single object by its ID:

`code/hibernate_examples/src/AccessPatterns.java`

```
Quip quip = null;
Session sess = null;
try {
  sess = factory.openSession();
  quip = (Quip)sess.get(Quip.class, new Long(1));
} finally {
  sess.close();
}
```

Hibernate wants to ensure that your persistent classes are POJOs. Therefore, the persistent objects know nothing[2] about Hibernate. The actual API for persistence is provided through a Hibernate object, the Session.

Persistence methods are called on the Session, and the requested persistent type is passed in. This snippet also demonstrates the holy template for using Hibernate: Always use a finally block to close the session as soon as possible.[3]

---

2.   Purists might say "almost nothing" since the classes know about their IDs in the database.

3.   Don't make "close the session" into a pattern for copy/paste reuse. Instead, use something such as Spring's HibernateTemplate.

ActiveRecord is more intrusive, requiring that persistent types extend a common ancestor: ActiveRecord::Base. In return, models provide persistence directly, with no need for anything like the Session. Here's the ActiveRecord version:

```
code/rails_xt/samples/activerecord/access_patterns.rb
```
```
q = Quip.find(1)
```

Persistent behaviors are part of the persistent classes themselves, not a third entity. So, you call find() directly on Quip. Connection management is entirely implicit, so you do not need to close the connection. Here's one way that Hibernate might load all Quips.

Now that we have mentioned the need to close the session, we aren't going to keep showing that code in the text.

```
code/hibernate_examples/src/AccessPatterns.java
```
```
quips = sess.createCriteria(Quip.class).list();
```

In here it is with ActiveRecord:

```
code/rails_xt/samples/activerecord/access_patterns.rb
```
```
quips = Quip.find(:all)
```

Again, Hibernate is nonintrusive, placing the lookup method on the Session, while ActiveRecord uses Quip directly. There is another difference here as well. Where Hibernate's session has tons of different methods, ActiveRecord tends to use a smaller set of methods with a variety of optional arguments, such as the previous :all. This difference stems directly from the type system differences. Java APIs need different methods to handle different return types.

Next, let's apply some conditions to limit the results of the query. Hibernate exposes an object-oriented Criteria API to access the various conditions. For example, let's load some Persons, but only those with a first name of Justin. Sort them by last name, of course:

```
code/hibernate_examples/src/AccessPatterns.java
```
```
people = sess.createCriteria(Person.class)
            .add( Expression.eq("firstName", "Justin"))
            .addOrder(Order.asc("lastName"))
            .list();
```

Instead of method chaining, ActiveRecord applies the standard Ruby technique of allowing a hash of options:

```
code/rails_xt/samples/activerecord/access_patterns.rb
```
```
p = Person.find(:all,
            :conditions => "first_name = 'Justin'",
            :order => "last_name ASC")
```

Both of the previous code examples assume you are issuing a query using hard-coded conditions ("Justin" is a literal and is unchangeable by the user). If you need to query based on user input, the previous approaches are unsafe, because of the potential for SQL injection attacks.

The easiest way to avoid SQL injection attacks is to use explicitly parameterized queries instead of creating SQL statements through string concatenation. Assuming that name is an "unsafe" variable from user input, you would have the following:

`code/hibernate_examples/src/AccessPatterns.java`

```
Criterion c = Restrictions.sqlRestriction("{alias}.first_name = ?",
                           name,
                           Hibernate.STRING);
p = sess.createCriteria(Person.class).add(c).list();
```

In ActiveRecord, as you would now expect, this is accomplished with an optional parameter to find():

`code/rails_xt/samples/activerecord/access_patterns.rb`

```
p = Person.find(:all,
                :conditions => ["first_name = :fname", {:fname=>name}])
```

The :conditions option is set to an array of values. The first value in the array is the parameterized SQL fragment; it can contain any number of named parameters of the form :paramname. The rest of the array is a Ruby hash containing key/value pairs to set the parameters.

Several other options exist that we will not cover in detail. For example, you can specify :first instead of :all to return only the first result. If you can pass an array of indices as the first parameter, ActiveRecord will find all instances of the class whose primary key is in that list.

ActiveRecord also allows you to search for records via properties. For example, you can say this:

`code/rails_xt/samples/activerecord/access_patterns.rb`

```
p = Person.find_by_first_name('Justin')
ps = Person.find_all_by_first_name('Justin')
```

ActiveRecord creates a query automatically while still properly escaping the value of the condition. These finder methods are available for all properties, and all combinations of properties, on the object. They also take all the same options as the regular find method.

So you can also say this:

```
code/rails_xt/samples/activerecord/access_patterns.rb
```

```
p = Person.find_by_first_name_and_last_name('Justin', 'Gehtland')
p = Person.find_by_first_name('Justin', :order=>'last_name ASC')
```

Persisting Data

Saving changes to the database implies a lot of complexity, much of which we will cover later in this chapter. For example, how do you wrap your changes in a transaction (Section 4.8, *Transactions, Concurrency, and Performance*, on page 106)? When are validation rules applied (Section 4.5, *Validating Data Values*, on page 94)? How are changes cascaded across relationships (Section 4.7, *Transitive Persistence*, on page 102)? For now, we are going to focus on the simple task of communicating a simple change to a database row.

Inserting a New Record

In Hibernate, the path to creating a new record is fairly straightforward. Simply create an instance of the desired class. Since Hibernate works with POJOs, it does not matter how you create an object.

You can call a constructor, invoke a factory, or get the object from some other framework. The important task is to eventually associate the object with a session, such as by calling save():

```
code/hibernate_examples/src/AccessPatterns.java
```

```java
Person p = new Person();
p.setFirstName("Dave");
p.setLastName("Thomas");
sess = factory.openSession();
sess.save(p);
sess.flush();
```

ActiveRecord allows a similar approach, but you call save() directly on the model object:

```
code/rails_xt/samples/activerecord/access_patterns.rb
```

```ruby
p = Person.new
p.first_name = 'Dave'
p.last_name = 'Thomas'
p.save
```

The save() method is configured to return false if the record could not be saved. If you prefer to have an exception thrown in the case of failure, use the save!() method instead. (We'll look at getting more specific information about a failure in Section 4.5, *Validating Data Values*, on page 94.)

Joe Asks...

Where Do All Those Finders Come From?

ActiveRecord finders appear to have a near infinite number of methods, once you take into account all combinations of possibilities:

```
Person.find_by_first_name
Person.find_by_last_name
Person.find_by_middle_name
Person.find_by_first_name_and_middle_name
Person.find_by_first_name_and_last_name
# etc. etc.
```

The trick is method_missing(). If a Ruby class implements method_missing(), it will be called for any method name that does not match any specific method. For example, this code:

`code/rails_xt/samples/activerecord/do_anything.rb`

```ruby
class DoAnything
  def method_missing(name, *args)
    puts "I can do anything, even #{name}"
  end
end

d = DoAnything.new
d.jump
d.dance
d.find_by_first_name_and_last_name
```

will output the following:

```
I can do anything, even jump
I can do anything, even dance
I can do anything, even find_by_first_name_and_last_name
```

The method_missing approach is similar to writing an Invocation-Handler in Java and using the handler to create a dynamic proxy. Like InvocationHandlers, method_missing should be used sparingly. Programs that rely heavily on method_missing() can easily confound both developers and developer tools.

Hibernate uses write-behind for SQL inserts. Rather than writing to the database immediately, Hibernate accumulates pending updates and does them all in one round-trip, where possible. ActiveRecord does not offer this level of abstraction; calls such as save() do what they say immediately.

You never need to write an initializer for an ActiveRecord object. Active-Records always accept a hash of properties, so you can create and initialize objects in a single line of code:

`code/rails_xt/samples/activerecord/access_patterns.rb`

```
p = Person.new :first_name=>'Dave', :last_name=>'Thomas'
p.save
```

If that still looks like too much code, you can combine new() and save() in a single step by calling create() or create!():

`code/rails_xt/samples/activerecord/access_patterns.rb`

```
p = Person.create :first_name=>'Dave', :last_name=>'Thomas'
```

You can even combine find() and create() in a single step. Methods that begin with find_or_create will find an existing record, if possible, and create one otherwise:

`code/rails_xt/samples/activerecord/access_patterns.rb`

```
p = Person.find_or_create_by_first_name_and_last_name 'Dave', 'Thomas'
```

Updating an Existing Record

The most common pattern for data modification, Hibernate style, is simple. Retrieve a record from the database, detach from the session, allow a user to make modifications, then persist those modifications:

code/hibernate_examples/src/AccessPatterns.java

```
//p is a Person detached from a prior session
sess = factory.openSession();
sess.saveOrUpdate(p);
p.setMiddleName("Brian");
sess.flush();
```

The slightly tricky part here is remembering to attach to the session. Several methods do this; saveOrUpdate() is the easiest to use because you do not have to know if the object already exists in the database.

ActiveRecord reuses the save() method for simple updates. Just as with Hibernate's saveOrUpate(), ActiveRecord's save() "does the right thing," choosing to insert or update based on whether the object already exists in the database:

code/rails_xt/samples/activerecord/access_patterns.rb

```
# p is a person from somewhere
p.middle_name = 'Brian'
p.save!
```

ActiveRecord provides a shortcut method for updating a specific record when you don't have the instance hanging around. Instead of loading the entity, updating its values, and then saving it, you can call update(), which takes an ID and a hash of properties and values to save:

```
Person.update(2, :middle_name=>'Brian')
```

A similar approach is to call update_attributes(). Given an instance, this method will set several attributes and commit the change to the database. This is convenient in a Rails controller method:

code/rails_xt/app/controllers/people_controller.rb

```
@person = Person.find(params[:id])
if @person.update_attributes(params[:person])
  # update succeeded...
```

Here you see the simplicity that results from an end-to-end naming convention. In a single line of code, parameters are extracted from a web form, assigned to an object, and committed to the database.[4]

---

4. Direct conversion from form parameters to model attributes raises a security issue. We show how Rails addresses this issue in Section 10.4, *#1. Unvalidated Input*, on page 278.

Deleting a Record

Hibernate provides a single simple mechanism for deleting an object. Call session.delete(), and pass in the persistent object you want to delete:

code/hibernate_examples/src/AccessPatterns.java

```
sess = factory.openSession();
Person p = (Person) sess.get(Person.class, new Long(2));
sess.delete(p);
sess.flush();
```

Hibernate will, upon session flush, issue the delete statement to remove that record from the database. Without issuing a custom query, this is the sum total of available options for deleting records in Hibernate.

ActiveRecord, on the other hand, provides many different strategies for deleting records. The most obvious is to call destroy() on the instance you want deleted. This causes ActiveRecord to immediately issue the delete statement required to remove the record:

code/rails_xt/samples/activerecord/access_patterns.rb

```
p = Person.find(2)
p.destroy
```

This eliminates the underlying record, but the in-memory instance p is still around if you need to reference the original values. The in-memory instance is frozen so you will not accidentally mistake it for a live object. (See Section 3.2, *Mutable and Immutable Objects*, on page 55 for a description of Ruby freezing.)

There is a parallel class-level destroy() method that takes an ID or an array of IDs as its argument.

For each ID passed, destroy() first loads the given object and then calls its destroy() method. This may seem like overkill, but this gives lifecycle callbacks the chance to run. For example, you might have a filter that prevents deletion because of some security constraint. (See Section 4.6, *Lifecycle Callbacks*, on page 97.)

4.5 Validating Data Values

Declarative validation is a powerful addition to an object model. Instead of writing code, you can simply declare constraints, which can then be enforced at various points in the object's life cycle. For example, here are some model constraints declared using the Hibernate Validator:

```
code/hibernate_examples/src/User.java
```
```java
@NotNull
@Length(min=3,max=40)
public String getLogin() {
  return login;
}
```

Even if you have never used Java 5 annotations, it is pretty obvious what these validation rules do. The login property cannot be null and must have a length from 3 to 40 characters.

Here is a similar validation in ActiveRecord:

```
code/rails_xt/app/models/user.rb
```
```ruby
validates_presence_of        :login, :email
validates_length_of          :login, :within => 3..40
```

Again, login cannot be nil and must have a length from 3 to 40 characters.

Hibernate validations are declared immediately before the property they reference. ActiveRecord validations explicitly name the properties they reference, so the previous code can constrain both login and email from the same line. ActiveRecord validations can be declared anywhere in the model class but are usually declared at the top.

Once you have declared some validations, you can explicitly validate an object. In Hibernate, ClassValidator.getInvalidValues() will return an array of all the invalid values on an object:

```
code/hibernate_examples/src/Validations.java
```
```java
User u = new User();
ClassValidator v = new ClassValidator(User.class);
InvalidValue[] errors = v.getInvalidValues(u);
```

In ActiveRecord, validation methods such as errors are invoked on the model objects themselves:

```
$ script/console
Loading development environment.
>> u = User.new
>> u.valid?
=> false
>> u.errors[:login]
=> ["is too short (minimum is 3 characters)", "can't be blank"]
```

Calling valid?() populates the errors hash. Keys are property names, and values are the validation errors.

Which Layer Does Validation?

When writing a web application in Java, you can tackle validation in one of two ways:

- You can validate form input on the way in from the client.

- You can validate persistent properties.

Examples of form validation include the Spring Validator. At the persistence layer, you might use Hibernate's Validator. Unfortunately, these layers are not connected. If you need to do similar validations in both layers, you will have to explicitly invoke the validator. For example, Hibernate's Validator can be applied automatically at the data object level but must be invoked manually in the web tier. (This could easily be improved with AOP, and we hope to remove this paragraph in a future release of the book.)

Rails, as a unified development stack, gives you a single, standard place to express your validation rules. These rules are described in your model classes, applied at persistence time, and reported all the way back to the web view layer.

In addition to explicit validation, O/RM frameworks should do implicit validation before saving a record. In Hibernate, trying to save an invalid object throws an exception:

`code/hibernate_examples/src/Validations.java`

```
assertThrows(PropertyValueException.class, new Callable() {
  public Object call()
      throws Exception {
    User u = new User();
    return sess.save(u);
  }
});
```

In ActiveRecord, save() will return false for an invalid object, and save!() will throw an exception:

```
>> u.save
=> false
>> u.save!
ActiveRecord::RecordInvalid: Validation failed: ...
```

At the time of this writing, ActiveRecord validation has a significant limitation. Error messages are reported in English, and there is no internationalization facility in Rails. Teams adopting Rails either pull in a third-party internationalization library or accept the cost of rolling their own internationalization.

See http://wiki.rubyonrails.org/rails/pages/Internationalization for advice to get started.

4.6 Lifecycle Callbacks

Most of the time, model classes are used like any other classes. In particular, model instances do not need to be constantly aware of the O/RM layer. However, in certain circumstances, objects may actually want to know what the O/RM layer is doing. For example, the Rails XT application's User class needs to take special care with its password-related properties. Users edit their passwords, but the database does not store passwords. To improve security, the database stores only the hashes of passwords.

At some point in time, a User needs to convert its password into a hash and discard the password. When should this happen? This should happen immediately before saving the User. But Users have no idea when they are about to be saved—that is the O/RM framework's job.

Enter lifecycle interfaces. O/RM frameworks provide a variety of lifecycle interfaces so that objects can receive notification of container events. Hibernate provides several different lifecycle techniques. For example, Hibernate's event system can hook into any of Hibernate's session methods. Here's how you could use events to manage Users's passwords and hashes:

`code/hibernate_examples/src/UserEventListener.java`

```
Line 1   public class UserEventListener extends DefaultSaveOrUpdateEventListener {
           public void onSaveOrUpdate(SaveOrUpdateEvent event)
               throws HibernateException {
             Object o = event.getObject();
     5       if (o instanceof User) {
               try {
                 ((User) o).hashPassword();
               } catch (NoSuchAlgorithmException e) {
                 throw new HibernateException(e);
    10         }
             }
             super.onSaveOrUpdate(event);
           }
         }
```

Consistent with Hibernate's philosophy, the lifecycle callback is not on the User model itself. Instead, a SaveOrUpdateEventListener interface acts as a hook for all save or load events on the session. (Similarly named interfaces exist for the other session methods.) Since the hook will see load and save events for all model types, we use an **if** statement to narrow down to Users (line 5). The actual business of the event listener is simply to ask the model object to hash its password (line 7), and the remaining code is boilerplate. Hibernate event listeners must be registered. There is an API for this, but it is more common to use the XML configuration file. For example:

`code/hibernate_examples/config/hibernate.cfg.xml`

```
<event type="save-update">
  <listener class="UserEventListener"/>
</event>
```

In ActiveRecord, lifecycle methods are usually added to the model classes themselves:

`code/rails_xt/app/models/user.rb`

```
before_save :encrypt_password
```

The before_save method is invoked directly on the User class and takes the name of a method to be called before a save. (Similarly named methods exist for all the other interesting methods in the persistence life cycle). In fact, the before_save takes several other forms as well. You can also pass a block:

```
before_save do
  #encrypt here
end
```

Instead of calling the class method before_save, you can implement an *instance* method, also named before_save:

```
def before_save
  #encrypt here
end
```

With any of the previous techniques, saving a user will automatically hash the password. You can easily verify this in script/console:

```
>> u = User.new
>> u.login = 'Tom'
>> u.password = u.password_confirmation = 'wombat'
>> u.email = 'contact@relevancellc.com'
>> u.crypted_password       => nil
>> u.save
>> u.password               => nil
>> u.crypted_password       => "81f8a1a1c0f9b92d74c5f65c8d0d5164772fc60a"
```

ActiveRecord will also let you decouple lifecycle methods, moving the lifecycle methods into a class separate from the model class. We don't think this is necessary for the User class, so we have not made this change in the Rails XT application.

But, it is easy enough to make a temporary change in script/console and see how external lifecycle methods work. Just pick an arbitrary class, and have it define before_save(). Since we are outside the model class, the method will take a model argument:

```
>> class SomeLifecycleCallback
>>   def before_save(model)
>>     puts "about to save instance of #{model.class}"
>>   end
>> end
```

Now, we can associate SomeLifecycleCallback with a User by using yet another variant of before_save():

```
>> class User; before_save SomeLifecycleCallback.new; end
```

To verify that SomeLifecycleCallback is called, simply save a (valid!) User:

```
>> u = User.find(:first)
>> u.save
about to save instance of User
```

What if you want to register a callback for all models, more like Hibernate's event system? Easy. Simply add SomeLifecycleCallback to ActiveRecord::Base:

```
>> class ActiveRecord::Base; before_save SomeLifecycleCallback.new; end
```

Now all kinds of model objects get SomeLifecycleCallback:

```
>> p = Person.find(:first)
>> q = Quip.find(:first)
>> p.save
about to save instance of Person
>> q.save
about to save instance of Quip
```

ActiveRecord's lifecycle callbacks are a pleasure to use. They are simply Ruby code and require no separate configuration.

Lifecycle callbacks are naturally loosely typed and loosely coupled. As a result, lifecycle callbacks feel natural in dynamic languages such as Ruby.

4.7 Associations and Inheritance

Throughout this chapter so far, we have made a simple association: One row in one table implies one instance of one class. Nontrivial systems are more complex. On the database side, databases are normalized and different tables are linked by foreign keys. On the object side, classes are related by inheritance and aggregation.

A major task of any O/RM framework is to make relationships in the data model accessible to the object model, even if the metaphors and terminology are different. The following sections describe some of the most common database relations and how they become visible in Hibernate and ActiveRecord objects.

One-to-Many Relationships

In a one-to-many relationship, a single row in one table is associated with an arbitrary number of rows in a second table. The second table has a foreign key column that refers to the primary key in the first table.

The Rails XT application has a one-to-many relationship from people to quips. The quips table has an author_id column that references the id column in the people table.

To expose this relationship at the object level in Hibernate, we start by creating JavaBeans properties that associate Quips with Persons:

```
code/hibernate_examples/src/Quip.java
private Person author;
public Person getAuthor() {
  return author;
}
public void setAuthor(Person author) {
  this.author = author;
}
```

And the opposite direction, here is Persons to Quips:

```
code/hibernate_examples/src/Person.java
private Set quips;
public Set getQuips() {
  return quips;
}
public void setQuips(Set quips) {
  this.quips = quips;
}
```

Next, we tell Hibernate about the relationships. On the "one" side, we add lines to person.hbm.xml:

`code/hibernate_examples/config/person.hbm.xml`

```xml
<set name="quips" inverse="true" cascade="all">
  <key column="author_id"/>
  <one-to-many class="Quip"/>
</set>
```

For the "many" side, we update quip.hbm.xml:

`code/hibernate_examples/config/quip.hbm.xml`

```xml
<many-to-one name="author" column="author_id" class="Person"/>
```

In ActiveRecord, the relationship between Quips and People is declared directly in the model source code. A Person has many Quips:

`code/rails_xt/app/models/person.rb`

```ruby
has_many :quips, :foreign_key=>'author_id'
```

The ActiveRecord code reads almost like documentation. The foreign_key key specifies that the foreign key for the join is author_id. In keeping with Rails' preference for convention, there is a reasonable default for foreign_key: the singular name of the table plus _id. If we had named the database column person_id instead of author_id, the foreign_key option could have been omitted. In the Hibernate implementation, we wrote bean accessors to traverse the relationships. In ActiveRecord, these methods are generated dynamically based on the has_many declaration. At runtime we can say things like this:

`code/rails_xt/sample_output/has_many.irb`

```
>> p = Person.create :first_name=>'Justin', :last_name=>'Gehtland'
=> (...description of p...)
>> p.quips
=> []
>> q = p.quips.create :text=>'Have fun storming the castle!'
=> (...description of q...)
>> p.quips.empty?
=> false
>> p.quips
=> [(...description of q...)]
>> p.quips.find(:first)
=> (...description of q...)
```

We did not write any code for the quips, create, empty?, or find methods. These convenience methods, plus several others, are created automatically by has_many.

On the Quip side, we declare the relationship in the opposite direction using belongs_to:

```
code/rails_xt/app/models/quip.rb
```

```ruby
belongs_to :author, :class_name=>'Person', :foreign_key=>'author_id'
```

Again, the foreign_key is necessary to override the default setting. In this case a second override is also needed. ActiveRecord guesses the class name for the owning instance from the foreign_key, which leads to the class name Author. The class_name overrides this and selects the correct class, Person.

Just as with has_many, ActiveRecord automatically creates a set of accessor methods for a belongs_to relationship. In the previous example, the calls to the author, nil?, and create_author methods demonstrated some of the methods that belongs_to has added to Quip.

Transitive Persistence

Here is some code that exercises the one-to-many relationship between Persons and Quips.

```
code/hibernate_examples/src/Relationships.java
```

```java
Line 1  sess.beginTransaction();
   -    Person person = new Person();
   -    person.setFirstName("John");
   -    Quip q = new Quip();
   5    q.setText("A stitch in time...");
   -    q.setAuthor(person);
   -    HashSet hs = new HashSet();
   -    hs.add(q);
   -    person.setQuips(hs);
  10    sess.save(person);
   -    sess.getTransaction().commit();
```

The usage of the Person and Quip classes is straightforward. Notice that we did need to set the association in both directions: setAuthor in line 6 and setQuips in line 9. Since the objects are POJOs, setting up the relation in both directions is our responsibility.

The call to save(person) poses an interesting question. What should actually get saved? A literal-minded O/RM would simply save the person, implicitly forgetting the associated quips. Another alternative is *transitive persistence*: when you save an object, the framework saves all related objects.

transitive persistence

In Hibernate, either alternative is possible—but you cannot tell which by looking at the code. In our sample project, saving a person will also save any quips, thanks to the following configuration line in person.hbm.xml:

```
<set name="quips" inverse="true" cascade="all">
```

The cascade property can take various values so that different operations cascade differently. Moreover, cascade can be set differently for different relationships. For bidirectional relationships, cascade can be different in one direction than in the other. Finally, if you don't want to worry about the cascade settings, you can always call session.save explicitly for each object.

ActiveRecord's approach to transitive persistence is simpler and less flexible. Each relationship type has a cascade rule, and these rules are fixed. A save operation will cascade from one to many:

```
>> p = Person.new :first_name=>'Lewis'
>> p.add_quips Quip.new(:text=>'Twas brillig...')
>> p.save
>> p.quips[0].new_record?    => false
```

Saving the Person saved the Quip automatically. But saves will not cascade from the many to the one:

```
>> p = Person.new :first_name=>'Mr.'
>> p.add_quips Quip.new(:text=>'I pity the fool...')
>> p.quips[0].save
>> p.new_record?              => true
```

Hibernate's support for transitive persistence is superior, although its usage can be confusing.

One-to-One, Many-to-Many, Polymorphic, and Through Associations

The one-to-many discussion in the previous section is representative of the general approach to associations, both in Hibernate and in Active-Record. Rather than fell more trees, we'll sum up and offer a few practical observations:

- In Hibernate, associations are described in XML, and then appropriate getter and setter methods are coded into POJOs.

- In ActiveRecord, associations are described in Ruby code in the model classes themselves. That's all you have to do; ActiveRecord will create accessor methods for you.

- With Hibernate, you have to do a lot of repetitive work. You end up describing an association in three places: the data schema, the model classes, and the Hibernate configuration. Hibernate developers often use code generation to reduce the amount of repetition involved, or developers on Java 5 may choose to use annotations.

- With ActiveRecord, there is less repetition: You create only the data schema and the model classes. The "configuration" is in a more appealing language: Ruby instead of XML. However, more consolidation is still possible. ActiveRecord could infer much more from the schema. We hope that future versions of both ActiveRecord and Hibernate will infer more from the database schema.

through associations

polymorphic associations

In addition to one-to-many, ActiveRecord also supports the other common associations: one-to-one and many-to-many. And ActiveRecord supports *through associations* that pass through an intermediate join table. ActiveRecord also support *polymorphic associations*, where at least one side of the association allows more than one concrete class. For more about these relationship types, see *Agile Web Develpment with Rails* [TH06].

Modeling Inheritance in the Data Tier

In previous sections, we discussed associations—relationships from the data world that O/RM tools propagate into the object world. We can also go in the opposite direction. Inheritance is a concept from the object world that O/RM frameworks can map to the data world.

Since inheritance is used to model hierarchy, we will use a hierarchy you may remember from grade school: celestial bodies. Under the base class CelestialBody, one might find Star and Planet, to name a few. Here is a simplified table definition:

code/rails_xt/db/migrate/005_create_celestial_bodies.rb
```
create_table :celestial_bodies do |t|
  # shared properties
  t.column :name, :string
  t.column :type, :string
  # star properties
  t.column :magnitude, :decimal
  t.column :classification, :char
  # planet properties
  t.column :gas_giant, :boolean
  t.column :moons, :int
end
```

The schema defines only one table, but our associated object model has three classes. How can the O/RM layer know which type to create?

The easiest solution is to add a *discriminator column* to the table schema. The discriminator column simply tells the O/RM which concrete class to instantiate for a particular data row. In Hibernate, you declare the discriminator in the configuration file:

```
code/hibernate_examples/config/celestialbody.hbm.xml
```

```xml
<discriminator column="type" type="string"/>
```

Then, certain values of the discriminator associate with a particular subclass and its properties:

```xml
<subclass name="Planet" discriminator-value="Planet">
  <property name="moons" type="integer"/>
  <property name="gasGiant" column="gas_giant" type="boolean"/>
</subclass>
```

You define Planet and Star as you would any other persistent class. (You do not have to declare a property for the discriminator.) The only novelty is that queries against CelestialBody may return a variety of different concrete classes:

```
//List may contain Stars or Planets
List list = sess.createQuery("from CelestialBody").list();
```

ActiveRecord will store an object's class name in the type column, if one exists. When retrieving objects from the database, ActiveRecord uses the type to create the correct class:

```
>> s = Star.new :name=>'Sol', :classification=>'G'
>> s.save
>> o = CelestialBody.find_by_classification 'G'
>> o.name       => "Sol"
>> o.class      => Star
```

Since ActiveRecord uses a zero-configuration, zero-code approach, it has no way of knowing which columns are appropriate for which classes. As a result, you can set any attribute for any subclass. You can give planets a classification:

```
>> p = Planet.create :name=>'Jupiter', :gas_giant=>true
>> p.classification = 'a very big planet!'
```

Or you can let stars have moons:

```
>> s = Star.create :name=>'Antares', :classification=>'M', :magnitude=>0.9
>> s.moons = 250
```

Dynamic language supporters consider this flexibility a feature, not a bug. However, if you want to guarantee that planets never get star properties, simply add a validation:

`code/rails_xt/app/models/planet.rb`

```ruby
class Planet < CelestialBody
  validates_each :magnitude, :classification do |obj, att, value|
    obj.errors.add att, 'must be nil' if value
  end
end
```

The validates_each method registers a block that will be called once each for the attributes classification and magnitude. Now, planets are a bit better behaved:

```
>> p = Planet.create!(:name=>'Saturn', :classification=>'A ringed planet')
ActiveRecord::RecordInvalid: Validation failed: Classification must be nil
```

single table inheritance

The technique of using one table to support many model classes is called *single table inheritance*, or *table per class* hierarchy. Hibernate supports some other approaches, such as table per subclass. With table per subclass, inheritance is spread across multiple tables, and Hibernate does the bookkeeping to join the parts back together.

ActiveRecord does *not* support table per subclass. In practice, this does not matter much. Having the O/RM provide powerful support for inheritance is important in Java, because inheritance itself is important. In Java, the inheritance hierarchy is often central to an application's design. On the other hand, idiomatic Ruby programs are duck-typed, and the "is-a" relationships of the inheritance hierarchy are relatively less important. In fact, the class hierarchy is often almost entirely flat. In the hundreds of ActiveRecord classes we have put into production, we have rarely felt the need for even single table inheritance, much less any more exotic techniques.

4.8 Transactions, Concurrency, and Performance

In many applications, the database owns the data, so the performance and the correctness of the database are paramount. Part of the goal of O/RM frameworks is to shield programmers from the complexity of the database. Indeed, much of the programming with a good O/RM design can focus on the business logic, leaving the "hard stuff" to the O/RM.

But that is *much* of the programming, not all. Programmers still have to worry about three (at least!) data-related tasks:

- Related units of work must be grouped together and succeed or fail as a unit. Otherwise, the combinations of partial failures create an explosion of complexity. This problem is solved with transactions.

- The "read for update" scenario must be optimized to balance concurrent readers with data integrity. By far the best first step here is optimistic locking.

- For performance reasons, navigation through the object model should aim for one database operation (or less) per user operation. The danger to avoid is something closer to one database operation *per row* in some table. The most common of these problems is the well-known N+1 problem.

Next we will show how ActiveRecord handles transactions, optimistic locking, and the N+1 problem.

Local Transactions

Hibernate includes a Transaction API that maps to the transactional capabilities of the underlying database. Here is an example that groups multiple operations into a single transaction:

code/hibernate_examples/src/Validations.java

```java
public void saveUsersInTx(User... users) {
  Session sess = HibernateUtil.sf.getCurrentSession();
  Transaction tx = sess.beginTransaction();
  try {
    for (User user: users) {
      sess.save(user);
    }
    tx.commit();
  } catch (HibernateException e) {
    tx.rollback();
    throw e;
  }
}
```

The saveUsersInTx method loops over an array of user objects, attempting to save each one. These users have the declarative validations described in Section 4.5, *Validating Data Values*, on page 94. If all the users are valid, each save will succeed, and the tx.commit will write all the users in the database. But if any individual users are invalid, the Validator will throw a HibernateException. If this happens, the call to tx.rollback will undo any previous saves within the transaction. In fact, "undo" is not quite the right word. The other saves will simply never happen.

Here is the ActiveRecord version:

code/rails_xt/app/models/user.rb

```
def User.save(*users)
  User.transaction do
    users.each {|user| user.save!}
  end
end
```

Any ActiveRecord class, such as User, has a transaction method that starts a transaction on the underlying connection. Commit and rollback are implicit. Exceptions that exit the block cause a rollback. Normal exit from the block causes a commit. The rules are simple and easy to remember.

ActiveRecord also supports transactional semantics on the objects themselves. When you pass arguments to transaction, those arguments are also protected by a transaction. If the database rolls back, the individual property values on the model objects roll back also. The implementation is a clever demonstration of Ruby, but in practice this feature is rarely used. In web applications, ActiveRecord instances are usually bound to forms. So, we want them to hold on to any bad values so that the user can have a chance to correct them.

All Other Transactions

Hibernate's transaction support goes far beyond the local transactions described previously. The two most important are container-managed transactions and distributed transactions.

With container-managed (a.k.a. declarative) transactions, programmers do not write explicit transactional code. Instead, application code runs inside a container that starts, commits, and aborts transactions at the right times. The "right times" are specified in a configuration file, usually in XML. ActiveRecord provides no support for container-managed transactions, and we rarely miss them. (Anything that can be done with container-managed transactions can also be done with programmatic transactions.)

Distributed transactions manage data across different databases. And, they manage data even across databases, message queues, and file systems. ActiveRecord provides no support for distributed transactions, and when we miss them, we miss them acutely. *Rails is currently unsuitable for systems that must enforce transactional semantics across different databases.* But chin up! The JRuby team (http://www.jruby.org) is working to make JRuby on Rails viable. Once it is, we will have access to Java's transaction APIs.

Optimistic Locking

Imagine a world without optimistic locking.

Jane: *I'd like to see available flights between Raleigh-Durham and Chicago.*

Computer: *Here you go!*

John: *Can you help me plan a trip from Chicago to Boston?*

Computer: *Sorry, Jane is making travel plans right now. Please ask again later.*

Many application scenarios are read-for-update: Look at a list of available flights and seats, and then buy some tickets. The problem is balancing data integrity and throughput. If only Jane can use the system (or a particular table or a particular row in a table), then data integrity is assured, but John is stuck waiting. If you let John and Jane use the system, you run the risk that they will make conflicting updates.

You can employ many tricks to balance data integrity and throughput. One of the simplest and most effective is optimistic locking with a version column in the database. Each data row keeps a version number column. When users read a row, they read the version number as well. When they attempt to update the row, they increment the version number. Updates are conditional: They update the row only if the version number is unchanged. Now both John and Jane can use the system. Every so often, John will try to update a row that has just been changed by Jane. To prevent Jane's change from being lost, we ask John to start over, using the new data. Optimistic locking works well because update collisions are rare in most systems—usually John and Jane both get to make their changes.

Optimistic locking is trivial in Hibernate. Define a column in the database and an associated JavaBean property in your model object. Usually the JavaBean property is called version:

`code/hibernate_examples/src/Person.java`
```java
private int version;
public int getVersion() { return version;}
public void setVersion(int version) {
  this.version = version;
}
```

In the Hibernate configuration file for Person, associate the version property with the version column in the database. If the database column is named lock_version, like so:

`code/hibernate_examples/config/person.hbm.xml`

```
<version name="version" column='lock_version'/>
```

then Hibernate will populate the version column when reading a Person and will attempt to increment the column when updating a Person. If the version column has changed, Hibernate will throw a StaleObject-StateException. ActiveRecord approaches locking in the same way, with one additional twist. If you name your column lock_version, ActiveRecord does optimistic locking automatically. There is no code or configuration to be added to your application.

All the tables in the Rails XT application use lock_version. Here's what happens when both John and Jane try to reset the same user's password at the same time. First, Jane begins with this:

`code/rails_xt/test/unit/user_test.rb`

```
aaron = User.find_by_email('aaron@example.com')
aaron.password = aaron.password_confirmation = 'setme'
```

Elsewhere, John is doing almost the same thing:

```
u = User.find_by_email('aaron@example.com')
u.password = u.password_confirmation = 'newpass'
```

Jane saves her changes first:

```
aaron.save
```

Then John tries to save:

```
u.save
```

Since Jane's change got in first, John's update will fail with a Active-Record::StaleObjectError.

If your naming convention does not match ActiveRecord's, you can override it. To tell ActiveRecord that the User class uses a column named version, you would say this:

```
class User < ActiveRecord::Base
  set_locking_column :version
end
```

You can turn off optimistic locking entirely with this:

```
ActiveRecord::Base.lock_optimistically = false
```

Sometimes existing data schemas cannot be modified to include a version column. Hibernate can do version checking based on the entire record if you set optimistic-lock="all". ActiveRecord does not support this.

Preventing the N+1 Problem

The N+1 problem is easy to demonstrate. Imagine that you want to print the name of each person, followed by each author's quips. First, get all the people:

```
$ script/console
>>people = Person.find(:all)
```

Now, iterate over the people, printing their names and their quips:

```
>> people.each do |p|
?>    puts p.full_name
?>    p.quips do |q|
?>      puts q.text
>>    end
>> end
```

This code works fine and is easy to understand. The problem is on the database side. After trying the previous code, refer to the most recent entries in log/development.log. You will see something like this:

```
Person Load (0.004605)   SELECT * FROM people
Person Columns (0.003437)   SHOW FIELDS FROM people
Quip Load (0.005988)   SELECT * FROM quips WHERE (quips.author_id = 1)
Quip Load (0.009707)   SELECT * FROM quips WHERE (quips.author_id = 2)
```

Our call to Person.find triggered the Person Load.... Then, for each person in the database, you will see a Quip Load.... If you have N people in the database, then this simple code requires N+1 trips to the database: one trip to get the people and then N more trips (one for each person's quips).

Database round-trips are expensive. We know in advance that we want all the quips for each person. So, we could improve performance by getting all the people, and all their associated quips, in one trip to the database. The performance gain can be enormous. The N+1 problem gets worse quickly as you have more data or more complicated relationships between tables.

SQL (Structured Query Language) excels at specifying the exact set of rows you want. But we use O/RM frameworks such as Hibernate and ActiveRecord to avoid having to deal with (much) SQL. Since the N+1 problem is so important, O/RM frameworks usually provide ways to avoid it. In Hibernate, you can add a hint to your query operation to specify what other data you will need next. If you are getting the people but you will be needing the quips too, you can say this:

`code/hibernate_examples/src/TransactionTest.java`

```java
Criteria c = sess.createCriteria(Person.class)
                  .setFetchMode("quips", FetchMode.JOIN);
Set people = new HashSet(c.list());
```

The setFetchMode tells Hibernate to use SQL that will bring back any associated quips. The resulting list will repeat instances of Person to match each Quip, so we use the HashSet to narrow down to *unique* people.

With ActiveRecord, you can specify relationships to preload with the :include option:

```
>> p = Person.find(:all, :include=>:quips)
```

If you want the control possible with raw SQL, you can do that too. In Hibernate, here is the code:

`code/hibernate_examples/src/TransactionTest.java`

```java
SQLQuery q = sess.createSQLQuery("SELECT p.* FROM PEOPLE p")
                 .addEntity(Person.class);
Set people = new HashSet(q.list());
```

And in ActiveRecord, here it is:

```
>> p = Person.find_by_sql("SELECT * from people")
```

4.9 Conserving Resources with Connection Pooling

Hibernate and other Java OR/M frameworks all manage connection pooling in some fashion. Hibernate comes with a default connection pooling mechanism and is easily configurable to use third-party pool managers. Hibernate requires this flexibility because of the wide variety of application types in which it can be used. ActiveRecord, on the other hand, was designed for a single application type: web applications. Any decent web server is already going to provide built-in pooling in the form of thread pooling; ActiveRecord simplifies the connection pooling problem by offloading to the thread pooler of the web server.

This means although Hibernate assigns connections into a (presumably thread-safe) external pool of connections, ActiveRecord assigns open connections into thread-local storage. All requests to the server are dispatched to one of those worker threads, and the ActiveRecord classes bound to those threads will share the open connections found there. As long as ActiveRecord is used in a production-quality web server, this pattern works.

However, if you attempt to use ActiveRecord in another setting, say a hand-rolled distributed application or behind a RubyQT front end, then the open-connection-per-thread strategy is likely to fail. Depending on how threads are created, pooled, or abandoned, the database connections may not be harvested in a timely fashion or at all. If the threads are abandoned and the connections are left in an open but inaccessible state, then eventually the database will run out of available connection resources, thereby shutting down the application.

These scenarios are rare; ActiveRecord was built for Rails, and Rails was built for the Web. To appease the rest of the world, though, a patch is in the works that provides a more robust connection pooling strategy.

For many people, ActiveRecord is the crowning achievement of Rails. It does not provide a kitchen sink of O/RM services, but it delivers the "Active Record" design pattern with an API that is clean, simple, and beautiful. Now that you have access to data, it is time to move your attention to how you can operate on that data through a web interface.

4.10 Resources

Composite Primary Keys for Ruby on Rails. . .
. . . http://compositekeys.rubyforge.org/
The composite_primary_keys plugin lets you deal with composite primary keys in a Rails application.

Crossing Borders: Exploring ActiveRecord. . .
. . . http://www-128.ibm.com/developerworks/java/library/j-cb03076/index.html
Bruce Tate does a nice job introducing ActiveRecord, as well as comparing it to various options in Java.

iBatis . . . . http://ibatis.apache.org/
iBatis is a data mapper framework. A data mapper might be better than the "Active Record" design pattern if you need much more control at the SQL level. iBatis has been ported to Ruby and so is an option if you need to write a Rails application that accesses legacy data schemas.

Chapter 5

Coordinating Activities with ActionController

Controllers coordinate the activities of views and models in the MVC paradigm. Controllers are responsible for the following:

- Collecting input from the user
- Creating model objects to handle the user's request
- Selecting the appropriate view code to render

Along the way, controllers are responsible for logic that is associated with the user request (as opposed to with a specific model object). Such logic includes the following:

- Authentication and authorization
- Business rules that involve multiple model objects
- Auditing
- Error handling

In addition to these responsibilities, most web application frameworks give controllers a web-specific responsibility as well. Web controllers provide an object model wrapper for the idioms of the Web: URLs, HTTP requests, headers, cookies, and so on. At the controller level, web applications are explicitly *web* programming. (By contrast, the model layer code is much more likely to be reusable outside of a web app.) In Rails, the ActionController library implements the controller layer. In this chapter, we will introduce ActionController by comparing it to a Struts application. We will start with basic CRUD and then drill in to more advanced issues such as session management, filters, and caching.

5.1 Routing Basics: From URL to Controller+Method

To access a web application, you need a URL. For our Struts sample application, the people list view lives at /appfuse_people/editPerson.html? method=Search. How does this URL get routed to running code in a Java web application? Typically, the first part of the name (appfuse_people) identifies a .war file or directory on the server that corresponds to a particular web application. Java applications often include an Ant task to copy the application code and resources to the appropriate directory on the server.

`code/appfuse_people/build.xml`

```xml
<target name="deploy-web" depends="compile-jsp" if="tomcat.home"
    description="deploy only web classes to servlet container's deploy directory

    <echo message="Deploying web application to ${tomcat.home}/webapps"/>
    <copy todir="${tomcat.home}/webapps/${webapp.name}">
        <fileset dir="${webapp.target}"
            excludes="**/web-test.xml,**/web.xml,**/*-resources.xml"/>
    </copy>

</target>
```

For a Struts application, the next part of the name (editPerson.html) is pattern matched to the Struts ActionServlet via a servlet and servlet-mapping elements in web.xml. Many Struts applications use the distinctive .do suffix; in our example, we have followed AppFuse's lead in simply using .html:

`code/appfuse_people/web/WEB-INF/web.xml`

```xml
<servlet>
  <servlet-name>action</servlet-name>
  <servlet-class>org.apache.struts.action.ActionServlet</servlet-class>
  <load-on-startup>2</load-on-startup>
</servlet>

<servlet-mapping>
  <servlet-name>action</servlet-name>
  <url-pattern>*.html</url-pattern>
</servlet-mapping>
```

These two steps do not exist in Rails development. Rails does not run more than one web application within a process—if you want multiple web applications, you run them in separate processes. Since *all* Rails code is routed to the ActionController layer, you don't have to take a separate configuration step to specify "I want to use ActionController." Rails applications also do not copy files into the web server during development. During development, Rails code is written and executed in a single directory tree. This is part of the reason that Rails application development is so interactive: changes take effect immediately, without a deploy step.

Most Java developers find ways to simplify these two steps. Frameworks such as AppFuse create the appropriate build.xml and web.xml settings for you. Inspired in part by Rails, many Java developers now run their development code from the same directory, avoiding part of the overhead of the compile/deploy cycle.

The more important part of routing happens within the Struts Action-Servlet and Rails ActionController. Struts uses settings in struts-config.xml to convert editPerson.html?method=Search into a method call:

```
<action
  path="/editPerson"
  type="com.relevancellc.people.webapp.action.PersonAction" ...
```

The path attribute matches editPerson to the class named by the type attribute: PersonAction. Finally, the query string ?method=Search leads us to the search method on PersonAction.

The Rails URL for the people list view is /people/list. Just as with Struts, Rails uses routing to convert this URL into a method on an object. In Rails, the routing is described not with XML but with Ruby code. Here is a simple routing file:

code/people/config/routes.rb

```
ActionController::Routing::Routes.draw do |map|
  map.connect ':controller/:action/:id'
end
```

The :controller portion of the route maps the first portion of the URL to a controller class. A standard convention for capitalization and class naming is used, so people becomes PeopleController. The mechanism is general, so this routing entry also implies that a URL that begins with foo will attempt to find a (nonexistent in this case) FooController. The :action portion of the route maps the second location component to a method. So, list invokes the list method. Again, the mechanism is general, so /people/foo would attempt to find a nonexistent foo method on the PeopleController. Finally, the :id maps to an id parameter, which is optional. In methods such as create and update that need an object to operate on, the id is conventionally a primary key.

Many opponents of Rails have criticized this default routing because they do not like the implied naming scheme. This entirely misses the point. Rails default routing makes *trivial things trivial*. It is easy to bring up a Rails server with a bunch of controllers that use this default route. The design philosophy is "pay as you go." The default routing gives you something simple, generic, and free. If you want more control, you can have that too, but you have to write some routing configuration, just as you do in Struts. You will see more advanced routing in Section 5.6, *Routing in Depth*, on page 133.

5.2 List and Show Actions: The R in CRUD

Now that we can route from URLs to code, let's look at the code. In our Struts application, /appfuse_people/editPerson.html?method=Search takes us to the search method of PersonAction:

```
code/appfuse_people/src/web/com/relevancellc/people/webapp/action/PersonAction.java
public ActionForward search(ActionMapping mapping, ActionForm form,
                            HttpServletRequest request,
                            HttpServletResponse response)
   throws Exception {
  PersonManager mgr = (PersonManager) getBean("personManager");
  List people = mgr.getPeople(null);
  request.setAttribute(Constants.PERSON_LIST, people);
  return mapping.findForward("list");
}
```

The signature of the method contains specific parameters for accessing the web object model (request and response) and the Struts object model (mapping and form). The object model is then used to load the people, and forward to the view, through the following steps:

1. On line 5, we look up the manager object that will actually do the work.

2. On line 6, we get the people object that will be rendered in the view.

3. On line 7, we add the people to the request, which makes the people available to the view.

4. Finally on line 8, we select the view that should render the list.

Behind the scenes is a lot of layering. The manager in its turn delegates to a DAO, which actually does the data access. The manager and DAO layers require two Java source files each: an interface to the layer and at least one implementation. In addition, the connections between layers are configured using Spring Dependency Injection. At the end of the chain, here is the code that does the work:

```
code/appfuse_people/src/dao/com/relevancellc/people/dao/hibernate/PersonDaoHibernate.java
public List getPeople(Person person) {
  return getHibernateTemplate().find("from Person");
}
```

If you understand how this all works in Struts, the transition to Rails is straightforward. A typical Rails controller does the same steps. This is not obvious at first, because at every step, the Rails approach makes a different stylistic choice. Here is the code:

```
code/people/app/controllers/people_controller.rb
def list
  @search = params[:search]
  if @search.blank?
    @person_pages, @people = paginate :people, :per_page => 10
  else
    query = ['first_name = :search or last_name = :search',
            {:search=>@search}]
    @person_pages, @people = paginate :people,
                                :per_page => 10, :conditions=>query
  end
end
```

The Rails list has no parameters! Of course, the same kinds of information are available. The difference is that the request and response objects are member variables (with accessor methods) on the controller. The Java philosophy here is "Explicit is better. It is easy to read a Struts action and see what objects you should be working with." The Rails philosophy is "Implicit is better, at least for things that are common. This is a web app, so requests and responses are pretty common! Learn them once, and never have to type or read them again."

The Rails list does not delegate to intermediate layers. There is no manager or DAO layer, just a call to paginate, which in turn directly accesses ActiveRecord. This is certainly an important difference, and we want to be careful in laying out why we think both the Java and Rails strategies make sense. Imagine the following conversation between Rita the Rails developer and Jim the Java developer:

Rita: *Why do you bother with all those layers?*

Jim: *The layers make it easier to test the code and to reuse the code in different contexts. For example, the manager layer has no web depen-*

dencies, so that code can be reused in a Swing application or over an RMI connection.

Rita: *Still, it must take forever to write all that extra code.*

Jim: *It isn't so bad. We have much more elaborate IDE support in the Java world. Plus, tools such as AppFuse or Maven can be used to do a lot of the boilerplate work. Aren't you worried that your Rails app is a dead end and that your code is inflexible and untestable?*

Rita: *Not at all. I am building the layers I need right now. If I need more layers later, it is much easier to add them. Dynamic typing makes it much easier to plug in new code or execute the existing code in a new context.*

Jim: *But with dynamic typing, how do you make sure your code works? I am used to the compiler making sure that variables are of the correct type.*

Rita: *We validate our code with unit tests, functional tests, integration tests, black-box tests, code reviews, and code coverage. Do you do the same?*

Jim: *You bet!*

In short, the Java approach (lots of layers, dependency injection, good tooling) is a reasonable response to Java's class-centric, statically typed object model. The Ruby approach (layers on demand, less tooling) is a reasonable approach to Ruby's object-centric, dynamically typed object model.

The Rails list method creates person_pages and people variables, but it does nothing to make these variables available to the view. Again, the difference is that Rails does things *implicitly*. When you create instance variables in a controller method, they are automatically copied into the view using reflection. This approach takes advantage of the fact that Ruby classes are open, and this approach can pick up arbitrary variables at any time.

Finally, the Rails code does not appear to select a view to render. Again, this is because Rails provides an implicit default behavior. When you exit a controller method, the default behavior is to render a view template file named app/views/{controllername}/{methodname}.rhtml. As you will see next, Rails provides a render method that you can use to override this behavior.

Now that you have seen the list action, you will look at the code for showing an edit form for a single person. Our Struts implementation uses a single action named edit for both the "new" and "update" varieties:

```
code/appfuse_people/src/web/com/relevancellc/people/webapp/action/PersonAction.java
public ActionForward edit(ActionMapping mapping, ActionForm form,
                          HttpServletRequest request,
                          HttpServletResponse response)
    throws Exception {
  PersonForm personForm = (PersonForm) form;
  if (personForm.getId() != null) {
    PersonManager mgr = (PersonManager) getBean("personManager");
    Person person = mgr.getPerson(personForm.getId());
    personForm = (PersonForm) convert(person);
    updateFormBean(mapping, request, personForm);
  }
  return mapping.findForward("edit");
}
```

This code goes through the same series of steps you saw earlier: Call into another layer to get the object, put the object into request scope, and select the mapping to the view. The novel part is interacting with the form bean. The form is an instance of PersonForm. The form bean represents the web form data associated with a person. Because the form is functionally a subset of a Person model, the form bean class can be autogenerated. You can accomplish this with an XDoclet tag at the top of the Person class:

```
@struts.form include-all="true" extends="BaseForm"
```

To display an edit form, the edit action needs to copy data from the model person to its form representation. The convert method does this. You could write individual convert methods for each model/form pair in an application. A far simpler approach is to use JavaBean introspection to write a generic convert method. Our approach uses a generic convert method that is included in AppFuse.

The Rails equivalent uses two actions: new and edit:

```
code/people/app/controllers/people_controller.rb
def edit
  @person = Person.find(params[:id])
end

def new
  @person = Person.new
end
```

The Rails version does the same things but in a different way. In Rails applications, there is no distinction between model objects and form beans; ActiveRecord objects serve both purposes. As a result, there is no form argument or convert step. The Rails version has two methods because Rails applications typically render "new" and "edit" with two different templates. (This is not as redundant as it sounds; the two templates delegate to a single partial template that actually draws the form.)

5.3 Create, Update, and Delete Actions

Create, update, and delete actions tend to have more interesting code because they alter state. As a result, they have to deal with validation, status messages, and redirection. Here is a Struts action method that will save or update a person:

`code/appfuse_people/src/web/com/relevancellc/people/webapp/action/PersonAction.java`

```java
public ActionForward save(ActionMapping mapping, ActionForm form,
                          HttpServletRequest request,
                          HttpServletResponse response)
    throws Exception {
  ActionMessages messages = new ActionMessages();
  PersonForm personForm = (PersonForm) form;
  boolean isNew = ("".equals(personForm.getId()));
  PersonManager mgr = (PersonManager) getBean("personManager");
  Person person = (Person) convert(personForm);
  mgr.savePerson(person);
  if (isNew) {
    messages.add(ActionMessages.GLOBAL_MESSAGE,
        new ActionMessage("person.added"));
    saveMessages(request.getSession(), messages);
    return mapping.findForward("mainMenu");
  } else {
    messages.add(ActionMessages.GLOBAL_MESSAGE,
        new ActionMessage("person.updated"));
    saveMessages(request, messages);
    return mapping.findForward("viewPeople");
  }
}
```

Let's begin by considering the happy case where the user's edits are successful. Much of this code is similar to previous examples; the new part is the addition of a status message. In line 5 we create an Action-Messages instance to hold a status message, and in lines 12–14 and 17–19 we save the ActionMessages into the request so they can be rendered in the view.

Here is the Rails version of update:

```
code/people/app/controllers/people_controller.rb
def update
  @person = Person.find(params[:id])
  if @person.update_attributes(params[:person])
    flash[:notice] = 'Person was successfully updated.'
    redirect_to :action => 'show', :id => @person
  else
    render :action => 'edit'
  end
end
```

The actual update happens on line 3. update_attributes is an ActiveRecord method that sets multiple attributes all at once. Like its cousins create and save, update_attributes automatically performs validations. Since the params[:person] hash contains all the name/value pairs from the input form, a single call to update_attributes does everything necessary to update the @person instance.

Like the Struts update, the Rails version of update sets a status message. In line 4, the message "Person was successfully updated." is added to a special object called the *flash*. The flash is designed to deal with the fact that updates are generally followed by redirects. *flash*

So, saving a status into a member variable does no good—after the redirect, the status variable will be lost. Saving into the session instead will work, but then you have to remember to remove the status message from the session later. And that is exactly what the flash does: saves an object into the session and then automatically removes the status message after the next redirect.

The flash is a clever trick. Unfortunately, the data that is typically put into the flash is not clever at all. Out of the box, Rails does not support internationalization, and status messages are stored directly as strings (usually in English).

Contrast this with the Struts application, which stores keys such as "person.added." The view can later use these keys to look up an appropriately localized string. The lack of internationalization support is one of the big missing pieces in Rails. If your application needs internationalization, you will have to roll your own or use a third-party library.

After a successful update operation, the controller should redirect to a URL that does a read operation. This makes it less likely that a user will bookmark a URL that does an update, which will lead to odd results later. Some possible choices are a show view of the object just edited, a list view of similar objects, or a top-level view. The Struts version does the redirect by calling findForward:

```
return mapping.findForward("mainMenu");
```

To verify that this forward does a redirect, you can consult the struts.xml configuration file. Everything looks good:

```
<global-forwards>
  <forward name="mainMenu" path="/mainMenu.html" redirect="true"/>
  <!-- etc. -->
</global-forwards>
```

Where Struts uses findForward for both renders and redirects, Rails has two separate methods. After a save, the controller issues an explicit redirect:

```
redirect_to :action => 'show', :id => @person
```

Notice that the redirect is named in terms of actions and parameters. Rails runs its routing table "backward" to convert from actions and parameters back into a URL. When using default routes, this URL will be /people/show/(some_int).

Now that you have seen a successful update, we'll show the case where the update fails. Both Struts and Rails provide mechanisms to validate user input.

In Struts, the Validator object automatically validates form beans, based on declarative settings in an XML file. Validations are associated with the form. To specify that the first name is required, you can use XML like this:

`code/appfuse_people/snippets/person_form.xml`

```
<form name="personForm">
  <field property="firstName" depends="required">
      <arg0 key="personForm.firstName"/>
  </field>
  <!-- other fields -->
</form>
```

The original intention of the discrete validation language was separation of concerns. Sometimes it is more convenient to keep related concerns together. Instead of writing the validation.xml file by hand, we generate the validations with XDoclet annotations in the Person model class in this way:

```
code/appfuse_people/src/dao/com/relevancellc/people/model/Person.java
/**
 * @hibernate.property column="first_name" length="50"
 * @struts.validator type="required"
 */
public String getFirstName() {
  return firstName;
}
```

During an Ant build step, the struts.validator annotation generates the appropriate lines in the validation.xml file. (In Java 5 and later, annotations provide a simpler and more integrated annotation mechanism.) In Rails, there's no separate form bean, and the validations are declared on the Person model class directly. You have already seen this in Section 4.5, *Validating Data Values*, on page 94:

```
code/people/app/models/person.rb
class Person < ActiveRecord::Base
  validates_presence_of :first_name, :last_name
end
```

Both the Struts version and the Rails version handle a validation error in the same way: Render the page again, with error messages marking the form fields that need to be corrected. In Struts, this redirection is handled in the Validator. Form beans such as PersonForm extend a Struts class, org.apache.struts.validator.ValidatorForm. The ValidatorForm class provides a validate method. The Struts framework calls validate automatically, and if any item fails validation, the form page is rendered again. The Rails approach is more explicit. When you call save or update_attributes on an ActiveRecord model, a boolean false may indicate a validation failure. If this happens, you can use render to render the edit action again:

```
code/people/snippets/update_fails.rb
if @person.update_attributes(params[:person])
  # ...success case elided...
else
  render :action => 'edit'
end
```

The validation errors are stored in the errors property on the @person object, so you do not need to do anything else to pass the errors to the form view. Section 6.5, *Building HTML Forms*, on page 156 describes how validations are rendered in the view.

The standard create and update actions in Rails do not demonstrate any additional platform features, so we will speak no more of them.

5.4 Tracking User State with Sessions

The Web is mostly stateless. In other words, HTTP requests carry with them all the information needed to locate/generate a response. State-lessness simplifies the interaction model between clients and servers and helps web applications to scale. It is easy to add "dumb" caches, proxies, and load balancers. Such intermediaries do not have to know anything about the previous state of the conversation, because *no previous state exists*.

Programmers can make the Web stateful by adding server-side sessions. Instead of having the entire conversation "in the open" in the request and response traffic, clients gradually build up state on the server. The server associates this state with a unique key, which it passes to the client (typically via HTTP cookies). This stateful view of the web produces a much more complicated picture. Intermediaries such as caches cannot return a cached value for a stateful URL, because an URL no longer uniquely identifies a resource. To generate the correct response, you now need an URL, the client's cookie, and the associated (application-specific) state on the server.

This sounds like an airtight argument against sessions, and it would be if scalability was the sole objective. The catch is that sessions can be very useful. Sessions are commonly used for all kinds of purposes:

- Sessions maintain user identity information for authentication and authorization purposes.

- Sessions store state in progress, where users have made intermediate decisions but have not made a final commitment. The ubiquitous "shopping cart" is a good example.

- Sessions are sometimes used to store user-interface preferences, including locale.

You have already seen one use of the session. In the update scenario set out in Section 5.3, *Create, Update, and Delete Actions*, on page 122, both the Struts and Rails applications used the session to keep status information alive long enough to survive a client-side redirect. In this section, we will look in more detail at the session API. But remember the scalability issue, and avoid session data where feasible.

In Java, the session is a property of the request object:

code/appfuse_people/src/web/com/relevancellc/people/webapp/filter/LocaleFilter.java

```
HttpSession session = request.getSession(false);
```

The session object exposes a simple API for managing name/value pairs. The following code is storing a Locale instance in the user's session:

code/appfuse_people/src/web/com/relevancellc/people/webapp/filter/LocaleFilter.java

```
session.setAttribute(Constants.PREFERRED_LOCALE_KEY, preferredLocale);
```

In Rails, the session is a property of the controller instance. Like its Java counterpart, the Rails session exposes a simple API for managing name/value pairs. The following code is from the acts_as_authenticated plugin:

code/rails_xt/lib/authenticated_system.rb

```
def store_location
  session[:return_to] = request.request_uri
end
```

The store_location method is called when we redirect a user to login. The current URL is stored under the :return_to key in the session. Then, after a successful login, we can redirect the user back to where she was headed and clear the session value:

code/rails_xt/lib/authenticated_system.rb

```
def redirect_back_or_default(default)
  session[:return_to] ? redirect_to_url(session[:return_to]) \
                      : redirect_to(default)
  session[:return_to] = nil
end
```

The Java and Rails session APIs have an annoyance in common: Both manage name/value collections without using language idioms already suited to the purpose. In Java servlets, the session does not implement HashMap, and in Rails the session does not implement all the methods of a Hash. But other than this minor nit, both APIs are easy to learn and use. The interesting part of sessions is not the API but the underlying issues of concurrency and scalability, which we will turn to next.

In Java, more than one user action can be active in a single servlet process. As a result, access to the session object must be protected with thread synchronization primitives. This is trickier than most people think, and even synchronization may not be enough. Brian Goetz, the lead author of *Java Concurrency in Practice* [Goe06], points out that the following simple code example is broken, *regardless* of any concurrency primitives you might add:

```
Foo foo = session.getAttribute("foo");
foo.setBar(newBar);
```

The problem is that the session mechanism doesn't know the session has changed, because it doesn't know that foo has changed. To avoid this problem, you need to reset attributes that are already in the session:

```
Foo foo = session.getAttribute("foo");
foo.setBar(newBar);
//make sure that session knows something changed!
session.setAttribute("foo", foo);
```

Rails does not suffer from this problem, because *Rails always resaves the session, regardless of whether the session has changed.* This eliminates a subtle source of bugs, but it makes sessions even more expensive. Every use of a Rails session implies a read and a write of the session store. When you tune for performance, you will want to disable sessions wherever they are not needed. You can turn off sessions in a controller with the following:

```
session :off
```

Or, you can do it with this on a per-action basis:

```
session :off, :only => %w[index list rss]
```

Session performance and scalability depends greatly on how sessions are stored. In Rails, as in Java web frameworks, you can use a number of different options for session storage. Here are a few rules to get you started:

- The default session store uses files on the file system. This is suitable for development but is undesirable for most deployment scenarios.

- You can use ActiveRecord to store the sessions in the database. To turn this on for a project, create and run a migration to add the sessions table:

  ```
  rake db:sessions:create
  rake db:migrate
  ```

  Then, uncomment the following line in your environment.rb:

  code/rails_xt/config/environment.rb

  ```
  config.action_controller.session_store = :active_record_store
  ```

Use ActiveRecord session storage until profiling shows that you have a performance issue, and then consult the resources at the end of this chapter.

5.5 Managing Cross-Cutting Concerns with Filters and Verify

It is possible to build complex web applications with nothing more than the basic CRUD actions described in the previous sections. It's possible but wasteful.

Often, program logic will need to apply to multiple actions or even multiple controllers. These elements are called *cross-cutting concerns*. Descriptions of cross-cutting concerns often cite security, logging, and transactions. In addition to these, validation and redirection rules may sometimes be generic enough for a cross-cutting approach.

cross-cutting concerns

Let's begin with logging. If you want to log that a particular action is called, you can simply add a call to the method itself. In the Struts application, you could do this:

code/appfuse_people/src/web/com/relevancellc/people/webapp/action/PersonAction.java
```
public ActionForward delete(ActionMapping mapping, ActionForm form,
                            HttpServletRequest request,
                            HttpServletResponse response)
   throws Exception {
 if (log.isDebugEnabled()) {
   log.debug("Entering delete method");
 }
```

You could do the same thing in Rails:

code/people/app/controllers/people_controller.rb
```
def destroy
  logger.debug('Entering delete method')
```

If you wanted to log *all* action methods, this approach would be tedious. Instead, you might choose to use a servlet filter to add logging. To define a servlet filter, you create an instance of javax.servlet.Filter whose doFilter method gets a chance to process requests before and after they are routed to a servlet.

Here is a Filter that will log the request URI before dispatching the request:

code/appfuse_people/src/web/com/relevancellc/people/webapp/filter/LoggingFilter.java

```
public void
doFilter(ServletRequest req, ServletResponse resp, FilterChain filterChain)
    throws IOException, ServletException {
  if (log.isDebugEnabled()) {
    HttpServletRequest r= (HttpServletRequest)req;
    log.debug("Entering " + r.getRequestURI());
  }
  filterChain.doFilter(req, resp);
}
```

To associate this filter with some set of URLs, you also need to give the filter a name in web.xml:

code/appfuse_people/web/WEB-INF/web.xml

```
<filter>
  <filter-name>loggingFilter</filter-name>
  <filter-class>com.relevancellc.people.webapp.filter.LoggingFilter</filter-class
</filter>
```

With this name, you can associate the loggingFilter with some specific URLs. To log any calls related to people, you would add the following to web.xml:

code/appfuse_people/web/WEB-INF/web.xml

```
<filter-mapping>
  <filter-name>loggingFilter</filter-name>
  <url-pattern>/appfuse_people/*</url-pattern>
</filter-mapping>
```

In Rails, you can create filter methods within the controller itself. To add logging before every action on the PeopleController, add the following line to PeopleController:

code/people/app/controllers/people_controller.rb

```
before_filter do |controller|
  logger.debug "About to handle #{controller.action_name}"
end
```

The before_filter block is invoked before every action method. Let's look at the various ways this differs from the servlet filter approach. First, the servlet filter has explicit parameters for the request and response. The Rails before_filter has a controller block parameter. The request and response are available through methods on controller.

The servlet filter's doFilter method also has a third parameter, filterChain. The filterChain forwards processing on to the next filter in the chain (or to the servlet if this is the last filter in the chain). In Rails, passing control to the next filter in the chain is implicit, based on the return value of before_filter. If a Rails before_filter returns true, control passes to the next filter. If a before_filter returns false, processing completes.

The servlet filter approach gives each filter an explicit name, where the previous before_filter uses an anonymous block. As an alternative, you can pass a symbol to before_filter, naming a method to be invoked as a before filter. Here is a before_filter with a named log_action:

```
code/people/app/controllers/people_controller.rb
```
```
before_filter :log_action
def log_action
  logger.debug "About to handle #{self.action_name}"
end
```

The servlet filter can apply to a subset of URLs, based on the filter-mapping configuration in web.xml. In Rails, you can apply a before_filter to a subset of actions, by using the :only and :except options. This before_filter logs only the index and show actions:

```
code/people/app/controllers/people_controller.rb
```
```
before_filter :log_action, :only=>[:index,:show]
```

This before_filter uses except to log all actions except index:

```
code/people/app/controllers/people_controller.rb
```
```
before_filter :log_action, :except=>[:index]
```

In addition to before_filter, Rails controllers can also use around_filter and after_filter. As their names suggest, these methods execute around and after controller actions, respectively.

Because the servlet filter is applied at the URL level, it is possible to filter across multiple servlets. If you changed the filter-mapping's url-pattern from /appfuse_people/* to /*, the loggingFilter would apply to all URLs. In Rails, you can affect multiple controllers by moving code to the ApplicationController class at app/controllers/application.rb. ApplicationController is a base class for all controllers, so methods declared there are available to all controllers. Likewise, filters on the ApplicationController class apply to all controllers.

It is worth nothing that servlet filters and Rails filters are not applied at quite the same point in time. Servlet filters are evaluated against the incoming URL, before that URL is converted into an action on a controller. (In fact, the URL may never be converted into an action on a controller, because not all servlets use MVC.) In Rails, the filters are applied at the controller/action level, after the URL has been evaluated against the routing table. In our experience, this distinction has made little difference in practice. Servlet filters and Rails filters tend to be used for the same kinds of tasks. For example, security constraints in Spring ACEGI are enforced by a servlet filter, and in the Rails acts_as_authenticated plugin they are enforced by a before_filter. See Chapter 10, *Security*, on page 267 for details.

One of the most common uses of filters is to redirect requests to a more appropriate endpoint. Rails has specific support for this use case via the verify method. verify takes a single hash, with a set of options that establish prerequisites for an action:

- :except contains the actions to which this verify does not apply.
- :flash contains keys that must be in the flash.
- :method contains the allowed HTTP methods (such as :get).
- :only contains the actions to which this verify applies.
- :params contains keys that must be present in the parameters.
- :session contains keys that must be in the session.
- :xhr can be set to true to require Ajax or to false to forbid it.

The same arguments hash specifies what to do if the conditions are not met:

- :render specifies a template to render.
- :redirect_to specifies a URL to redirect to, using the same arguments as url_for.
- :add_flash adds name/value pairs to the flash.

The Rails scaffold provides a good example of verify. The Rails scaffold defines a common set of actions: show, edit, create, new, list, update, and destroy. Some of these actions alter application state and should require an HTTP POST. Here is the verify:

`code/people/app/controllers/people_controller.rb`

```
verify :method => :post, :only => [ :destroy, :create, :update ],
       :redirect_to => { :action => :list }
```

If a user tries to reach create, update, or delete with any verb other than POST, he will be redirected to GET the list action.

5.6 Routing in Depth

As seen in Section 5.1, *Routing Basics: From URL to Controller+Method*, on page 116, the default Rails route does quite a bit of work. From :controller/:action/:id, you can handle an infinite number of possible controllers, methods, and IDs without ever adding another route. But, your application's structure is directly exposed in every URL. In this section, we will show several examples where design requirements introduce a bit more indirection between URLs and controller code.

First, we will introduce a small bit of terminology. For routing purposes, a URL is composed of *components* separated by dividers. The default route has three components, divided by a slash. Routing converts these components into a controller, an action, and possibly some parameters to the action.

components

Let's start with the login and logout URLs in the Rails XT application. These URLs points to the AccountController's login and logout methods. You will see how these methods work in Section 10.1, *Authentication with the acts_as_authenticated Plugin*, on page 268; for now, our concern is only with the URLs. The users think /account/login is excessive and want to use simply /login instead. Ditto for logout. We add the following lines to routes.rb:

```
code/rails_xt/config/routes.rb
```

```
map.connect 'login', :controller=>'account', :action=>'login'
map.connect 'logout', :controller=>'account', :action=>'logout'
```

The first argument to connect is a *static component*: 'login'. This component exactly matches the same component occurring in the URL. The second argument is a hash specifying the controller and action to call.

static component

Why doesn't the default route specify a controller and action? The default route is composed of components preceded by a colon, such as :controller. These *dynamic components* match any component and assign a named value based on the match. So, :controller matches foo and selects the foo controller. Let's add a route that shows recently edited quips. To see the twenty most recently modified, use /quips/recent/20. If no number is specified, the default should be ten.

dynamic components

```
code/rails_xt/config/routes.rb
```

```
map.connect 'quips/recent/:count',
            :defaults => {:count => '10'},
            :requirements => {:count => /\d+/},
            :controller=>'quips', :action=>'recent'
```

Joe Asks. . .

How Do You Test Routing?

Rails has built-in assertions for testing routing. assert_recognizes asserts that a URL is recognized as you expect, and assert_generates asserts that a set of arguments generate a specific URL. You can test both directions at once with assert_routing. Here is the test code for the routes covered in this section:

code/rails_xt/test/functional/routing_test.rb

```ruby
require File.dirname(__FILE__) + '/../test_helper'

class RoutingTest < Test::Unit::TestCase
  def test_default_route
    assert_routing '/quips/show/1',
      :controller=>'quips', :action=>'show', :id=>'1'
  end

  def test_account_routes
    assert_routing 'login',
      :controller=>'account', :action=>'login'
    assert_routing 'logout',
      :controller=>'account', :action=>'logout'
  end

  def test_recent_routes
    assert_routing '/quips/recent/20',
      :controller=>'quips', :action=>'recent', :count=>'20'
    assert_routing '/quips/recent',
      :controller=>'quips', :action=>'recent', :count=>'10'
  end

  def test_conditional_routes
    assert_routing '/quips/edit/1',
      :controller=>'quips', :action=>'edit', :id=>'1'
  end
end
```

These are functional tests. Functional tests are covered in detail in Section 7.2, *Functional Testing*, on page 193. Routes are also implicitly tested by any test that uses URLs to access functionality, including integration tests (Section 7.4, *Integration Testing*, on page 199) and selenium tests (Section 6.10, *Black-Box Testing with Selenium*, on page 174).

This route demonstrates two new options: requirements and defaults. The requirements option constrains the possible values for a dynamic component. The :count, if specified, must be one or more digits. The defaults option fills in the value for a dynamic component if the component isn't present in the URL. If :count is omitted, params[:count] will be set to '10'. Our tireless users have one final request. The same URL should service both edit and update: /quips/edit. Here's the route:

```
code/rails_xt/config/routes.rb
map.edit 'quips/edit/:id',
         :conditions => {:method => 'get'},
         :controller=>'quips', :action=>'edit'
map.edit 'quips/edit/:id',
         :conditions => {:method => 'post'},
         :controller=>'quips', :action=>'update'
```

This route demonstrates two more features of routing: conditions and named routes. The :conditions clauses allows you to route on things other than just the URL. (This feature requires Rails 1.2.) Here we check the HTTP verb and route GETs one way and POSTs another.

Instead of map.connect, we create a *named route* by calling the arbitrary name map.edit. Named routes generate specially named methods that can be useful for organizing routes into related groups. For example, map.edit creates the method edit_url. You can use edit_url instead of url_for to make code easier to read.

named route

Here we have shown route recognition—how Rails converts URLs into controllers, actions, and parameters. The opposite direction, route generation, deals with how Rails converts controllers, actions, and parameters into URLs. Route generation is covered in Section 6.2, *Minimizing View Code with View Helpers*, on page 151.

5.7 Logging, Debugging, and Benchmarking

Web application frameworks tend to make heavy use of logging for diagnostics and troubleshooting. A good log file can help you reconstruct what happened when a problem occurs or even detect impending problems before they manifest. Web applications tend to make less use of GUI debuggers; nevertheless, a good GUI debugger can be invaluable when tracking a difficult problem. Finally, performance tuning is one of the last steps in developing an application. Simple benchmarking techniques can go a long way toward eliminating performance problems.

The techniques we discuss in this section are not unique to the controller layer. In fact, all these techniques touch the entire application. We chose to cover them here because the controller layer ties everything together. The individual pieces of a well-designed system are often fairly simple. It is when the pieces are pulled together by the controller that tricky and unexpected interactions occur. Logging, debugging, and benchmarking will help you understand these interactions.

Logging

log level

In Java, the de facto standard for logging is an open source project called log4j. To understand log4j, you need to deal with four basic concepts: log levels, appenders, layouts, and loggers. The *log level* specifies the urgency of the log message. Messages range from extremely urgent to informational. There tends to be a reverse correlation with message volume: There are very few urgent messages and potentially an avalanche of informational messages. Most Java developers use a set of predefined log levels:

FATAL

A fatal message is an application's last gasp before expiring in some disastrous way. There should not be many FATAL log entries.

ERROR

An error message indicates a serious condition that probably calls for human intervention (to restart a process, fix a bug, repair corrupt data, and so on).

WARNING

A warning message indicates a potential problem but no immediate error.

INFO

An informational message reports a normal event in a healthy application.

DEBUG

A debug message provides additional information that is useful when debugging a system. Debugging messages are like informational messages, but there may be a lot more of them, and they are usually disabled in production systems.

TRACE

A trace message is used for very fine-grained troubleshooting, like DEBUG but more so. We rarely use TRACE.

An *appender* is a destination to which messages are appended. In development, appenders are usually a console window, a local file, or both. In production, appenders may be more robust and write to a socket or database. A *layout* determines the format of the message, specifying what fields the message includes and how the fields are delimited. Log entries usually include a time stamp and some information about the source of the message, plus the message itself.

appender

layout

Appenders and layouts are configured for one or more *loggers*. Loggers provide named methods for logging messages at the various log levels and route those messages to some number of appenders and layouts. Loggers have names, which are usually associated with Java package names. Names are hierarchical and have a reasonable set of inheritance rules. This lets you say things like "I want all loggers to log messages that have a severity of WARNING (or greater), sending them to a file. I am currently debugging the com.foo package, so set the com.foo logger to severity DEBUG, sending messages to the console."

loggers

Log4j can be configured with a properties file or XML. We prefer the properties file, which is easier to read. Here is the basic appender and layout for the Struts People application:

`code/appfuse_people/web/WEB-INF/classes/log4j.properties`

```
log4j.appender.stdout=org.apache.log4j.ConsoleAppender
log4j.appender.stdout.layout=org.apache.log4j.PatternLayout
```

These lines request console output, with a standard format. The entire file is a few dozen lines and includes some extensions and refinements to these basics settings. The most important is the package-specific settings for log level:

`code/appfuse_people/web/WEB-INF/classes/log4j.properties`

```
log4j.logger.com.relevancellc.people=DEBUG
log4j.logger.com.relevancellc.people.webapp.filter=ERROR
log4j.logger.com.relevancellc.people.webapp.listener.UserCounterListener=WARN
log4j.logger.com.relevancellc.people.util=WARN
```

The com.relevancellc.people package contains our code. We set the level to DEBUG because we want to see quite a bit of information as we develop the application. The three subpackages under com.relevancellc.people contain generated code, which is presumably bug-free. We do not want be buried in detailed log messages from this code, so the log level is turned way down to WARN or ERROR. How did we choose between WARN and ERROR? In this case, we did not choose. When AppFuse created the skeleton of the application, these settings were already in place.

⫯⫰ Joe Asks...
What about JDK 1.4 Logging?

In addition to the log4j package, Java programmers also have access to an official Logging API, which was added to the Java SDK in JDK 1.4. This is a rare, embarrassing example of the community picking one thing (log4j) and the Java Community Process (JCP) picking something different. To make matters worse, there is a metaframework called Commons Logging that lets you code against a generic API and then plug in either log4j or JDK 1.4 logging. Logging is not complicated enough to need this much indirection!

The story of Java logging is an amusing anecdote about how not to write software, but it contributes nothing to the task of learning Ruby and Rails, so we will speak no more of it.

The effect of these settings is that we never see messages from these packages. No news is good news, so we accept the settings and move on.

To log a message, you will need a logger object. In Java, you typically instantiate a logger as a static member of a class:

```
code/appfuse_people/src/web/com/relevancellc/people/webapp/action/BaseAction.java
```

```
protected final Log log = LogFactory.getLog(getClass());
```

Then simply call methods on the logger. Loggers have method names for different log levels, so to log a debug message, use the following:

```
if (log.isDebugEnabled()) {
  log.debug("Entering delete method");
}
```

The call to log.isDebugEnabled is a performance optimization. If logging is disabled for the DEBUG level, then the call to log.debug will return without doing anything. We still pay the overhead of the method call, which is small, and the overhead of creating the arguments to debug, which might be nontrivial. By checking isDebugEnabled, we avoid making a needless call to debug.

Rails' support for logging is simpler and easier to use than log4j's but is less flexible. In Rails, you do not need to configure a logger. Instances of ActiveRecord and ActionController provide a logger method, with a pre-configured logger. The logger has named methods for different log levels, just as in Java. To log an INFO message, do the following:

code/rails_xt/app/controllers/people_controller.rb

```ruby
def destroy
  logger.info "Entering destroy method"
```

That is easy enough, but you will not see that kind of logging in a Rails application often. Rails includes a ton of information in its own logging statements, and this information is often sufficient enough that you do not need to make any additional calls to the logger. Here is the log output from creating a new person:

code/people/snippets/create_person.log

```
Processing PeopleController#create (for 127.0.0.1 at 2006-10-30 11:58:17) [POST]
  Session ID: 08ecf4526b2d1b38406396d58a538e02
  Parameters: {"commit"=>"Create", "action"=>"create",\
"controller"=>"people", "person"=>{"first_name"=>"Jean", "last_name"=>"Dough"}}
Person Columns (0.001395)   SHOW FIELDS FROM people
SQL (0.000290)   BEGIN
SQL (0.273139)   INSERT INTO people ('first_name', 'last_name')\
VALUES('Jean', 'Dough')
SQL (0.186078)   COMMIT
Redirected to http://localhost:3000/people/list
Completed in 0.47041 (2 reqs/sec) | DB: 0.46090 (97%) | \
  302 Found [http://localhost/people/create]
```

Rails logging gives you the following information for every request:

- The URL, host, time, and HTTP verb (line 1)

- The user's session ID (line 2)

- The request parameters, including controller and action (line 3)

- The SQL statements executed, with timing information (line 5)

- The templates rendered or redirects issued (line 10)

- The HTTP response code and total time to handle the request (line 11)

By default, Rails logging emits ANSI control sequences, which colorize the log lines for supported terminals. For all other viewers, these control sequences are just gibberish, so we usually turn them off in environment.rb:

code/people/config/environment.rb

```ruby
ActiveRecord::Base.colorize_logging = false
```

Rails log level names are almost the same as the log4j defaults: DEBUG, INFO, WARN, ERROR, and FATAL. (There is no TRACE.) These levels come from the Logger class in the Ruby standard library, which Rails uses by default. The development and test environments set the log level to DEBUG, and the production environment uses INFO. You can override these settings in the environment-specific .rb file. For example, this line sets the production log level to WARN:

> code/people/config/environments/production.rb

```
config.log_level = :warn
```

By default, Rails logging is "clean"—it shows the message only, without any of the other context to which you may be accustomed. However, the Logger class provides a format_message that you can override to include additional information. Rails redefines format_message on Logger itself. We will overcome this by subclassing Logger and providing our own format_message:

> code/rails_xt/config/environment.rb

```
class BetterLogger < Logger
  Format = "[%s#%d] %5s -- %s: %s\n"
  def format_message(severity, timestamp, msg, progname)
    Format % [timestamp, $$, severity, progname, msg]
  end
end
```

Thanks a lot, Perl.

This is basic sprintf-style formatting. The only puzzler is the variable $$. That's Ruby for the current process ID. To make BetterLogger the default logger for the application, we must add a line to environment.rb. While we are there, we will set the progname that will appear in log output:

> code/rails_xt/config/environment.rb

```
config.logger = BetterLogger.new "#{RAILS_ROOT}/log/#{RAILS_ENV}.log"
config.logger.progname = 'rails_xt'
```

Rails logging has a couple of nice features that take advantage of Ruby blocks. Instead of passing a string to a log method, you can pass a block. The result of running the block will be the message to be logged. Instead of using the following:

```
# bad Ruby style!
if logger.info?
  logger.info expensive_message
end
```

you can simply say this:

```
logger.info {expensive_message}
```

The block semantics guarantee that expensive_message will evaluate only if the INFO level is enabled. For example, this logger call avoids the call to inspect unless DEBUG logging is enabled:

```
code/rails_xt/app/controllers/people_controller.rb
def edit
  @person = Person.find(params[:id])
  logger.debug {"Found person #{@person.inspect}"}
end
```

In several places, Rails uses a silence idiom to adjust the log level for the duration of the block. When silence is called, the log level is boosted (usually to ERROR), squelching log messages. Rails uses this to hide irrelevant details from the log. For example, the ActiveRecord implementation of session stores silences logging so that your logging will show ActiveRecord messages for your domain objects but not for session objects:

```
code/rails/actionpack/lib/action_controller/session/active_record_store.rb
def update
  if @session
    ActiveRecord::Base.silence { @session.save }
  end
end
```

The place where Rails' default logging falls far short of log4j is in supporting a variety of appenders (log message destinations). Fortunately, there is a log4r project[1] that is inspired by log4j. If you need more capable logging than what we have shown here, you can trivially switch to log4r. Because of Ruby's duck typing, you do not need an adapter layer such as Java's Commons Logging.

Benchmarking

Rails includes three tools to help benchmark application performance: script/performance/benchmarker, script/performance/profiler, and the controller method benchmark. To put them through their paces, consider the following question: Can the Rails XT application be made to handle 5,000 logins per second?

The benchmarker command measures the elapsed time for some Ruby code, running in the environment of your application. We are not aware of any major performance problems in the sample applications, but we

---

1. http://log4r.sourceforge.net/

know that security functions are often slow. Let's try authenticating a user[2] in the Rails XT application:

```
$ script/performance/benchmarker 'User.authenticate("quentin","test")'
          user       system       total       real
#1      0.010000    0.000000    0.010000 (  0.000836)
```

The numbers (reported in seconds) are pretty small, so let's try running the benchmark fifty times in a row:

```
$ script/performance/benchmarker 50 'User.authenticate("quentin","test")'
          user       system       total       real
#1      0.020000    0.010000    0.030000 (  0.090123)
```

It appears that our system will have no trouble authenticating quite a few more than fifty users in a second. For many applications this is good enough.

But our proposed goal is much higher: We want to authenticate 5,000 users in a second. Plus, the benchmarker measured only the API call, not the progression through the web stack before and after the key method call. Should we add more web servers, try to optimize the authenticate method, use some native code, or give up on a Ruby-based approach?

To answer these questions, we need to know where User.authenticate is spending its time. Enter the profiler. The profiler instruments the code to tell us which methods authenticate calls and the relative time spent in each:

```
$ script/performance/profiler 'User.authenticate("quentin","test")' 50
Loading Rails...
Using the standard Ruby profiler.
  %   cumulative   self              self     total
 time   seconds   seconds  calls  ms/call  ms/call  name
 5.78     0.10      0.10      51    1.96    29.41   ActiveRecord::Base#method_missing
 5.20     0.19      0.09    1229    0.07     0.10   Hash#[]
 5.20     0.28      0.09     354    0.25     0.25   Kernel.==
 4.62     0.36      0.08      50    1.60    12.00   ActiveRecord::Base#find_every
 4.62     0.44      0.08      21    3.81     4.29   Gem::GemPathSearcher#matching_file
 4.62     0.52      0.08      50    1.60     4.00   Enumerable.each_with_index
 4.62     0.60      0.08      50    1.60    14.00   ActiveSupport::Deprecation.silence
 4.62     0.68      0.08      77    1.04     2.21   Class#new
 4.05     0.75      0.07      50    1.40     5.40   ActiveRecord::Base#construct_condi
 4.05     0.82      0.07     200    0.35     0.35   ActiveRecord::Base#current_scoped_
 ... about 100 more lines of decreasing importance ...
```

---

2. The security API we use here is discussed in detail in Chapter 10, *Security*, on page 267. The quentin/test combination comes from our fixture data.

Note the following points here:

- Everything took much longer under the profiler than the bench-marker. This is not a problem; it merely indicates the overhead of profiling. (As a rule of thumb, the benchmarker gives useful absolute numbers, and the profiler gives useful relative numbers.)
- There is no "smoking gun" method that dominates the elapsed time. If we start optimizing Ruby code, or even switching to native code for some methods, we expect percentage improvements, not order-of-magnitude improvements.
- That we see Class.new and Gem::GemPathSearcher#matching_file makes us suspicious that we are seeing start-up costs that are not representative of the application's long-run behavior.

Given the last point, let's run the profiler again, but for 500 iterations instead of just 50:

```
$ script/performance/profiler 'User.authenticate("quentin","test")' 500
Loading Rails...
Using the standard Ruby profiler.
  %   cumulative  self              self     total
 time   seconds   seconds  calls ms/call ms/call  name
 5.46    0.73      0.73   11129    0.07    0.08   Hash#[]
 4.57    1.34      0.61     501    1.22   24.35   ActiveRecord::Base#method_missing
 3.97    1.87      0.53     501    1.06    2.14   Benchmark.measure
 3.29    2.31      0.44    2501    0.18    0.32   ActiveRecord::Base#connection
 2.47    2.64      0.33     500    0.66    6.82   ActiveRecord::Base#construct_finde...
 2.32    2.95      0.31    2000    0.15    0.19   ActiveRecord::Base#current_scoped_...
 2.02    3.22      0.27     500    0.54    1.84   User#authenticated?
 2.02    3.49      0.27     500    0.54    3.08   ActiveRecord::Base#add_conditions!
 1.95    3.75      0.26    1000    0.26    0.48   User#encrypt
 1.95    4.01      0.26     500    0.52    1.86   ActiveRecord::Base#construct_condi...
```

That looks more realistic. All the dominant methods are directly related to the operation we are trying to evaluate. Some further observations are as follows:

- Encryption is not an issue. Even if User#encrypt could calculate an SHA1 hash *instantly*, we would see only a 2 percent increase in speed overall.
- We might benefit by replacing ActiveRecord with a custom SQL implementation.
- The calls column suggests that each call to User.authenticate triggers five calls to get the connection. It might be worth looking at the code path to see whether that number could be reduced.

We should step back for second. Although the profiler results suggest some possible optimizations, *we would not bother trying any of them.* The optimizations are likely to make the code more complex, error-prone, and difficult to maintain. Plus, nothing in the profiler results convinces us that the code would not scale to a second web server. In many scenarios, that second server will be far cheaper than the development effort to make the code perform on one server.

The key question here is whether the authentication scales. Can we increase throughput and lower response time by simply adding hardware? We can get a partial answer to this question from ActionController's benchmark method.

benchmark takes three arguments and a block. The block is executed, and timing information is written to the log, as controlled by the three arguments: a message to include in the log, a log level, and a silence argument, which disables any logging inside the block being benchmarked. You could call benchmark yourself:

```
code/rails_xt/app/controllers/examples_controller.rb
def benchmark_demo
  self.class.benchmark "log message here" do
    # add some expensive operation you want to test
    render :text=>'<h1>Hello world</h1>'
  end
end
```

In practice this is rarely necessary. Rails already benchmarks all sorts of interesting activities. Most importantly, Rails benchmarks both the total time to process a request, and the time spent in the database.

If we believe that the application can scale perfectly linearly (an unlikely ideal), then we have this:

```
M = 5000 / R
```

In this equation, R is the number of requests per second on a single machine, and M is the number of web tier machines we will need.

Let's switch to production mode and run a production-quality server (Mongrel). We will load the production database with our sample data.[3]

```
RAILS_ENV=production rake db:migrate
RAILS_ENV=production rake db:fixtures:load
RAILS_ENV=production mongrel_rails
```

---

3. Be careful about doing this on real projects, where the production database data is important!

Now, we can log in through the web interface and then review the performance numbers in the Rails log. Here is what we saw on a development laptop (2.16GHz MacBook Pro, 2GB RAM, random developer stuff running in the background):

```
Processing AccountController#login (for 127.0.0.1 at 2006-10-31 13:05:04) [POST]
  Session ID: 80dcc7858d5fcef6385f50a0e90e9f94
  Parameters: {"commit"=>"Log in", "action"=>"login",\
    "controller"=>"account", "login"=>"quentin", "password"=>"[FILTERED]"}
Redirected to http://localhost:3000/quips
Completed in 0.00262 (381 reqs/sec) | DB: 0.00038 (14%)\
| 302 Found [http://localhost/login]
```

Two numbers jump out. First, the 381 requests per second. If that is the best we can do, then we will need 5000/381, or about 14 web servers to allow 5,000 logins per second. Second, the database (DB) proportion of that time was low, only 14 percent. Notice that 14 percent tells us nothing about how loaded the MySQL process was, only how long we had to wait for it. This suggests that we could have at least five to six web servers hitting the database simultaneously with no loss of throughput, and quite possibly more.

We have not seen Rails deployments with as many as fourteen web servers in front, so we would not cavalierly assume that there are no problems lurking there. But we have seen Rails deployments with four or even eight web servers. Given the numbers we have shown here, would you be willing to bet that you could handle 5,000 logins per second with eight web servers? This simple exercise has us within a close order of magnitude, and we have not done any optimizations yet. We are confident it would be possible.

How does this all compare with the Java options for profiling? If profiling is your chief concern, Java beats Ruby hands down. Java has more profiling tools and better profiling tools. Both commercial and open source options exist. Because the Java platform includes a virtual machine specification with documented profiling hooks, it beats Ruby profiling not only in practice but in concept.

That said, we have not missed Java's cool profilers while writing Ruby and Rails applications. We rarely used them in Java and rarely use their lesser cousins in Ruby. In our experience, *most well-tested, well-factored applications are already fast enough.* When they are not fast enough, the solutions usually require only two tools: observation of the application and log files and a little bit of pencil-and-paper reckoning. In an aggregate thirty-plus years of software development, we have done performance tuning of some form on almost every application we have ever developed. In 95 percent of them, we never wanted or needed a profiler.

Debugging

As Java developers, we are accustomed to powerful GUI debuggers for our applications. In Ruby, support for debugging is primitive. We have tried a few open source and commercial debuggers. They are all so slow that we never bother to launch them.

We rarely miss the debugger, because our development method uses a variety of different tests to catch program errors. But "rarely" is not the same thing as "never," and a good GUI debugger for Ruby would be appreciated.

Until the mythical GUI debugger arrives, you can use a console-based alternative. Rails includes a console-based debugger based on the ruby-breakpoint[4] library. To use this debugger, simply add a breakpoint statement anywhere in your code. To see breakpoint in action, consider this buggy code:

`code/rails_xt/samples/debug_me.rb`

```ruby
class Widget
  attr_accessor :name
  def initialize(value)
    name = value
  end
end
w = Widget.new('zipper')
puts w.name
```

You might expect this code to print "zipper"; however, it prints "nil"—to find out why, let's add a breakpoint at the end of initialize:

`code/rails_xt/samples/debug_me.rb`

```ruby
def initialize(value)
  name = value
  breakpoint
end
```

When the program reaches the breakpoint, it will start an irb session. You can use this session to inspect or modify program values. We will show the current instance_variables so you can see what happened to our name:

---

4. http://ruby-breakpoint.rubyforge.org/

```
$ ruby samples/debug_me.rb
Executing break point at samples/debug_me.rb:19 in 'initialize'
irb(#<Widget:0x2a8c2d8>):001:0> instance_variables
=> ["@__bp_file", "@__bp_line"]
```

The variables prefixed with @__bp are used internally by the breakpoint
library and do not concern us. More important, there is no @name variable. The next part to look at is local_variables:

```
irb(#<Widget:0x2a8c2d8>):002:0> local_variables
=> ["value", "name", "_"]
irb(#<Widget:0x2a8c2d8>):003:0> value
=> "zipper"
```

Gotcha! Ruby is treating name as a local variable. Ruby is interpreting
our name= to mean "Set the name local variable," when we were mistakenly expecting "Call the name= method." Now that we understand the
problem, we can continue past the breakpoint by typing exit (all platforms), Ctrl-D (Unix), or Ctrl-Z (Windows). Then, we will correct the code
to use self.name= to avoid ambiguity:

code/rails_xt/samples/debug_me.rb
```
def initialize(value)
  self.name = value
end
```

It is worth pointing out that instance_variables and local_variables are
not special debugging commands. These are regular Ruby methods,
available at any time in any Ruby program.

Java GUI debuggers will let you debug a local program, but they will
also let you connect to a server process. This can be helpful in tracking
down problems that manifest only at the level of the entire system. The
breakpoint library can do the same. If you set a breakpoint in a Rails
server process, the breakpoint library will call out to a remote debugger. You can launch the remote debugger with the script/breakpointer
command included in every Rails application. Don't forget to remove
breakpoints from production code!

Additional instructions for debugging with breakpoint are available on
the Rails Wiki.[5] Intrepid Rubyists are also debugging Ruby applications using gdb; see _why's blog post[6] for a summary of a few different
approaches.

---

5. http://wiki.rubyonrails.org/rails/pages/HowtoDebugWithBreakpoint
6. http://redhanded.hobix.com/inspect/theRubyGdbArmsRaceNowAtAStandoff.html

5.8   Resources

A Look at Common Performance Problems in Rails. . .
. . . http://www.infoq.com/articles/Rails-Performance
Stefan Kaes on finding and fixing Rails performance problems.

Regaining Control of Rails Logging. . .
. . . http://dazuma.blogspot.com/2006/10/regaining-control-of-rails-logging.html
Advice on how to log more structured information and how to filter and search
your Rails logs.

Roll your own SQL session store. . .
. . . http://railsexpress.de/blog/articles/2005/12/19/roll-your-own-sql-session-store
Stefan Kaes's custom SQL session store, which offers better performance than
ActiveRecord-based sessions.

Sessions N Such http://errtheblog.com/post/24
Chris Wanstrath explains turning off sessions in Rails.

Under the hood: Rails' routing DSL. . .
. . . http://weblog.jamisbuck.org/2006/10/2/under-the-hood-rails-routing-dsl
First in a series of articles describing Rails routing from the implementation
up. Routing is already extremely flexible; armed with this information, you can
extend it any way you like.

Using memcached for Ruby on Rails Session Storage. . .
. . . http://railsexpress.de/blog/articles/2006/01/24/
using-memcached-for-ruby-on-rails-session-storage
Stefan Kaes's test results using memcached. Stefan regularly updates his blog
with new test results, so in addition to this article, make sure you read his most
recent entries.

Chapter 6

Rendering Output with ActionView

ActionView is the view in Rails' approach to MVC. ActionView takes the objects created by the controller and renders output, usually as HTML or XML. ActionView is bundled with ActionController in a Ruby gem called ActionPack, which is included in Rails. Together with ActiveRecord, ActionView and ActionController form the core of Rails.

Although it is possible to render content directly from the controller, almost 100 percent of Rails applications use ActionView. ActionView supports many different approaches to rendering through a pluggable template mechanism. ActionView ships with three styles of templates. Embedded Ruby (ERb) templates are stored in .rhtml files and use a mix of markup and embedded Ruby to build dynamic content. Builder templates are stored as .rxml files and use pure Ruby to build XML output. JavaScript templates are stored as .rjs files and use a Ruby API to build JavaScript output.

It is easy to add new template types, either your own or from third parties. To demonstrate this we will also look at Markaby, a third-party gem that uses pure Ruby to render HTML.

Java web applications employ a slew of techniques to write dynamic view code: inline Java, tag libraries, the JSTL expression language, and the Object Graph Notation Language. In ActionView, most of these roles are filled by plain old Ruby code in the form of helpers. Like tag libraries, Rails helpers reduce the amount of code in the view. However, Rails helpers do not try to hide their Rubyness.

Rails is rightly famous for its Ajax support. We can only begin to cover the Ajax API in the short space we have here, and we use a sampling of the various APIs to demonstrate the key concepts. We also cover acceptance testing with Selenium. Selenium is not part of Rails, or even Rails-specific, but it has an important role in ensuring quality. Selenium allows you to write, record, step through, and play back tests in the browser, exercising your entire application.

6.1 Creating Basic .rhtml Files

In Java web applications, JavaServer Pages (JSPs) are the norm for basic page rendering. JSPs include static content, plus chunks of code dynamic. To execute code in a JSP, place it inside <% %>. To execute Java code and write the result into the page, use <%= %> instead. Here is a "Hello, World" page that includes your name (if it was available in the query string):

> code/java_xt/snippets/hello.jsp

```
<h1>Hello</h1>
<% if request.getParameter('name') %>
Welcome, <%= request.getParameter('name') %>
<% end %>
```

In ActionView, the JSP role is filled by .rhtml files. Rails evaluates .rhtml files using Embedded Ruby (ERb), a templating library that is part of the Ruby standard library. If you know the JSP syntax, ERb should look familiar:

> code/people/app/views/people/hello.rhtml

```
<h1>Hello</h1>
<% unless request.params['name'].blank? %>
Welcome, <%= request.params['name'] %>
<% end %>
```

In both JSP and ActionView, view code can access the same web object model seen by the controller: the request (as shown in the previous examples), the response, the session, and so on. Therefore, it is possible to build entire applications inside the view template. Don't do this. In both JSP and Rails, doing significant coding in the view is a Bad Thing. The combination of HTML markup and template code is difficult to read, test, and maintain. The only code in the view layer should be code dedicated to the formatting of output.

Both JSPs and ActionView have mechanisms to reduce the "codiness" of view templates. In JSP, there are declarations and tag libraries. Action-View provides helpers, layouts, and partials.

6.2 Minimizing View Code with View Helpers

Rather than doing direct Java coding in a JSP, many Java programmers prefer to use *tag libraries*. Tag libraries are custom markup backed by Java code. Tag libraries require a bit more work to create: you have to implement the code in Java, create a tag library descriptor, and then configure the page (or the web application) to make the tag library available. The advantage is clean syntax in the view. Rather than mixed markup and Java code, you can have pure markup.

tag libraries

One of the most common tag libraries is the JSTL core library, which includes tags for control flow and output. Using these tags, the JSP "Hello, World" example becomes as follows:

```
code/appfuse_people/web/pages/hello.jsp
```

```
<%@ taglib uri="http://java.sun.com/jstl/core" prefix="c" %>
<h1>Hello</h1>
<c:if test="not empty request.name">
  Welcome, <c:out value="request.name"/>

</c:if>
```

All the Java code has been replaced by tags. The c:if tag replaces an if statement, and the c:out tag replaces the JSP output expression. This has two goals. First, the tags are intended to be more readable than the Java code, particularly to page designers who may be editing the view code. Second, the tags allow a level of validation that does not require parsing Java code (or understanding Java stack traces). The downside is two new syntaxes to learn: the custom tag vocabulary and the *expression language* that is used, for example, to create the boolean expressions in c:if's test attribute.

expression language

The JSP world includes a huge number of tag libraries that you can add to your project: formatting tags, tags that help create HTML markup, tags that access user credentials from the session, and more. Action-View does not have a direct equivalent to tag libraries. Instead, Action-View provides built-in *view helpers*. ActionView includes dozens of helper methods, which are automatically available to all .rhtml pages. In addition, Rails adds formatting helpers to the Ruby classes for strings, numbers, and dates.

view helpers

6.3 Writing Custom Helpers

The built-in ActionView helpers are extremely useful but cannot cover every possible situation. So, Rails provides a standard place for your own helpers. The app/helpers directory contains a helper file for each controller in your application. When you use script/generate to create a controller FooController, Rails also creates a helper file, app/helpers/ foo_helper.rb. This code is automatically included in all of FooController's views.

Because Rails includes so many built-in helpers, simple web applications may not need many (or any) custom helpers. You'll know when and if you need them. When you see the same code repeated in multiple places in your view, it is time to write a helper.

As a simple example, imagine that the users of the Rails XT application want a politeness filter for quips. Their specific requirement states that when the politeness filter is on, four-letter words should render as !@#$. We'll add this capability as a helper in QuipsHelper:

`code/rails_xt/app/helpers/quips_helper.rb`

```ruby
module QuipsHelper
  # See http://en.wikipedia.org/wiki/Bowdler
  def bowdlerize_four_lettered(str)
    h(str.to_s.gsub(/\b\w{4}\b/, '!@#$'))
  end
  alias_method :bfl, :bowdlerize_four_lettered
end
```

The implementation is probably a bit more literal than intended, but we like to code to spec. We are automatically doing HTML escaping (the h method) because we are lazy and don't want to have to call both h and bfl all over our views. We have given the method a meaningful name and a short alias. This strikes a good balance between our desire to have self-documenting names and the fact that this particular method may be used quite a lot. With the helper in place, a show view for quips can be as simple as this:

`code/rails_xt/app/views/quips/filtered_show.rhtml`

```erb
<% for column in Quip.content_columns %>
<p>
  <b><%= column.human_name %>:</b> <%=bfl @quip.send(column.name) %>
</p>
<% end %>
<%= link_to 'Edit', :action => 'edit', :id => @quip %> |
<%= link_to 'Back', :action => 'list' %>
```

Joe Asks...

How Do You Test Custom Helpers?

Rails automatically creates test/unit for model code and creates test/functional for controller code. There is no corresponding test/helper for helper code. Don't let that bother you; just make your own. Here is a Rake task that you can add to lib/tasks to manage your helper tests:

`code/rails_xt/lib/tasks/test_helpers.rake`

```ruby
namespace :test do
  desc "Run the helper tests in test/helpers"
  Rake::TestTask.new(:helpers => [ :prepare_test_database ]) do |t|
    t.libs << "test"
    t.pattern = 'test/helpers/**/*_test.rb'
    t.verbose = true
  end
end
task :default => [ 'test:helpers' ]
```

And here is an example test for the bfl method from the main text. Notice that we stub out any required Rails helpers (such as h) to decouple the test from Rails.

`code/rails_xt/test/helpers/quips_helper_test.rb`

```ruby
require File.dirname(__FILE__) + '/../test_helper'
require 'quips_helper'

class QuipsHelperTest < Test::Unit::TestCase
  include QuipsHelper

  # handmade stub method
  def h(s); s; end

  def test_bfl
    assert_equal 'safely sized words', bfl('safely sized words')
    assert_equal '!@#$ and !@#$', bfl('darn and drat')
  end
end
```

6.4 Reuse with Layouts and Partials

include directive

View templates often need to share code. In JSP, you can move common code into a separate .jsp file and then use an *include directive*. The include directive is often used to compose the key elements of the page, such as headers, footers, menus, status messages, and content. For example, here is a JSP page from the Struts sample application, edited to show only the basic page structure:

```
<div id="page">
  <div id="header" class="clearfix">
    <jsp:include page="/common/header.jsp"/>
  </div>
  <div id="content" class="clearfix">
    <div id="main">
      <jsp:include page="/common/messages.jsp" %>
      <!-- main content here! -->
    </div>
    <div id="nav">
      <div class="wrapper">
        <jsp:include page="/WEB-INF/pages/menu.jsp"/>
      </div>
    </div>
  </div>
  <div id="footer" class="clearfix">
    <jsp:include page="/common/footer.jsp"/>
  </div>
</div>
```

The jsp:include tag pulls in the header, messages, navigation, and footer. You can then reuse these JSP fragments across multiple pages. Action-View does something similar. Two things, in fact: *layouts* and *partials*. A layout is a template that is automatically rendered around the main content of a page. A partial is a template that is explicitly invoked from another template. Pages automatically use a layout, if one is available.

layouts

partials

By default, the layout for a controller named Foo is a template named app/views/layouts/foo.html. If a controller-specific layout is unavailable, ActionView will automatically use app/views/layouts/application.html, if it exists. The PeopleController in the Rails XT application demonstrates layouts and partials in action:

`code/rails_xt/app/views/layouts/people.rhtml`

```
<html>
<head>
  <title>People: <%= controller.action_name %></title>
  <%= stylesheet_link_tag 'scaffold' %>
</head>
```

```
<body>
<%= render :partial=>'header' %>
<p style="color: green"><%= flash[:notice] %></p>
<%= @content_for_layout %>
<%= render :partial=>'/shared/footer' %>
</body>
</html>
```

As you can see here, the layout is usually responsible for rendering the head section of the document. Inside the body, the @content_for_layout variable contains the main content for an action.[1] For example, when rendering /people/list, @content_for_layout would usually contain the rendered output from app/views/people/list.rhtml.

The calls to render :partial let us reuse common templates for the header and footer of the page. To distinguish partials from complete pages, they are named with a leading underscore. Thus, the header partial points to app/views/people/_header.rhtml. Partials such as headers and footers are often shared across all controllers. The app/views/shared directory holds such shared partials, which can be accessed with names such as '/shared/footer'. Note that the underscore is omitted in the call to render but present on the file system.

Every partial has a local variable named after the partial. You can pass this local variable to a partial with the :object option. You can also set local variables with the :locals option:

`code/rails_xt/app/views/examples/call_partials.rhtml`

```
<%= render :partial=> 'listmaker',
          :object=> 'My Todo List',
          :locals => {:items => ['climb Everest', 'swim Channel']} %>
```

Inside the partial, listmaker will be 'My Todo List', and items will be ['climb Everest', 'swim Channel']. The partial might look like this:

`code/rails_xt/app/views/examples/_listmaker.rhtml`

```
<h1><%= listmaker %></h1>
<ol>
  <% items.each do |item| %>
  <li><%= item %></li>
  <% end %>
</ol>
```

The do...end loop in the partial is one way to render a collection. It is ugly, and most web applications render many collections. ActionView

---

1. More recent versions of Rails use yield instead of @content_for_layout.

provides a better way. When calling a partial, specify the :collection option. The partial will execute once for each item in the collection, setting the template variable to each item in turn. Using collection partials, you could improve the previous two examples as follows:

code/rails_xt/app/views/examples/call_collection_partials.rhtml

```
<h1>My Todo List</h1>
<ol>
<%= render :partial=> 'listmaker2',
           :collection => ['climb Everest', 'swim Channel'] %>
</ol>
```

The partial is now simply as follows:

code/rails_xt/app/views/examples/_listmaker2.rhtml

```
<li><%= listmaker2 %></li>
```

6.5 Building HTML Forms

Struts includes a page construction tag library to build HTML forms. In our sample application, page construction tags are prefixed with html. Here is the Struts code to render the input elements for a person's first and last names:

code/appfuse_people/web/pages/personForm.jsp

```
<li>
    <label for="firstName" class="desc">First Name </label>
    <html:errors property="firstName"/>
    <html:text property="firstName" styleId="firstName"
       styleClass="text medium"/>
</li>
<li>
    <label for="lastName" class="desc">Last Name </label>
    <html:errors property="lastName"/>
    <html:text property="lastName" styleId="lastName"
       styleClass="text medium"/>
</li>
```

You should notice several points here. First, there is a seamless back-and-forth between custom tags and plain HTML. The label tags are HTML, but the html-prefixed tags invoke custom code. The html:errors tag looks up error messages on a named form property. The html:text tag generates an HTML input type="text". The styleId and styleClass attributes become id and class attributes on the generated input elements.

The Rails scaffold code for editing the properties of a person lives at app/views/people/_form.rhtml:

`code/people/app/views/people/_form.rhtml`

```
<p><label for="person_first_name">First name</label><br/>
<%= text_field 'person', 'first_name'  %><%= error_message_on 'person',
    'first_name' %></p>

<p><label for="person_last_name">Last name</label><br/>
<%= text_field 'person', 'last_name'  %><%= error_message_on 'person',
    'last_name' %></p>
```

Where the Struts version used page construction tags, the Rails version uses built-in form helpers. The error_message_on method emits validation errors. The text_field method takes two arguments here. Rails combines the two arguments to create a parameter name, so text_field 'person', 'first_name' becomes a parameter named person[first_name]. When the parameters are submitted to the server, Rails automatically converts parameters named in this fashion into a hash. This is convenient, since ActiveRecord constructors take a hash argument.

The Struts form validation has two features absent in Rails:

- Validations can be checked with client-side JavaScript.
- Error messages are internationalized.

If you need these features in your Rails application, you will have to find a plugin or roll your own. We have found that Rails has advantages in other areas that outweigh these deficiencies, but it is important to be aware of them when estimating development effort for a project. Rails includes form helper methods for every kind of HTML form input. Here are some examples of form helpers:

`code/rails_xt/app/views/examples/forms.rhtml`

```
<h2>Form Fields Bound To Query Params</h2>
<%= start_form_tag %>
<table>
<tr>
 <td><label for="sample_text">Text</label></td>
 <td><%= text_field :sample, :text %></td>
</tr>
<tr>
 <td><label for="sample_password">Passsword</label></td>
 <td><%= password_field :sample, :password, {:style=>'color:blue;'} %></td>
</tr>
<tr>
 <td><label for="sample_area">Text Area</label></td>
 <td><%= text_area :sample, :area, {:size=>'10x10'} %></td>
</tr>
</table>
<%= end_form_tag %>
```

On line 6, you see the two-argument version of a form tag helper. The first argument is an instance variable name, and the second argument is the name of an accessor on that instance. Rails will populate the initial value from the instance variable and will convert the query string arguments into a hash named for the instance variable. On line 10, you see the three-argument version. The third argument is a hash that is converted into attributes on the tag. Here we set a CSS style.

On line 14, you see another three argument helper. This time, however, the third argument is not an HTML attribute. The argument is size=>'10x10', but a proper textarea expects rows and cols. Here Rails has provided a shortcut. You can specify separate rows and cols if you want, but Rails has special-cased the options handling for text_area_tag to convert size arguments into rows and cols. As you are writing view code, look out for helpers such as these that can simplify common tasks.

Rails form helpers are validation aware. If a model object has validation errors, the Rails form helpers will put form tags for invalid data inside a <div class="fieldWithErrors">. You can then use CSS styles to call attention to errors. (The Rails scaffold adds a red border). Several other form helpers are worth mentioning, and we'll get to them shortly. First, we have to do something about all the ugly HTML code we just showed you. Each one of those form fields looks the same: Each is wrapped in tr and td, and each is preceded by a label. The HTML around each field is extremely repetitive. Surely there must be a better way!

Rails provides the form_for helper to reduce the repetitiveness of form code. The previous form looks like this if you use form_for:

`code/rails_xt/app/views/examples/form_for.rhtml`

```
<h2>Form Fields Bound To Query Params</h2>
<% form_for :sample do |f| %>
<table>
<tr><td><label for="sample_text">Text</label></td>
<td><%= f.text_field :text %></td></tr>
<tr><td><label for="sample_password">Password</label></td>
<td><%= f.password_field :password, {:style=>'color:blue;'} %></td></tr>
<tr><td><label for="sample_area">Text Area</label></td>
<td><%= f.text_area :area, {:size=>'10x10'} %></td></tr>
</table>
<% end %>
```

Notice that form_for uses an ERb evaluation block (<% %>) instead of an ERb output block (<%= %>). form_for takes a block parameter, which is the form object. In the block, you can use the block parameter and omit the first argument to each field helper; for example, you'd use f.text_field instead of text_field :sample.

That is not much of an improvement so far. The real power of form_for comes in conjunction with form builders. A form builder gets to override how each form element is built. Here is a custom form builder that automatically generates all the tr, td, and label goo around our HTML fields:

`code/rails_xt/app/helpers/tabular_form_builder.rb`

```
class TabularFormBuilder < ActionView::Helpers::FormBuilder
  (field_helpers - %w(hidden_field)).each do |selector|
    src = <<-END_SRC
      def #{selector}(field, *args, &proc)
        "<tr>" +
          "<td><label for='\#{field}'>\#{field.to_s.humanize}:</label></td>" +
          "<td>" + super + "</td>" +
        "</tr>"
      end
    END_SRC
    class_eval src, __FILE__, __LINE__
  end
  def submit_tag(value)
    "<tr>"+
      "<td> </td>"+
      "<td><input name='commit' type='submit' value='#{value}'/></td>"+
    "</tr>"
  end
end
```

This code looks a bit tricky, but what it does is not that complex. The call to field_helpers returns all the field helper names. Then, the src string creates a new definition for each method that includes the formatting we want. Finally, submit_tag is special-cased because we do not want a label for submit tags.

To use our custom form builder, we need to pass a named option to the third parameter for form_for. We will capture this in a new helper method named tabular_form_for:

`code/rails_xt/app/helpers/application_helper.rb`

```
require 'tabular_form_builder'
module ApplicationHelper
  def tabular_form_for(name, object, options, &proc)
    concat("<table>", proc.binding)
    form_for(name, object, options.merge(:builder => TabularFormBuilder), &proc)
    concat("</table>", proc.binding)
  end
end
```

The calls to concat are the ERb version of puts, and the call to form_for sets the :builder to be our TabularFormBuilder.

Using the TabularFormBuilder, our form code simplifies to the following:

```
code/rails_xt/app/views/examples/tabular_form_for.rhtml
<h2>Tabular Form For</h2>
<% form_for :sample, @sample do |f| %>
<%= f.text_field :text %>
<%= f.password_field :password, {:style=>'color:blue;'} %>
<%= f.text_area :area, {:size=>'10x10'} %>
<% end %>
```

That is an enormous improvement in readability. And although the FormBuilder code looks tricky, you do not have to start from scratch. We pasted the src block from the FormBuilder base class and tweaked it until we liked the results.

Sometimes you want a form that is not associated with a model object. Methods such as text_field assume an associated model object, but Rails has a second set of methods that do not scope query parameters to a particular object. Instead of text_field, you use text_field_for. Similarly named methods exist for all the other form input types.

6.6 Building HTML with Markaby

In the Java world, JSPs are the most controversial piece of the MVC web stack. JSPs are often despised and sometimes replaced entirely. We could spend an entire book debating the reasons for this and comparing various alternatives.

But the underlying turmoil here comes from a simple fact. The view layer is where programmers, interaction designers, and graphic designers all have to work together. These groups have different goals, different skills, and different tools. JSP syntax exists, in part, because Java syntax is alien to designers and cannot be processed by pure-HTML tools. But from there you start to get a sense that you are peeling an onion. JSP tag libraries exists because JSP is too Java-like. Templating engines such as Velocity[2] exist because JSP tag libraries are too arcane, and they require new Java code to support even the simplest dynamic tasks. Tapestry[3] components hide inside attributes of regular HTML tags and should be able to "play nice" with HTML tools.

Many people find this creative chaos distressing—why isn't there one right way to create dynamic views? We find the variety to be healthy,

---

2. http://jakarta.apache.org/velocity/
3. http://tapestry.apache.org/

for two reasons: First, it validates the separation of the model, view, and controller. The point of separation is to allow each layer to vary independently of the others, and in practice this objective is realized more often in the view than anywhere else. Second, the variety of view choices is competition, and it spurs new innovation. You can tell the Java web world is healthy by the variety and ongoing development of view technologies.

Ditto for Rails. Most Rails programs use the built-in .rhtml templates, to be sure. But a growing minority use third-party templating libraries. Here we will show you one of these libraries, Markaby.[4] Markaby has a pure-Ruby syntax that makes view code cleaner and easier to read than .rhtml files. If your view code is developed and maintained by Ruby programmers, Markaby may be perfect for you. To install Markaby as a Rails plugin, use this:

```
script/plugin install http://code.whytheluckystiff.net/svn/markaby/trunk
```

You can also install Markaby as a gem: gem install markaby. If you install Markaby as a gem, you will have to manually register Markaby as the template handler for files with the .mab extension:

`code/rails_xt/config/environment.rb`
```
require 'markaby'
require 'markaby/rails'
ActionView::Base::register_template_handler('mab',
  Markaby::ActionViewTemplateHandler)
```

Here is the Rails scaffold layout written in Markaby:

`code/rails_xt/app/views/layouts/astro.mab`
```
html do
  head do
    title action_name
    stylesheet_link_tag 'scaffold'
  end
  body do
    p flash[:notice], :style=>"color: green"
    self << @content_for_layout
  end
end
```

- Line 1 demonstrates generating an element. Simply call the element by name, passing a block for anything that should nest inside the element.

---

4.   http://code.whytheluckystiff.net/markaby/

- Line 3 shows how to set the content of an element, simply by passing it as a string.
- Line 4 demonstrates calling a Rails helper. Rails helpers are presumed to be output-generating and are written automatically.
- Line 7 shows creating HTML attributes, by passing them as a Ruby hash.
- Line 8 demonstrates writing content directly, by concatenating onto self.

To demonstrate a few more of Markaby's features, here is a simple show template:

```
code/rails_xt/app/views/astro/show.mab
```

```
div.planet! do
  for column in Planet.content_columns
    p do
      span.emphasis column.human_name
      h(@planet.send(column.name))
    end
  end
end
link_to 'Edit', :action => 'edit', :id => @planet
link_to 'Back', :action => 'list'
```

- Line 1 shows generating an element ID. Any method with a bang becomes the ID of its element, so div.planet! turns into <div id="planet">.
- Line 4 shows how to add a CSS class. Any method with no other obvious meaning becomes a CSS class, so span.emphasis turns into <span class="emphasis">.

As Markaby demonstrates, alternative view templates are alive and well in the Rails world. See the references for pointers to some others.

6.7 Caching Pages, Actions, and Fragments

At the risk of overgeneralization, you could say that the Java world caches models, and the Rails world caches views. Because there is no broadly used mechanism for caching views in Java, this section will cover Rails only, without any comparison to Java.

Caching is a performance optimization, and Rails makes it easy to apply caching at the right moment in the development process. Caching should be done only after you have the application working and in the presence of performance measurements that indicate the need. (More than half the Rails applications we have built never use caching at all. Yes, it is easy to add, and in many cases the applications would run faster. But we never build it until there is a demonstrated need.)

ActionView provides three levels of caching: page, action, and fragment. Page caching causes entire pages to be cached. Turning on page caching is trivial. In a controller, list the actions to be cached, like this:

code/people/app/controllers/people_controller.rb

```
caches_page :show, :edit
```

When Rails first renders an action that is page cached, it copies the results into the public directory. Subsequent requests for the page *do not encounter Rails at all.* Since the page is now in the public directory, it is returned like any other static resource. The performance of cached pages is as good as it gets. Unfortunately, cached pages are often inappropriate. Any page that has per-user behavior (like security checks), that has per-user state (sessions), or that changes over time cannot be cached.

If your application requires per-user behavior such as a security check, you can use cached actions instead of cached pages. The syntax is almost the same:

code/rails_xt/app/controllers/quips_controller.rb

```
caches_action :show, :edit
```

When Rails first renders a cached action, it saves the results. Instead of saving the page in the public directory, Rails caches the page at a location unknown to the web server (tmp/cache by default). Subsequent requests enter the controller layer, where all before filters (such as security checks) execute. If the before filters return successfully, Rails renders the page from the cache without executing the action code. Cached actions do not get nearly the performance boost of cached pages, but they keep access control intact.

If your web application produces different content for different users, then even action caching is not an option. Even something as simple as a status line saying "Logged in as 'Stu' for 2 hours" means that every user's page is different, and action caching is not an option. Enter fragment caching. If you can identify a part of a page that is generic and slow to render, it is a candidate for fragment caching.

Imagine that we want to cache a controller's show action. This time, our page layout includes per-user data, so we cannot cache the entire action. Instead, in the show.rhtml we can wrap the output in a cache do...end:

```
code/rails_xt/app/views/people/show.rhtml
```
```
<% cache :fragment=>'show' do %>
<% for column in Person.content_columns %>
<p>
  <b><%= column.human_name %>:</b> <%=h @person.send(column.name) %>
</p>
<% end %>
<%= link_to 'Edit', :action => 'edit', :id => @person %> |
<%= link_to 'Back', :action => 'list' %>
<% end %>
```

The fragment cache is colocated with the action cache and uses the same naming convention. This means name collisions can occur. More important, a single view might have multiple fragments to cache. Therefore, you should always give fragments a unique name by passing a name/value pair to cache do. Rails interprets the name value/pairs like arguments to url_for. We prefer to use a key name that is not used anywhere else in our application's routing, and that clearly indicates a fragment. Therefore, "fragment" is a decent name, as used previously.

When Rails first encounters the cache method, it renders the code inside the block and saves it in the cache. Subsequent requests do not execute the block, because cache checks the cache first and uses the cached content if present.

You have seen how to turn on page, action, and fragment caching. That is the easy part. The hard part is making sure that cached items are invalidated when data changes. Several possible approaches exist:

- Don't worry about it, and let the application display stale information. This is probably a bad idea in most applications.

- Clean the cache from outside Rails, using a background process that deletes the caches files, perhaps on a timer.

- Manually expire cached items. Whenever a controller saves modifications that invalidate a cache, call expire_page, expire_action, or expire_fragment explicitly.

- Use a Rails sweeper (a form of the Observer design pattern) to expire pages based on model changes.

We recommend the sweeper approach, because it cleanly separates caching from the rest of your program logic. Here's how to use sweepers to manage the various cache examples we created earlier in this section. First we will take care of the page caching on the People application's PeopleController. In the models directory, we create a PersonSweeper:

```
code/people/app/models/person_sweeper.rb
```
```
class PersonSweeper < ActionController::Caching::Sweeper
  CACHED_ACTIONS = ['show', 'edit']
  observe Person
  def expire_cache_for_instance(inst)
    CACHED_ACTIONS.each do |action|
      expire_page(:controller=>'people', :action=>action, :id=>inst)
    end
  end
  alias_method :after_save, :expire_cache_for_instance
  alias_method :after_destroy, :expire_cache_for_instance
end
```

Here's how it works:

1. On line 1, the class extends ActionController::Caching::Sweeper to tell Rails that this is a cache sweeper.

2. On line 3, the observe call tells Rails what model class to observe.

3. On line 1, we expire the show and edit views associated with a Person that has changed.

4. Starting on line 9, we make sure expire_cache_for_instance gets called for both after_save and after_destroy. Since the signatures are an exact match, we use alias_method.

With rendering and page caching under your belt, you are ready to build a beautiful web application. Wait a minute, the marketing department has asked us to change the previous sentence to end with "beautiful Web 1.0 application."

As a matter of principle, we refuse to use the "Web #.#" buzzword. Nevertheless, web development is changing, slowly, for the better. Users now expect more from the Web than just pages as still life. Modern web applications should be able to dynamically update parts of a single page, issue multiple background requests, use visual effects to highlight changing information, and provide input options beyond plain old forms. In short, they now want web applications to provide interfaces as rich and varied as traditional desktop applications. That is the promise of Ajax.

How Do You Test Caching?

Because Rails does not ship with any assertions to test caching, many Rails developers might skip this step. Don't. A broken caching implementation can return bad data and violate security policies. The Rails Cache Test Plugin* makes it easy to test caching. Here is a simple test for the page caching in the People sample application:

code/people/test/integration/person_caching_test.rb

```ruby
require "#{File.dirname(__FILE__)}/../test_helper"

class PersonCachingTest < ActionController::IntegrationTest
  fixtures :people
  def test_caching
    assert_cache_pages('/people/show/1', '/people/edit/1')
  end
  def test_expiry
    assert_expire_pages('/people/show/1', '/people/edit/1') do
      post '/people/destroy/1'
    end
  end
end
```

On line 6, assert_cache_pages takes a list of pages and verifies that GETting each page causes the page to be cached. On line 9, assert_expire_pages runs a block of code and then verifies that each page in its argument is removed from the cache.

The Rails Cache Test Plugin also includes support for other HTTP verbs and for testing action and fragment caching.

---

*. http://blog.cosinux.org/pages/page-cache-test

6.8 Creating Dynamic Pages with Ajax

Ajax (*Asynchronous JavaScript and XML*) has taken the Web by storm. The term was coined by Jesse James Garrett in February 2005, and by September 2006 a survey[5] reported that almost 70 percent of respondents[6] were already using or planning to use Ajax techniques.

Part of the reason for this success is vagueness in defining the term *Ajax*. Ajax has become one of those buzzwords that expands to mean just about anything you are doing on the Web. For this book, we will

---

5. http://www.ajaxian.com/by/topic/survey/
6. http://www.surveymonkey.com/DisplaySummary.asp?SID=2402465\&U=240246533425

use the term *Ajax* to mean *any web application technique that breaks the page metaphor of the Web and runs without any additional software on modern browsers.*

This definition expands on the original XML to include a variety of different data formats: XML, HTML, the JavaScript Object Notation (JSON), and plain text at the very least. Also, any technique for introducing asynchrony meets this definition: the typical XMLHttpRequest object plus various tricks using frames, script tags, and image tags.

JavaScript Libraries: Prototype and Scriptaculous

At the center of any Ajax architecture lies one or more JavaScript libraries. These libraries run in the client browser, respond to user input, submit asynchronous requests, process server responses, and update the user interface.

In theory, these libraries are decoupled from your server-side framework. Since all the actual communication in Ajax is over HTTP, any Ajax client code should coexist with any well-written server code. In practice, this is partially true. The most popular Ajax libraries are indeed used with different server-side stacks. According to a recent survey, Prototype is the most popular Ajax framework. We have seen Prototype used on projects with Rails, .NET, Java, and PHP back ends.

Despite the logical separation of Ajax and server-side frameworks, there is pressure toward integrated solutions. If a server-side framework includes custom tags or helper methods that generate code for a particular Ajax framework, then it will be easier to use that framework.

This is in fact the case with Rails. Rails includes helper methods that specifically target two JavaScript frameworks: Prototype and Scriptaculous. Because these helper methods are so easy to use in Rails, most Rails projects will pick these libraries without further consideration.

To include Ajax in a Rails application, the first step is to include script tags for the Prototype and Scriptaculous libraries. Since script tags are usually included in the head of an HTML document, the best place to include these tags is a controller's layout:

code/rails_xt/app/views/layouts/quips.rhtml

```
<%= javascript_include_tag :defaults %>
```

The defaults symbol is special-cased to include all of Rails' default Java-Script libraries, so the previous line of code translates to the following:

```
<script src="/javascripts/prototype.js?1149008954" type="text/javascript">
</script>
<script src="/javascripts/effects.js?1149008954" type="text/javascript">
</script>
<script src="/javascripts/dragdrop.js?1149008954" type="text/javascript">
</script>
<script src="/javascripts/controls.js?1149008954" type="text/javascript">
</script>
<script src="/javascripts/application.js?1149008954" type="text/javascript">
</script>
```

The file application.js is for any custom JavaScript you write. If you need more JavaScript files, you can pass a string to javascript_include_tag:

`code/rails_xt/app/views/layouts/quips.rhtml`

```
<%= javascript_include_tag 'mylibrary' %>
```

This renders the following:

```
<script src="/javascripts/mylibrary.js?" type="text/javascript"></script>
```

Rails Ajax Helpers

Now that we have our client-side JavaScript libraries available, we can make our application's pages more usable. Let's start with the show and edit actions of the scaffold. Instead of making the user change pages to switch from show to edit mode, why not just let him use one page for both purposes? Here's one possible approach: When the mouse hovers over a property value in the show action, the text becomes hot and changes color. Clicking the text dynamically opens a tiny edit form for that single field, which then uses Ajax to make the update to the server.

We picked this exact design for one reason: Scriptaculous supports it, and Rails includes a helper that makes it trivial. We have added the InPlaceEditor to the Quips show action:

`code/rails_xt/app/views/quips/show.rhtml`

```
<% for column in Quip.content_columns %>
<p>
  <b><%= column.human_name %>:</b>
  <%= in_place_editor_field "quip", column.name %>
</p>
<% end %>
```

That's it. The only difference from a non-Ajax view is the call to in_place_editor_field, which shows the current value of particular column and then adds JavaScript to do everything else: highlight the field on mouseover, show the edit form, submit an edit via Ajax, and update the field based on the server response. Here's the resulting HTML for one column, reformatted for readability:

```
code/rails_xt/sample_output/in_place.html
```
```html
<span class="in_place_editor_field"
        id="quip_text_1_in_place_editor">This is quip 1</span>
<script type="text/javascript">
//<![CDATA[
new Ajax.InPlaceEditor('quip_text_1_in_place_editor',
                        '/quips/set_quip_text/1')
//]]>
</script>
```

The Ajax.InPlaceEditor is a Scriptaculous object. As you might guess from the HTML, Scriptaculous has its own set of naming conventions that govern the HTML class and id attributes, as well as the parameters you pass to Ajax.InPlaceEditor. If you use the Rails helpers, you do not have to learn or worry about these naming conventions.

The second parameter to Ajax.InPlaceEditor is the server URL to call, /quips/set_quip_text/1. In standard Rails routing, this implies a set_quip_text action on the QuipsController. More generally, we will need actions for every column, named like set_quip_[colname]. Where do these names come from? Again, a single-line helper method does everything. In the controller:

```
code/rails_xt/app/controllers/quips_controller.rb
```
```ruby
in_place_edit_for :quip, :text
```

The arguments to in_place_edit_for are the model and column names that should allow in-place editing. Here we allow editing for a quip's :text.

As a slightly more complex example, let's add a search view for quips. As the user types characters into a search form, the results will update automatically, à la GoogleSuggest. First, we will need a search action on the controller:

```
code/rails_xt/app/controllers/quips_controller.rb
```
```ruby
def search
  @quips = Quip.find_text_like(params[:search])
  render :partial=>'search_results' if request.xhr?
end
```

The call to find_text_like presumes a class method on Quip that will find text like some value:

`code/rails_xt/app/models/quip.rb`

```
def self.find_text_like(value)
  find(:all, :conditions=> "text LIKE " +
      ActiveRecord::Base.connection.quote("%#{value}%"))
end
```

The call to render :partial lets the one search action handle both Ajax and non-Ajax requests. If request.xhr? returns true, the request was made via Ajax. We don't want to render the entire page, just the changed part, which we plan to place in a partial named _search_results.rhtml. Otherwise, we fall out of the method, and Rails automatically renders search.rhtml.

Now we need to create a search.rhtml that will show a collection of quips, plus a form to submit a search string:

`code/rails_xt/app/views/quips/search.rhtml`

```
<h1>Search quips</h1>
<%= image_tag 'loading.gif', :id=>'spinner',
            :style=>"display:none; float:right;" %>

<% form_tag do %>
  <%= text_field_tag 'search', @search %>
  <%= observe_field :search,
                    :frequency => 0.5,
                    :update => 'search-results',
                    :complete=>"Element.hide('spinner')",
                    :before=>"Element.show('spinner')",
                    :with=>"'search=' + encodeURIComponent(value)",
                    :url=>{:action=>'search'} %>
  <image>
<% end %>
<div id="search-results">
<%= render :partial=>'search_results' %>
</div>
<%= link_to 'List', :action => 'list' %>
```

We initially created this file by copying and pasting the template for the show action, show.rhtml. Then we made the following changes:

- The image_tag shows an animated GIF as a progress indicator so the user can tell we are making an asynchronous call. Since there is no Ajax call at first, this image is set to :style=>"display:none".
- There is a form for the search operation, containing a search field.

- Inside the form there is a call to the observe_field helper. This is where the Ajax happens and is described in more detail in a moment.
- The actual table is not rendered here but in a partial named search_results.
- The partial is wrapped with a div id="search-results".

The call to observe_field takes a single required argument, plus a large number of optional arguments. The ones we use here are as follows:

- :search is the ID of the field to observe. It refers to the text_field_tag.
- :frequency is how often (in seconds) to check the field for changes. Smaller values are more responsive but put more load on the server. (Zero is a special case causing the field to be checked when you exit the control.)
- :update is the DOM ID to update with the results of the Ajax call. This is why we needed to wrap the partial with a known DOM ID.
- :complete and :before specify JavaScript to execute before and after the Ajax call. This shows and hides the progress indicator.
- :with specifies the query string for the Ajax request. The call to encodeURIComponent is JavaScript.
- :url specifies the server URL to call, using standard Rails url_for arguments.

Planning for Ajax

These two examples have only scratched the surface of Rails' Ajax support. Besides in_place_editor_field, there are helpers for other user interface enhancements, including drag and drop. Besides observe_field, there are helpers to handle almost everything that can happen in a browser interface: links, forms, button clicks, timers, and so on.

Complete coverage of these features (and their many optional arguments) would take about half a book. Rather than do that, we will revisit these two examples to make some general points about Ajax design and about Ajax implementation in Rails.

First, we will talk about the design side. The two examples we have shown here demonstrate things that might be useful in some situations but certainly not in all. Adding an InPlaceEditor presumes you want to allow edits one field at a time.

Although this is convenient, you should avoid this in several situations:

- Many users may not recognize that the in-place editor even exists. You may need to add more visual indication or to train users in some way.
- Some model objects have validation constraints that span multiple fields or multiple rows. Allowing per-field edits may put these objects in an invalid state or make some valid states unreachable.
- In-place editing puts more demand on the server.

degradable

A huge design concern is users without Ajax-enabled browsers. In our examples, everything will still work with Ajax disabled—you can verify this by disabling JavaScript in your browser. But this *degradable* Ajax required some up-front thinking that we did not mention when we first presented the examples. The in-place editing example is usable without Ajax because the Edit links are all still there. If Ajax is unavailable, simply go from Show to Edit mode with a plain old page transition.

The search example works without Ajax because of the way we coded the controller. If JavaScript is turned off, then the form observer will of course not work. But, a user can still submit the form the old-fashioned way by pressing Enter. The form will post to the same URL that the Ajax call would have, /quips/search. However, the call to request.xhr? will return false, and Rails will render search.rhtml in response. We could make the non-Ajax case even clearer by including a submit button in the search form and then use JavaScript to hide the button in Ajax-aware environments. Rails makes degradable Ajax possible, as long as you are careful.

The two examples we have shown here demonstrate some most important themes of Rails Ajax development:

- Rails helper methods hide the details of Prototype and Scriptaculous. As long as you stay within the capabilities of the helper methods, you do not really have to understand the JavaScript. (We think you should, though.)
- Degradable Ajax is possible if you are careful. One easy approach is to have the same controller methods do double-duty and branch on request.xhr?.
- Ajax helpers methods tend to take a few required parameters and many optional ones via a final Hash argument. Many of the option names are shared across several methods, reducing the amount you have to learn.

- Many of the Rails Ajax helpers encourage a style of Ajax that depends on returning HTML fragments (as opposed to the XML suggested by the acronym AJAX). This style simplifies the incremental addition of Ajax features to an existing web application but may be less useful if you are building a more thoroughly Ajaxified application.

Another approach to Ajax development is to send JavaScript code in response to Ajax requests. Although this might sound like an unlikely approach, Rails includes a clever JavaScript generation mechanism that allows you to write page updates in Ruby code. The next section will show you how.

6.9 Rendering JavaScript with RJS

RJS (Rails JavaScript) lets you update pages by programming against a page object on the server. This page object, written in Ruby, is actually a code generator that converts Ruby code into JavaScript, which Rails returns to the client for execution there. This sounds complex, but the usage is surprisingly simple. As an example, we will create a better search action called better_search.

The better_search action will work just like search but will also report the number of items returned. This report will live in a separate partial. From the main view file, better_search.rhtml, we will reference this partial:

`code/rails_xt/app/views/quips/better_search.rhtml`

```
<div id="search-count">
<%= render :partial=>'search_count'%>
</div>
```

The partial itself is simple enough:

`code/rails_xt/app/views/quips/_search_count.rhtml`

```
Found <%= @quips.size %> matching your request.
```

Now for the challenge: After the user triggers a search, two different divs should update: the search-results div containing the table and the search-count div with the result count. If you tried to use the observe_field with an :update option, you would have two choices:

- Wrap the two divs in a higher-level HTML element, and :update that.
- Issue two separate Ajax requests, one for each element.

Both of these choices are poor. In our simple example, it might be easy enough to group the elements together, but in general you may need to update many more than two elements. By the time you group them all together you are updating the entire page, which rather defeats the point of Ajax. The second choice is even worse. The two Ajax requests decompose a single user action into two server actions. Because Ajax is asynchronous, these actions might succeed or fail separately. Or they might both succeed, but one response might be lost. Either way, the user interface ends up in an incorrect state. Better yet, given that most calls succeed, the symptoms will be difficult to reproduce. (Translation: It will work on your machine and fail on your most important user's machine.)

RJS comes to your rescue. With RJS, doing multiple updates is a snap. Here is an RJS template used by the better_search action:

code/rails_xt/app/views/quips/_search_update.rjs

```
page.replace_html 'search-results', :partial=>'search_results'
page.replace_html 'search-count', :partial=>'search_count'
page.visual_effect :highlight, 'search-count'
```

The previous replace_html methods take a DOM ID and a partial. Rails then generates JavaScript to replace the contents of each DOM ID with the result of rendering the partial. The call to visual_effect highlights the search count so that the user can tell something has changed.

From the controller, an RJS template is accessed like any other template. In fact, you cannot tell from the controller code what kind of template is in use:

code/rails_xt/app/controllers/quips_controller.rb

```
def better_search
  @quips = Quip.find_text_like(params[:search])
  render :partial=>'search_update' if request.xhr?
end
```

In addition to basic DOM updates, RJS includes methods for alerts, timers, redirects, and Scriptaculous drag and drop.

6.10 Black-Box Testing with Selenium

In a Rails application, the tests in test/functional are used to test controllers. They also test the view code to some degree, since the view templates are rendered when controller actions are invoked. These tests are *white-box* tests, because they have access to (and can test) internal

white-box

details of how the controllers and views work. These tests are covered in detail in Chapter 7, *Testing*, on page 181.

The opposite of white-box test is a black-box test. In black-box testing, the tests have no awareness of the internal workings of the program being tested. Black-box tests are often performed jointly by the developers and consumers of a system. When used in this way, black-box tests are *acceptance tests*. Acceptance tests are, quite literally, the measure of success of a system.

acceptance tests

Since acceptance tests know nothing of implementation details, acceptance testing tools are not specific to any language or library. We build acceptance tests for web applications with the open source tool Selenium.[7]

Testing a Rails application with Selenium usually involves three separate libraries:

- Selenium Core is the underlying Selenium engine. Selenium Core can run tests on about a dozen different browser platforms.

- The Selenium IDE is a Firefox extension for recording tests. Tests recorded in the Selenium IDE can then be run on other browers using Selenium Core.

- Selenium on Rails is a Rails plugin that provides a Ruby-based library for invoking Selenium. For substantial tests, this library is easier to work with than the test format produced by the Selenium IDE.

To see these libraries in action, follow the instructions on the Selenium home page for installing Selenium Core and the Selenium IDE. We will use the Selenium IDE to record a test for the People application.

1. After installing Selenium IDE, restart Firefox.

2. Run the People application against the test environment:

   ```
   RAILS_ENV=test script/server
   ```

3. Open Firefox, and navigate to the People index page, /people.

4. From the Firefox Tools menu, select Selenium Recorder to turn on the Selenium Recorder. Resize the browser window and the recorder so you can see both.

---

7. http://www.openqa.org/selenium/

5. Click the New Person link to create a new person. Notice that the recorder is recording your actions.

6. Click the Create button to create a new person. This should fail since the person has no name.

7. Select the error message "can't be blank" in the browser window. Right-click the selection, and choose Append Selenium Command | verifyTextPresent.

8. Enter a first name and last name, and click Create again.

9. Select the status message "Person was successfully created" and append another Selenium command to verify this text is present.

10. Switch to the Selenium Recorder, and save the test as test/selenium/people/create_person.html.

Use the Selenium IDE to run your test. The Play button at the top of the IDE will start a test, and you can run at three different speeds: Run, Walk, or Step. The Selenium IDE has several other features that we will not explicitly cover here:

- The command field is a pop-up window that lists all the (large) number of possible Selenium commands.
- The Log tab keeps log messages from past tests.
- The Reference tab documents the current command and automatically syncs with whatever command you have selected.

In a Rails application, the easiest way to run an entire test suite is to install the Selenium on Rails plugin:[8]

```
script/plugin install http://svn.openqa.org/svn/selenium-on-rails/selenium-on-ra
```

Navigate to the /selenium URL within your People application. The Selenium on Rails plugin implements this URL (in test mode only!) to provide a four-panel UI for running Selenium tests. You can see this UI in Figure 6.1, on the next page. The top-left panel shows your tests, the middle shows the current test, and the right panel provides an interface for single-stepping or running the tests. The large panel across the bottom contains your application so you can watch the tests as they run. Try running your test in Run mode and in Step mode. In Step mode you will need to click Continue to take each step.

---

8. We have found that the dash delimiter does not play well with Rails 1.2 RC1. Renaming the plugin to use underscores (selenium_on_rails) fixes the problem.

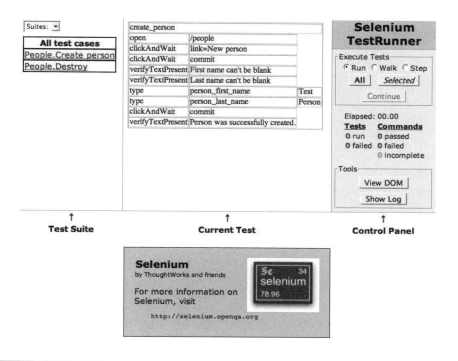

Figure 6.1: RUNNING TESTS WITH SELENIUM

If you opened the source for a saved Selenium IDE test, you would see an HTML file with a table. The individual test steps are formatted as table rows like this step, which navigates to the /people URL:

```
<tr>
        <td>open</td>
        <td>/people</td>
        <td></td>
</tr>
```

Selenium on Rails provides an alternative format for tests that uses Ruby syntax. This is convenient if you are writing more complex tests. To create a Selenium on Rails test, use the following generator:

```
./script/generate selenium your_test.rsel
```

This will create a test file named test/selenium/your_test.rsel. Fill in the test with RSelenese commands. (The RSelenese commands are documented in the RDoc for Selenium on Rails. You can generate this documentation by going to vendor/plugins/selenium-on-rails and executing rake rdoc.)

Here is an RSelenese test for logging in to the Rails XT application:

```
code/rails_xt/test/selenium/_login.rsel
setup :fixtures=>:all
open '/account/login'
type 'login', 'quentin'
type 'password', 'test'
click 'commit'
wait_for_page_to_load 2000
```

This test starts by loading all test fixtures and then navigates to the login page. After logging in, the test waits for up to 2,000 milliseconds to be redirected to a post-login page. Notice that this test's filename begins with an underscore. Borrowing from Rails view nomenclature, this is a partial test. Since all tests will need to log in, this test is invoked from other tests with the RSelenese command include_partial.

Selenium on Rails also includes a test:acceptance Rake task. You can use this task to run all of your Selenium tests.

6.11 Conclusions

The view layer is where programmers, interaction designers, and graphic designers meet. In the Java world, the view tier is often built around the assumption that programmers know Java and designers know HTML. Much effort then goes to creating a dynamic environment that splits the difference between Java and the HTML/scripting world. Tag libraries, the JSTL expression language, and OGNL all aspire to provide dynamic content *without* the complexity of Java syntax.

If we had to pick one phrase to summarize how the Rails approach differs, it would be "Ruby-centered simplicity." The vision is that everyone (including page designers) needs to know a little Ruby but nothing else. Since Ruby is a scripting language, it is already friendly enough for designers as well as programmers. As a result, there is no need for intermediaries such as tag libraries and custom expression languages. Everything is simply Ruby.

Neither approach is perfect. After all the effort to "simplify" Java into tags and expression languages, we have seen both programmers and designers struggle to understand what is happening on a dynamic page. If you have chosen a side in the dynamic vs. static languages debate, this is frustrating, *regardless of which side you are on*. The Java web tier mixes static, compiled code (Java) with dynamically evaluated code (tag library invocations, expression languages). To troubleshoot a Java web application, you need to have a thorough understanding of both worlds.

Troubleshooting Rails applications is no joy either. Things are simpler since there is only one language, but there are still problems. Tool support is minimal at present, although we expect Ruby's rising popularity to drive major tool improvements. Stack traces in the view are deep and hard to read, both in Ruby and in Java.

Since tracking down problems that have percolated all the way to the view is such a pain, we had better make sure that such problems are few and far between. Fortunately, Rails provides excellent support for testing, which is the subject of the next chapter.

6.12 Resources

HAML: HTML Abstraction Markup Language...
... http://unspace.ca/discover/haml/
HAML is an alternative templating engine for Rails.

Markaby Is Markup As Ruby........http://code.whytheluckystiff.net/markaby/
Markaby is a pure-Ruby approach to generating HTML markup. Obsessed with convenience and willing to employ as much idiomatic Ruby as necessary to get there.

Rails Cache Test Plugin........http://blog.cosinux.org/pages/page-cache-test
The Rails Cache Test Plugin provides assertions to test the caching of content and the expiration of cached content. The tests will work even with caching turned off (as it usually is in the test environment), because the plugin stubs out cache-related methods.

Selenium.....................................http://www.openqa.org/selenium/
Selenium is a testing tool for web applications. Selenium runs directly in the browser and is therefore suitable for functional and acceptance testing, as well as browse compatibility testing.

Selenium IDE........................http://wiki.openqa.org/display/SIDE/Home
Selenium IDE is a Firefox extension you can use to record, execute, and debug Selenium tests.

Selenium on Rails...................http://www.openqa.org/selenium-on-rails/
Selenium on Rails is a Rails plugin that provides a standard Selenium directory for a Rails project, Ruby syntax for invoking Selenium tests, and a Rake task for acceptance tests.

Chapter 7

Testing

Testing starts small, with *unit testing*. Unit testing is automated testing of small chunks of code (units). By testing at the smallest granularity, you can make sure that the basic building blocks of your system work. Of course, you needn't stop there! You can also apply many of the techniques of unit testing when testing higher levels of the system. *unit testing*

Unit tests do not directly ensure good or useful design. What unit tests do ensure is that *things work as intended*. This turns out to have an *indirect* positive impact on design. You can easily improve code with good unit tests later. When you think of an improvement, just drop it in. The unit tests will quickly tell you whether your "two steps forward" are costing you one (or more) steps back somewhere else.

The Test::Unit framework is part of Ruby's standard library. To anyone familiar with Java's JUnit, Test::Unit will look very familiar—these frameworks, and others like them, are similar enough that they are often described as the *XUnit frameworks*. Like JUnit, Test::Unit provides the following: *XUnit frameworks*

- A base class for unit tests and a set of naming conventions for easily invoking a specific test or a group of related tests
- A set of *assertions* that will fail a test (by throwing an exception) if they encounter unexpected results *assertions*
- Lifecycle methods (setup() and teardown()) to guarantee a consistent system state for tests that need it

In this chapter, we will cover Test::Unit and how Rails' conventions, generators, and Rake tasks make it easy to write and run tests. We'll also cover the custom assertions that Rails adds to Test::Unit and the three kinds of tests generated by Rails. Finally, we will explore some other tools regularly used to improve Rails testing: FlexMock for mock objects and rcov for code coverage.

7.1 Getting Started with Test::Unit

The easiest way to understand Test::Unit is to actually test something, so here goes. Imagine a simple method that creates an HTML tag. The method will take two arguments: the name of the tag and the (optional) body of the tag. Here's a quick and dirty implementation in Java:

`code/java_xt/src/unit/Simple.java`

```java
package unit;

public class Simple {
  public static String tag(String name) {
    return tag(name, "");
  }
  public static String tag(String name, String body) {
    return "<" + name + ">" + body + "</" + name + ">";
  }
}
```

And here is the similar code in Ruby:

`code/rails_xt/samples/unit/simple_tag_1.rb`

```ruby
module Simple
  def tag(name, body='')
    "<#{name}>#{body}</#{name}>"
  end
end
```

One way to test this code is to fire up irb, require() the file, and try some inputs:

```
irb(main):001:0> require 'simple_tag_1'
=> true
irb(main):004:0> include Simple
=> Object
irb(main):006:0> tag 'h1'
=> "<h1></h1>"
irb(main):007:0> tag 'h1', 'hello'
=> "<h1>hello</h1>"
irb(main):008:0> tag nil
=> "<></>"
```

This kind of interactive testing is useful, and it lets you quickly explore corner cases (notice that the result of tag nil is probably undesirable).

The downside of this interactive testing is that you, the programmer, must be around to do the interacting. That's fine the first time, but we would like to be able to automate this kind of testing. That's where unit testing and assertions come in.

Most Java developers write unit tests with JUnit. Although JUnit is not part of Java proper, its use is extremely widespread. You can download it at http://www.junit.org, or it is included with most Java IDEs and a wide variety of other projects. Here's a simple JUnit TestCase:

`code/java_xt/src/unit/SimpleTest.java`

```java
package unit;

import junit.framework.TestCase;

public class SimpleTest extends TestCase {
  public void testTag() {
    assertEquals("<h1></h1>", Simple.tag("h1"));
    assertEquals("<h1>hello</h1>", Simple.tag("h1", "hello"));
  }
}
```

JUnit relies on several conventions to minimize your work in writing tests. JUnit recognizes any subclass of TestCase as a container of unit tests, and it invokes as tests any methods whose names begin with test. Assertions such as assertEquals() that take two values list the expected value first, followed by the actual value. JUnit tests can be run in a variety of test runners, both graphical and console based (consult your IDE documentation or http://www.junit.org for details).

The equivalent Ruby TestCase is extremely similar:

`code/rails_xt/samples/unit/simple_tag_1_test.rb`

```ruby
require 'test/unit'
require 'simple_tag_1'

class SimpleTest < Test::Unit::TestCase
  include Simple
  def test_tag
    assert_equal("<h1></h1>", tag("h1"))
    assert_equal("<h1>hello</h1>", tag("h1", "hello"))
  end
end
```

Test::Unit recognizes any subclass of Test::Unit::TestCase as a container of unit tests, and it invokes as tests any methods whose names begin with test. As with JUnit, assertions such as assert_equal() that take two values list the expected value first, followed by the actual value. You can run the tests in an .rb file by simply pointing Ruby at the file:

```
$ ruby simple_tag_1_test.rb
Loaded suite simple_tag_1_test
Started
.
Finished in 0.001918 seconds.

1 tests, 2 assertions, 0 failures, 0 errors
```

When a test fails, you should get a descriptive message and a stack trace. For our Simple example, a test that expects tag names to be automatically lowercased should fail:

`code/java_xt/src/unit/FailingTest.java`

```java
public void testTag() {
    assertEquals("<h1></h1>", Simple.tag("H1"));
}
```

Here is the error report from the JUnit console:

```
junit.framework.ComparisonFailure:
Expected:<h1>
Actual  :<H1></H1>
        at unit.FailingTest.testTag(FailingTest.java:6)
        at sun.reflect.NativeMethodAccessorImpl.invoke0(Native Method)
        (...more stack...)
```

Here is the Ruby version of a failing test:

`code/rails_xt/samples/unit/failing_test.rb`

```ruby
require 'test/unit'
require 'simple_tag_1'

class FailingTest < Test::Unit::TestCase
  include Simple
  def test_tag
    assert_equal("<h1></h1>", tag("H1"))
  end
end
```

As with JUnit, the console output will report the failing method name, the cause of the problem, and some stack trace information:

```
$ ruby failing_test.rb
(...snip...)
  1) Failure:
test_tag(FailingTest) [failing_test.rb:8]:
<"<h1></h1>"> expected but was
<"<H1></H1>">.

1 tests, 1 assertions, 1 failures, 0 errors
```

When you are writing a test right now, in the present, you have the entire context of the problem in your brain. At some point in the future, refactoring may break your test. Take pity on poor Howard, the programmer who is running the tests that unlucky day. He has never looked at your code before this very moment, and he has no helpful context in *his* head. You can increase your karma by providing an explicit error message. In JUnit, use an alternate form of the assertEquals() method with an error message as the first argument:

If you don't believe in altruism, bear in mind that Howard might be you!

`code/java_xt/src/unit/SelfDocumentingTest.java`

```java
public void testTag() {
  assertEquals("tag should lowercase element names",
               "<h1></h1>", Simple.tag("H1"));
}
```

Now, the console report for a failing test will include your error message.

```
junit.framework.ComparisonFailure: tag should lowercase element names
Expected:<h1>
Actual   :<H1></H1>
         at unit.SelfDocumentingTest.testTag(SelfDocumentingTest.java:7)
         (...more stack...)
```

Watch out! This time, the Ruby version contains a surprise. You can add an optional error message, but it is the *last* parameter, not the first. This is inconsistent with JUnit but consistent with Ruby style: *Put optional arguments at the end.*

`code/rails_xt/samples/unit/self_documenting_test.rb`

```ruby
require 'test/unit'
require 'simple_tag_1'

class SelfDocumentingTest < Test::Unit::TestCase
  include Simple
  def test_tag
    assert_equal("<h1></h1>", tag("H1"),
                 "tag should lowercase element names")
  end
end
```

The console output will now include your explicit error message:

```
$ ruby self_documenting_test.rb
(...snip...)
  1) Failure:
test_tag(SelfDocumentingTest) [self_documenting_test.rb:8]:
tag should lowercase element names.
<"<h1></h1>"> expected but was
<"<H1></H1>">.
```

Next, let's test what should happen if the user passes a null/nil name to tag. We would like this to result in an exception. Early versions of Java and JUnit did not handle "test for exception" in an elegant way, but JUnit 4.*x* uses a Java 5 annotation to mark tests where an exception is expected. Here is a test that checks for an IllegalArgumentException:

JUnit 4 differs in several ways from many of the examples shown here. We are using older JUnit idioms where possible because we expect they are more familiar to most readers.

> code/junit4/src/unit/SimpleTest.java

```
@Test(expected=IllegalArgumentException.class)
public void nullTag() {
  Simple.tag(null);
}
```

Where JUnit uses a custom annotation, Test::Unit takes advantage of Ruby's block syntax:

> code/rails_xt/samples/unit/test_nil.rb

```
def test_nil_tag
  assert_raises (ArgumentError) {tag(nil)}
end
```

This test should fail, since we do not yet handle the **nil** case as intended:

```
$ ruby simple_tag_1_test_2.rb
Loaded suite simple_tag_1_test_2
Started
F.
Finished in 0.025861 seconds.

  1) Failure:
test_nil_tag(SimpleTest) [simple_tag_1_test_2.rb:11]:
<ArgumentError> exception expected but none was thrown.

2 tests, 3 assertions, 1 failures, 0 errors
```

Now we can fix the tag implementation to reject **nil**:

> code/rails_xt/samples/unit/simple_tag_2.rb

```
module Simple
  def tag(name, body='')
    raise ArgumentError, "Must specify tag" unless name
    "<#{name}>#{body}</#{name}>"
  end
end
```

After writing these unit tests, the tag method may still seem not very good. Perhaps you would like to see a tag() that handles attributes, does more argument validation, or makes clever use of blocks to allow nested calls to tag(). With good unit tests in place, it is easy to make speculative improvements. If your "improvement" breaks code some-where else, you will know immediately, and you will be able to undo back to a good state:

Assertions

Assertions are the backbone of unit testing. An assertion claims that some condition should hold. It could be that two objects should be equal, it could be that two objects should *not* be equal, or it could be any of a variety of more complex conditions. When an assertion works as expected, nothing happens. When an assertion fails to work, infor-mation about the failure is reported loudly. If you are in a GUI, expect a red bar or a pop-up window, with access to more detailed information. If you are in a console, expect an error message and a stack trace.

Both JUnit and Test::Unit provide several flavors of assertion. Here are a few key points to remember:

- Equality is not the same as identity. Use assert_equal() to test equality and assert_same() to test identity.
- **false** is not the same as **nil** (although **nil** acts as **false** in a boolean context). Use assert_nil() and assert_not_nil() to deal with **nil**.
- Zero (0) evaluates to **true** in a boolean context. Don't write code that forces anybody to remember this.
- Ruby uses raise for exceptions, so you test for exceptions with assert_raises. Do not call the assert_throws method by mistake! assert_throws is used to test Ruby's throw/catch, which (despite the name) is not used for exceptions.

You can write your own assertions, since they are just method calls. Typically your assertions will assert more complex, domain-specific conditions by calling one or more of the built-in assertions.

Lifecycle Methods

Often, several tests depend on a common setup. For example, if you are testing data objects, then all your tests may depend on a common database connection. It is wasteful to repeat this code in every test, so unit testing frameworks provide lifecycle callback methods.

JUnit defines setUp() and tearDown() methods, which are called auto-matically before and after each test. Similarly, Test::Unit defines setup()

and teardown() methods. To see them in action, consider this real example from the Rails code base: ActiveRecord's unit tests need to test threaded database connections.

The "threadedness" of ActiveRecord connections involves some global setup and teardown. So, any testing of threaded connections must be preceded by code to put ActiveRecord into a threaded state.

code/rails/activerecord/test/threaded_connections_test.rb
```
def setup
  @connection = ActiveRecord::Base.remove_connection
  @connections = []
  @allow_concurrency = ActiveRecord::Base.allow_concurrency
end
```

Notice that some original, pretest globals are saved in variables (@connection and @allow_concurrency). These values are then reset after the test completes:

code/rails/activerecord/test/threaded_connections_test.rb
```
def teardown
  # clear the connection cache
  ActiveRecord::Base.send(:clear_all_cached_connections!)
  # set allow_concurrency to saved value
  ActiveRecord::Base.allow_concurrency = @allow_concurrency
  # reestablish old connection
  ActiveRecord::Base.establish_connection(@connection)
end
```

You are likely to find that setup() is useful often to avoid duplicate code for similar start states. Since Ruby is garbage-collected, teardown() is used less often, typically for cleaning up application-wide settings.

To give an indication of their relative frequency, here are some simple stats from Rails:

```
$ ruby rails_stats.rb
631 .rb files
212 test classes
126 test setup methods
20 test teardown methods
```

The program that generates these stats is quite simple. It uses Ruby's Dir.glob to loop over files and regular expression matching to "guesstimate" the relative usage of setup() and teardown():

```
code/rails_xt/samples/rails_stats.rb
```

```
base ||= "../../rails" # set for your own ends
files = tests = setups = teardowns = 0
Dir.glob("#{base}/**/*.rb").each do |f|
  files += 1
  File.open(f) do |file|
    file.each do |line|
      tests += 1 if /< Test::Unit::TestCase/=~line
      teardowns += 1 if /def teardown/=~line
      setups += 1 if /def setup/=~line
    end
  end
end

puts "#{files} .rb files"
puts "#{tests} test classes"
puts "#{setups} test setup methods"
puts "#{teardowns} test teardown methods"
```

7.2 Rails Testing Conventions

Historically, Java frameworks have not imposed a directory structure or naming convention for tests. This flexibility means that every project tends to be a little different. When approaching a new project, you typically need to consult the Ant build.xml file to learn the project structure. Some programmers have found that this flexibility does more harm than good and now use Apache Maven (http://maven.apache.org/) to impose a common structure across projects.

Rails projects have a standard layout and naming conventions. As a result, most Rails projects look a lot like most other Rails projects. For example, application code lives in the app directory, and the corresponding test code lives in the test directory. This convention makes it easy to read and understand unfamiliar projects.

Rails' naming conventions are instantiated by the various generators. When you call script/generate, Rails creates stubbed-out versions of test classes, plus the environment they need to run. Rails initially supported two kinds of tests: unit tests for model classes and functional tests for controller classes. Since Rails 1.1, you can also generate a third kind of test called an *integration test*, which can test an extended user interation across multiple controllers and model classes.

integration test

The three kinds of tests are described in more detail in the following sections. Unlike most of the book, this chapter does not include Java code for comparison, because there is no equivalent Java framework that is in widespread use.

Unit Testing

Let's start by testing a Rails model class. We've cleaned up the output of the following script/generate to show only the new files created for the Person model:

```
script/generate model Person
    create  app/models/person.rb
    create  test/unit/person_test.rb
    create  test/fixtures/people.yml
    create  db/migrate/002_create_people.rb
```

The files app/models/person.rb and db/migrate/002_create_people.rb deal with the ActiveRecord model class itself and are covered in detail in Chapter 4, *Accessing Data with ActiveRecord*, on page 77. Here we are concerned with the files in the test directory. The unit test for the Person class is the file test/unit/person_test.rb, and it initially looks like this:

```
require File.dirname(__FILE__) + '/../test_helper'

class PersonTest < Test::Unit::TestCase
  fixtures :people

  # Replace this with your real tests.
  def test_truth
    assert true
  end
end
```

The first line requires (after the path-math) the file test/test_helper.rb. The test/test_helper.rb file is automatically created with any new Rails application and provides three useful things:

- A ready-made environment for your tests, including everything you are likely to need: environment settings, a live database connection, access to model classes, Test::Unit, and Rails' own extensions to Test::Unit.

fixtures

- Access to *fixtures*, that is, sample data for your tests. We will talk more about this in a minute.
- Any application-wide test helpers or assertions you might choose to write.

The remainder of the PersonTest is an empty unit test, waiting and hoping that your conscience will lead you to write some tests, except for

> ### ⚡ Joe Asks...
> #### Is Fixture Configuration Easy in Rails?
>
> We are not going to kid you. Configuring fixtures is a pain, no matter what language or tool you are using. But in Rails this cloud does have a bit of a silver lining. YAML is simpler than XML to work with and less verbose. The introduction of the ERb templating step lets us jump out to a serious programming language (Ruby) when configuration tasks start to get tedious.

one little thing—that line fixtures :people. This line makes fixture data available to your tests. Here's how it works....

Rails' fixture system looks for a fixture file corresponding to :people but located in the directory test/fixtures. This leads to a file named test/fixtures/people.yml, which is the other file originally created by script/generate. The initial version of people.yml looks like this:

```
# Read about fixtures at http://ar.rubyonrails.org/classes/Fixtures.html
first:
  id: 1
another:
  id: 2
```

This file is in the YAML format, covered in detail in Section 9.3, *YAML and XML Compared*, on page 245. Rails uses the leftmost (unindented) items to name Person objects: first and another. Rails uses the indented name/value pairs under each item to initialize model objects that are available to your tests. You can (and should) add name/value pairs as appropriate to create reasonable objects for your tests. Here is a more complete version of the people fixture:

`code/rails_xt/test/fixtures/people.yml`

```
first:
  id: 1
  first_name: Stuart
  last_name: Halloway
another:
  id: 2
  first_name: Justin
  last_name: Gehtland
```

To use a fixture in your test, call a method named after the plural form of your model class. So, the :first person is available as people(:first). You can then use this object as needed during a test:

code/rails_xt/test/unit/person_test.rb

```
def test_find_by_first_name
  assert_equal people(:first),
               Person.find_by_first_name('Stuart')
end
```

Rails is clever about injecting fixture objects into your database. During testing, Rails uses a test-specific database, so unit tests will not blow away your development (or production!) data. Since the fixtures provide a reliable initial setup, you will find that your model tests rarely need to implement a setup() method at all.

Managing Your Fixture Data

Unfortunately, fixture editing often gets more complex, repetitive, and prone to error. Here's a quips fixture on the way to disaster:

```
quip_1:
  id: 1
  author_id: 1
  text: This is quip 1
quip_2:
  id: 2
  author_id: 1
  text: This is quip 1
# 48 more...
```

Fortunately, Rails offers an elegant solution to this kind of repetition. Before handing your fixture to the YAML parser, Rails processes the file as an Embedded Ruby (ERb) template. ERb is Ruby's templating language, which means you can intersperse Ruby code in your templates.[1] With ERb, the quips fixture becomes this:

code/rails_xt/test/fixtures/quips.yml

```
<% (1..50).each do |i| %>
quip_<%= i %>:
  id: <%= i %>
  author_id: <%= 1+(i%2) %>
  text: This is quip <%= i %>
<% end %>
```

---

1. ERb is also used in Rails views; see Chapter 6, *Rendering Output with ActionView*, on page 149 for more ERb examples.

Verifying that the quips load correctly is easy enough. You can use a Rake task to load all fixtures and then use script/console and have a look around:

```
$ rake db:fixtures:load
(in /Users/stuart/FR_RAILS4JAVA/Book/code/rails_xt)
$ script/console
Loading development environment.
>> Quip.count
=> 50
```

Functional Testing

Now that you have seen a model test in action, let's look at testing a Rails controller.

```
$ script/generate controller People
      create   app/views/people
      create   app/controllers/people_controller.rb
      create   test/functional/people_controller_test.rb
      create   app/helpers/people_helper.rb
```

The file app/controllers/people_controller.rb is the controller itself and is covered in detail in Chapter 5, *Coordinating Activities with ActionController*, on page 115. Both app/views/people and app/helpers/people_helper.rb are view code, covered in Chapter 6, *Rendering Output with ActionView*, on page 149. That leaves the *functional test* file test/functional/people_controller_test.rb, which initially looks like this:

functional test

```
require File.dirname(__FILE__) + '/../test_helper'
require 'people_controller'

# Re-raise errors caught by the controller.
class PeopleController; def rescue_action(e) raise e end; end

class PeopleControllerTest < Test::Unit::TestCase
  def setup
    @controller = PeopleController.new
    @request    = ActionController::TestRequest.new
    @response   = ActionController::TestResponse.new
  end

  # Replace this with your real tests.
  def test_truth
    assert true
  end
end
```

As you can see, a functional test in Rails is nothing more than a unit test for a controller. Much of the code here is similar to the model test case, with two noteworthy differences:

- Controller tests reopen the controller to redefine rescue_action(). In production code, rescue_action() handles reporting and logging for unhandled exceptions. But in test code, we just want exceptions to bubble through and trigger test failures. This is a good example of the usefulness of open classes, discussed in Section 3.1, *Extending Core Classes*, on page 53.

- Controller tests have a setup() method, which establishes a @controller, plus a @request and @response that can be used to simulate interacting with an HTTP request.[2]

Test Automation with Rake

In the preceding examples in this section, we have run tests from a single .rb file. Rails applications also include Rake tasks to automate running a set of tests. (Rake is an automation tool similar to Ant and is covered fully in Chapter 8, *Automating the Development Process*, on page 217.) Here is how you would use the test:units Rake task to run all model tests:

```
$ rake test:units
(in /Users/stuart/FR_RAILS4JAVA/Book/code/rails_xt)
/opt/local/bin/ruby -Ilib:test\
"/opt/local/lib/ruby/gems/1.8/gems/rake-0.7.1/lib/rake/rake_test_loader.rb"\
"test/unit/person_test.rb" "test/unit/quip_test.rb"
Started
..
Finished in 0.315247 seconds.

2 tests, 2 assertions, 0 failures, 0 errors
```

The test:units task is one of several standard testing tasks, all of which are summarized in Figure 7.1, on the facing page.

At this point someone might argue that you have everything you need to test Rails applications. You have a testing framework (Test::Unit), an automation tool (rake), and a code generator that establishes simple, easy-to-remember naming conventions (script/generate). Most web application frameworks do not even do this much, but Rails goes much

---

2. "Stub" classes such as TestRequest and TestResponse are good examples of the benefit of duck typing, discussed in Section 3.7, *Duck Typing*, on page 70.

Test Task	Usage
default	Runs unit and functional tests
test	Runs unit and functional tests
test:functionals	Runs all functional (controller) tests
test:integration	Runs all integration tests (controller tests that can have multiple sessions across multiple controllers)
test:plugins	Tests third-party plugins used by this Rails application
test:recent	Runs tests for files changed in past ten minutes
test:uncommitted	Runs tests for files not yet committed to source control
test:units	Runs all unit tests

Figure 7.1: RAILS TESTING TASKS

further. In Section 7.3, *Rails Extensions to Test::Unit*, you will see that Rails provides extensions to Test::Unit and a generator (script/generate scaffold) to show you how to use them.

7.3 Rails Extensions to Test::Unit

The easiest way to get started with Rails' extensions to Test::Unit is to look at the tests you get for free with the Rails scaffold:

```
$ script/generate scaffold Person
```

Most of the scaffold code is examined in Section 1.2, *Rails App in Fifteen Minutes*, on page 2. Here, we will focus on one generated file, the functional test test/functional/people_controller_test.rb. We will take the People-ControllerTest class apart, line by line. First, the test includes fixtures:

code/rails_xt/test/functional/people_controller_test.rb

```
fixtures :people, :users
```

The scaffold generator assumes that the PeopleController deals with people, and it sets the fixtures accordingly. All but the most trivial applications will find that controllers sometimes interact with more than one model class. When this happens, simply add more other models to the fixtures line. For example:

```
fixtures :people, :widgets, :thingamabobs, :sheep
```

Next comes the setup method:

```
def setup
  @controller = PeopleController.new
  @request    = ActionController::TestRequest.new
  @response   = ActionController::TestResponse.new
end
```

Almost all functional tests simulate one (or more) web request/response cycles. Therefore, the @request and @response variables are instantiated for each test.

Now for a real test. The scaffold generates an index page that simply renders a list view of the model contents. Here's the test for the index page:

```
def test_index
  get :index
  assert_response :success
  assert_template 'list'
end
```

First, the get() method simulates an HTTP GET on a controller. The one-argument version seen here specifies a Rails action name. Then the Rails assertion assert_response :success asserts that the response is a success, that is, HTTP status 200. The Rails assertion assert_template 'list' asserts that the response was rendered from the list template.

As Java programmers, we are tempted to ask, "Where are the objects?" Maybe test_index() ought to look more like the following code, with explicit objects:

```
# hypothetical, with explicit objects
@controller.get :index
assert_equal :success, @response.status
assert_equal 'list', @response.template
```

The two previous examples are functionally equivalent. The difference is one of style. In Java, we tend to prefer to make objects explicit. In Ruby, but especially in Rails, we prefer to let the "obvious" thing be implicit where possible. Try reading both versions aloud to get a better sense of the difference. Next, the scaffold tests the list action:

```
def test_list
  get :list
  assert_response :success
  assert_template 'list'
  assert_not_nil assigns(:people)
end
```

Most of this code is familiar from test_index(). The novel part is the following:

```
assert_not_nil assigns(:people)
```

The assigns variable is special. If you create an instance variable in your controller, that variable will magically be available to your view template. The magic is actually quite simple: Rails uses reflection to copy controller variables into a collection, which is then copied back into the view instance. The collection is named assigns, so the previous assertion can be read "Assert that the controller created a non-nil variable named people."

Next, the scaffold tests the show action:

```
def test_show
  get :show, :id => 1
  assert_response :success
  assert_template 'show'
  assert_not_nil assigns(:person)
  assert assigns(:person).valid?
end
```

This test looks a little different, because the show method expects a specific person to show. Rails' default behavior is to identify specific model instances by adding an id to the URL, so the call to get() includes a second argument to pass in the id of a person:

```
get :show, :id => 1
```

The general form of get() can handle any possible context for a request:

```
get(action=nil, parameters=nil, session=nil, flash=nil)
```

How can we be sure that a person with an ID of 1 exists? Look to the fixture file test/fixtures/people.yml:

code/rails_xt/test/fixtures/people.yml

```
first:
  id: 1
  first_name: Stuart
  last_name: Halloway
```

The other bit of novelty in test_show() is the valid?() test:

```
assert assigns(:person).valid?
```

This is just ActiveRecord's standard support for validation, discussed in Section 4.5, *Validating Data Values*, on page 94. As you add validation methods to the Person class, the call to valid?() will automatically become smarter.

The scaffold's test_new() does not introduce any new concepts, so we'll skip it. Next, then, is test_create():

`code/rails_xt/test/functional/people_controller_test.rb`

```ruby
def test_create
  num_people = Person.count
  post :create, :person => {}
  assert_response :redirect
  assert_redirected_to :action => 'list'
  assert_equal num_people + 1, Person.count
end
```

This presents several new ideas. Unlike the methods discussed so far, create actually changes the database. This has several implications for our test. First, the test calls post() instead of get(), since the create() operation is not idempotent.[3] Second, we want to test that the database changes in an appropriate way. The following line:

```ruby
num_people = Person.count
```

captures the number of people before the create() operation, and the following line:

```ruby
assert_equal num_people + 1, Person.count
```

verifies that exactly one person is created. (If you want, you could perform a more rigorous test here and make sure that the new person matches the arguments passed in.)

A third implication of mutating operations such as create() is that we should not expect a :success response. Instead, a successful update redirects to the show action. The following lines:

```ruby
assert_response :redirect
assert_redirected_to :action => 'list'
```

verify that create() redirects correctly.

The remaining scaffold methods (test_edit(), test_update(), and test_destroy()) do not introduce any new testing concepts, although you may want to read them to cement your understanding of the scaffold.

---

3. An idempotent operation can be performed any number of times with no effect beyond the effect of executing once. Idempotent operations are very friendly to proxies and caches, because there is no harm (other than wasted bandwidth) in performing the operations an extra time, now and then. Idempotent operations have their own HTTP verb (GET).

> ### Why the Scaffold Redirects After a POST
>
> Redirecting after a POST makes it difficult for users to accidentally submit the same update twice. (You have probably seen the double-update problem in poorly written web applications. One symptom is the browser warning "You are about to resubmit a URL that contains POST data. Are you sure?")
>
> Rails applications typically do not suffer from the double-update problem, because a reasonably good solution (the redirect) is baked into the scaffold.

7.4 Integration Testing

Integration tests were added in Rails 1.1. You can create an integration test with the integration_test generator: *Integration tests*

```
script/generate integration_test QuipsSample
```

Integration tests start like other tests, by including the TestHelper and any necessary fixtures. The only difference is that they extend ActionController::IntegrationTest:

code/rails_xt/test/integration/quips_sample_test.rb

```
require "#{File.dirname(__FILE__)}/../test_helper"

class QuipsSampleTest < ActionController::IntegrationTest
  fixtures :quips, :users, :roles, :roles_users
```

At their simplest, integration tests look like an alternative syntax for functional tests:

```
def test_index_redirects_to_login
  get '/quips/index'
  assert_response :redirect
  follow_redirect!
  assert_response :success
  assert_template 'account/login'
end
```

In test_index_redirects_to_login, the call to get takes the actual URL, instead of the hash of routing arguments. This implicitly tests the routing code as well. If you don't want that, you can always pass the standard url_for arguments instead.

Where integration tests shine is in grouping the low-level testing primitives into recognizable user actions. To demonstrate this, let's write a test that demonstrates a hypothetical user (Quentin) logging in and destroying a quip. First, we write the test itself:

```
def test_quentin_deletes_post
  user_session(:login=>:quentin, :password=>:test) do |quentin|
    quentin.logs_in
    quentin.destroys_quip(1)
  end
end
```

The nice aspect of this syntax is its close resemblance to English: "Using credentials quentin/test, Quentin logs in and destroys Quip 1." Now we just have to make the syntax work.

Integration tests provide an open_session method that creates a session to represent a single user's interaction with the application. We can implement our user_session in terms of open_session:

```
def user_session(credentials)
  open_session do |sess|
    sess.extend UserActions
    sess.credentials = credentials
    yield sess
  end
end
```

The sess object returned by open_session implements all the integration test methods: get, post, assert_response, follow_redirect!, and so on. Of course, it does not implement our domain-specific methods logs_in and deletes_quip. Not to worry. In user_session we simply have sess extend a module named UserActions that provides these methods.

Finally, we create the private module UserActions to define our domain-specific methods:

```
private

module UserActions
  attr_accessor :credentials
  def logs_in
    post '/account/login', credentials
    assert_response :redirect
    follow_redirect!
    assert_response :success
    assert_template 'account/index'
  end
```

```
  def destroys_quip(id)
    post '/quips/destroy', :id=>id
    assert_response :redirect
    follow_redirect!
    assert_response :success
    assert_template 'quips/list'
  end
end
```

Now that we have logs_in and deletes_quip, we will probably reuse them in a bunch of other tests.

You may think we have worked through this entire example backward. We started from the top (recognizable user actions) and built the plumbing underneath. In many cases, it may be easier to start at the bottom and then compose the higher-level operations.

A nice feature of Ruby is that you can go both ways[4] (or any way in between). Sometimes starting from the top helps you create a better API: Forget about what is possible for a moment, and just write the best expression of your intent. Then leverage Ruby's flexibility to make the syntax work for you, instead of the other way around.

You might choose to supplement or replace integration testing with automated tests that run in the web browser. Testing in the browser evaluates the external interface of the system, without any knowledge or assumptions about the implementation details.

Selenium is an excellent open source framework for this kind of testing and is covered in Section 6.10, *Black-Box Testing with Selenium*, on page 174.

7.5 Rails Testing Examples

This section demonstrates several unit tests from the real world: Rails' own test suite. We have picked these tests to highlight specific ways in which the Ruby libraries or language lead to approaches that would be unusual or unthinkable in Java.

---

4. We'll be disappointed if this is not quoted out of context.

Testing the Inflector

The Inflector module implements all of Rails' clever management of names, such as conversions between singular and plural:

```
$ script/console
Loading development environment.
>> Inflector.pluralize "robot"
=> "robots"
>> Inflector.pluralize "pony"
=> "ponies"
>> Inflector.pluralize "sheep"
=> "sheep"
```

As you can imagine from this example, Inflector's unit tests need to cover normal plurals, plus a variety of special rules. You might expect the unit tests to look something like this:

> code/rails_xt/samples/unit/inflector_test.rb

```
# hypothetical
def test_pluralize
  assert_equal "searches", Inflector.pluralize("search")
  assert_equal "switches", Inflector.pluralize("switch")
  # etc.
end
```

The actual test code looks like this:

> code/rails/activesupport/test/inflector_test.rb

```
SingularToPlural.each do |singular, plural|
  define_method "test_pluralize_#{singular}" do
    assert_equal(plural, Inflector.pluralize(singular))
    assert_equal(plural.capitalize,
                 Inflector.pluralize(singular.capitalize))
  end
end

SingularToPlural.each do |singular, plural|
  define_method "test_singularize_#{plural}" do
    assert_equal(singular, Inflector.singularize(plural))
    assert_equal(singular.capitalize,
                 Inflector.singularize(plural.capitalize))
  end
end
```

The trick here is extracting data from code. Rather than embed a list of singulars and their plurals in the code, the Inflector tests extract the data into SingularToPlural. You should be able to guess the type of SingularToPlural, which is a Hash:

```
SingularToPlural = {
  "search"        => "searches",
  "switch"        => "switches",
  "fix"           => "fixes",
  # dozens more...
}
```

The SingularToPlural.each blocks call define_method() to create a new test method for each pair in SingularToPlural. define_method() works almost like def(), except you can use a runtime string value for the method name. This approach has two advantages over directly coding each assertion:

- The code is DRY. If the form of each assertion ever has to change, you can change one line of code, instead of dozens. In fact, we have already taken advantage of this by running the test in both directions, from plural to singular as well as from singular to plural.
- The SingularToPlural is easy to read, because it separates intent ("This is a map of singulars to plurals...") from implementation detail ("...that we can test with Test::Unit and Inflector").

The key Ruby features that enable Rails' approach are as follows:

- Literal syntax for key data types such as Hash. If you had to make method calls to populate the SingularToPlural object, you would harm both the readability and the DRYness.
- The ability to dynamically define methods with define_method(). Without this ability, you would have to *call* tests in a loop, instead of *creating* tests in a loop. Creating named tests is better because XUnit frameworks such as JUnit and Test::Unit report the name of the tests that fail.

How would you test an Inflector in Java? What would be different?

Silencing Warnings

Unit testing frameworks typically send output to the console. Even if you use a graphical wrapper (the famous green bar/red bar of JUnit), your tests will use the console when they are running unattended, in automated or continuous integration builds.

This use of the console poses a small problem. What if the program itself uses the console too? Your testing output will be mixed with the program output. This is particularly annoying because unit tests should be able to run in a "no news is good news" mode—absolute silence unless a failure has occurred. How do you get your program to shut up so its output does not distract your clean, green, no-output tests?

In Rails, this problem occasionally arises when test setup and teardown needs to cheat a little. The most common example in the Rails code base appears to be resetting constants. Usually, resetting constants is a bad idea and generates a warning. But resetting a constant may be exactly what you want to do when creating a sandbox for a particular test. Many Rails tests use (different) versions of a sample struct named Post. This doesn't cause any warnings, because conflicting versions of Post are created inside a silence_warnings block:

code/rails/actionpack/test/template/date_helper_test.rb

```
silence_warnings do
  Post = Struct.new("Post", :written_on, :updated_at)
end
```

The silence_warnings() method turns off warnings for the duration of a block. The block syntax is particularly nice here, because with the indentation you can guess what silence does without even knowing Ruby. Here's how it works:

code/rails/activesupport/lib/active_support/core_ext/kernel/reporting.rb

```
def silence_warnings
  old_verbose, $VERBOSE = $VERBOSE, nil
  yield
ensure
  $VERBOSE = old_verbose
end
```

silence_warnings() saves the current $VERBOSE level, sets $VERBOSE to nil, executes its block, and restores the original $VERBOSE level. You will find blocks are useful any time you need this kind of "wrapper" behavior.

Does the same idiom exist in Java? Sort of. Another place where a "wrapper" behavior is useful is when opening and closing database connections. In Java, the Spring frameworks wraps JDBC calls, so you don't have to manage a **finally** block and explicitly close() JDBC connections yourself:

```
//t is a Spring JDBCTemplate
List l = t.query("SELECT title FROM events", new RowMapper() {
  public Object mapRow(ResultSet rs, int i) throws SQLException {
    return rs.getString("title");
  }
});
```

Where in Ruby you would use a block, in Java you see a one-method interface (for example, RowMapper), plus an anonymous inner class to implement a single method (for example, mapRow()). Syntax matters. The anonymous inner class idiom is bulky enough that it often goes unused, even where it could greatly DRY the code. Ruby's blocks are appropriate in most places where an anonymous inner class would be used in Java.

7.6 Measuring Code Coverage with rcov

Code coverage measures the degree to which code is covered by tests. Code coverage has been around since the 1960s. In the Java world, code coverage is provided by open source tools such as Cobertura[5] and commercial products including Clover.[6] In the Ruby world, you can use the open source rcov[7] for code coverage. rcov is available as a gem, and you can install it via the following:

```
gem install rcov
```

The instrumentation required to measure code coverage can make your test run slower—a lot slower. To offset this, rcov includes a native extension that makes rcov run more than 100 times faster. You should definitely build these extensions. After installing rcov, navigate into your gems to where rcov is installed, and run the following:

```
ruby setup.rb
```

Once installed, rcov is available as a Rake task and as the command-line tool rcov. We will demonstrate the Rake task version. In the People sample application, there is a coverage task:

code/people/lib/tasks/rcov.rake
```
namespace 'rcov' do
  begin
    require 'rcov/rcovtask'
    Rcov::RcovTask.new do |t|
      t.name = 'test'
      t.libs << "test"
      t.test_files = FileList['test/**/*test.rb']
      t.verbose = true
      t.rcov_opts = ['-x', '^lib,^config/boot']
    end
  rescue LoadError
    # ignore missing rcov
  end
end
```

---

5. http://cobertura.sourceforge.net/
6. http://www.cenqua.com/clover/
7. http://eigenclass.org/hiki.rb?rcov

C0 code coverage information

Generated on Sun Oct 22 18:50:24 PDT 2006 with rcov 0.7.0

Name	Total lines	Lines of code	Total coverage	Code coverage
TOTAL	418	243	98.6%	97.5%
app/controllers/account_controller.rb	45	37	100.0%	100.0%
app/controllers/application.rb	11	5	100.0%	100.0%
app/controllers/people_controller.rb	58	43	100.0%	100.0%
app/controllers/quips_controller.rb	83	56	92.8%	89.3%
app/helpers/account_helper.rb	2	2	100.0%	100.0%
app/helpers/application_helper.rb	3	2	100.0%	100.0%
app/helpers/people_helper.rb	2	2	100.0%	100.0%
app/helpers/quips_helper.rb	2	2	100.0%	100.0%
app/models/celestial_body.rb	2	2	100.0%	100.0%
app/models/person.rb	38	19	100.0%	100.0%
app/models/quip.rb	13	9	100.0%	100.0%
app/models/role.rb	8	4	100.0%	100.0%
app/models/user.rb	73	50	100.0%	100.0%
config/environment.rb	56	6	100.0%	100.0%
config/routes.rb	22	4	100.0%	100.0%

Figure 7.2: AN RCOV REPORT SUGGESTS THAT TESTS ARE NEEDED

On 7, the test_files accessor specifies the tests to run. When the tests are run, rcov will generate a report showing which lines are covered. rcov automatically excludes certain files from this report (presumably you are not interested in code coverage for the Ruby standard library or for the tests themselves). We want to exclude even more files, so on line 9, the rcov_opts accessor excludes lib and config/boot. The rescue LoadError protects users who do not have rcov installed (the default behavior of Rails is to bomb out of Rake if an exception is unrescued while reading a task).

With the task in place, rake rcov:test will generate a set of HTML reports with an index page at coverage/index.html. At one point while developing the Rails XT application, the coverage index page looked like Figure 7.2.

These numbers look pretty good—it appears most lines are being tested. But the QuipsController has some uncovered lines. Clicking the name of the file shows covered lines in drab green and uncovered lines in red. The offending lines are shown in Figure 7.3, on the facing page. Aha! Somebody wrote the Ajax examples (search and better_search) without

```
31  #START: search
32  def search
33    @quips = Quip.find_text_like(params[:search])
34    render :partial=>'search_table' if request.xhr?
35  end
36  #END: search
37
38  #START: better_search
39  def better_search
40    @quips = Quip.find_text_like(params[:search])
41    render :partial=>'search_update' if request.xhr?
42  end
43  #END: better_search
```

Figure 7.3: AN RCOV FILE REPORT WITH COLOR-CODING

writing any tests. After adding the appropriate tests, another rcov run showed that all lines were covered.

We find code coverage to be an important part of the overall testing strategy, but the raw percentages are meaningless without context. Several factors can create artificially high (or low) coverage percentages:

- Methods that write methods (such as attr_accessor) create code without any corresponding source code lines. Since rcov is line-oriented, these methods are invisible.
- Line-oriented coverage missed other things as well. If a method combines multiple boolean expressions and then branches, simple line coverage does not guarantee that all the expressions are being tested.
- The choice of files to include (and exclude) from reporting can overwhelm significant data with irrelevant noise.

Rather than obsess over the absolute number, it is more useful to compare coverage numbers across libraries or across time. If some modules have consistently lower coverage than others, why is that? There may be a good reason, and it would be wise to document it. If a particular module's coverage is drifting up or down over time, does this indicate a real change in testing quality, or is it an artifact of something else? A particularly good use of coverage is in estimating the risk associated with change requests. If code has very high coverage, then work estimates in that code will probably be more reliable.

We have also found that code coverage testing has peripheral benefits. rcov will tend to run your tests in a different order than Rake. Since tests are supposed to be independent, running them in a different order should not matter. But our experience is that unintended dependencies tend to creep in, and rcov often flushes these out. One team we know has taken this to its logical extreme, adding a randomizer to Rake so that tests run in a different order every time.

7.7 Testing Interactions with Mock Objects

Up to this point, the examples in this chapter have been concerned with testing object state. Most tests are written this way:

1. Create an object to test.
2. Call methods on the object.
3. Assert that the object's state is valid.

This approach to testing can lead to issues when the object you want to test has nontrivial relationships with other objects. Imagine the following scenario:

1. Create an object A that you want to test.
2. Call some methods on A. Those methods call other methods on objects B and C.
3. Assert that A, B, and C are in a valid state.

mock objects

Oops. Now our test for A depends on the implementation details of B and C. Ideally, we want to test A in isolation. The solution to this dilemma is *mock objects*. A mock object performs two tasks. First, it replaces an object that we are not interested in testing. Second, it records calls made to that object. Later we can verify that the correct calls were made and in the correct order. Instead of testing state, we are testing interactions. The previous scenario becomes this:

1. Create an object A that you want to test.
2. Create mock objects for B and C.

expectations

3. Set your *expectations* for how B and C should be used.
4. Call some methods on A. Those methods call other methods on (mock!) objects B and C.
5. Assert that A is in a valid state.

Verify

6. *Verify* the mock objects. Verification compares your expectations with the actual calls made to B and C and fails the test if they do not match.

To see how mock objects are useful in practice, consider how you would write a test for the manager layer in our Struts sample application. Classes such as PersonManager delegate most of their work to instances in the DAO layer, such as PersonDao. To test PersonManager, we need to create a mock instance of PersonDao. Then we can set expectations on that mock, call some methods on a PersonManager, and verify that the PersonDao is used as expected.

Since the Java SDK does not include mock object support, the first step is to select a third-party framework. We will be using jMock,[8] a popular open source library:

```
code/appfuse_people/test/service/com/relevancellc/people/service/PersonManagerTest.java
```

```java
import org.jmock.Mock;
```

We instantiate our objects in the test setup:

```java
protected void setUp()
    throws Exception {
  super.setUp();
  personDao = new Mock(PersonDao.class);
  personManager.setPersonDao((PersonDao) personDao.proxy());
}
```

Next, we write the test:

```java
public void testGetPeople()
    throws Exception {
  List results = new ArrayList();
  person = new Person();
  results.add(person);
  personDao.expects(once()).method("getPeople")
      .will(returnValue(results));
  List people = personManager.getPeople(null);
  assertTrue(people.size() == 1);
  personDao.verify();
}
```

On line 6, we set the expectations for personDao. The getPeople method should be called once, returning a list of Person objects. Notice how the API calls read almost like English. Next, we invoke the personManager. Finally, on line 10, we verify that the personManager behaved as expected. In this case we are not testing any state at all; we are testing only that personManager interacted with personDao as expected.

---

8. http://www.jmock.org/

Like Java, Ruby does not ship with a mock object library. We will use FlexMock.[9] You can install FlexMock via RubyGems:

```
gem install flexmock
```

To make FlexMock available to all tests in a Rails application, require it in test_helper.rb:

> code/rails_xt/test/test_helper.rb

```
require 'flexmock'
```

Now for a test. The Rails XT sample application does not have a manager layer, so we will introduce a new feature in the controller layer. Instead of simply accessing all quips, users should be allowed to filter quips based on their preferences. Our application will store user preferences in the session and use a third-party API to filter content. The third-party API will be implemented through a @filter_service instance on the controller.

It is possible to call the FlexMock API via freestanding classes. It is much simpler, however, to just begin our test case by including FlexMock::TestCase:

> code/rails_xt/test/functional/quips_controller_test.rb

```
include FlexMock::TestCase
```

Adding FlexMock::TestCase gives us helper methods for creating mocks, and it automatically validates the mocks during teardown.

The QuipsController should provide a new method, list_with_user_filter. This method should return all quips, minus any that are rejected by the FilterService. Here is the test:

> code/rails_xt/test/functional/quips_controller_test.rb

```
def test_list_with_user_filter
  filter = flexmock("filter")
  filter.should_expect do |m|
    m.filter(Array,nil).returns([quips(:quip_1)])
  end
  @controller.instance_variable_set('@filter_service', filter)
  get :list_with_user_filter
  assert_equal [quips(:quip_1)], assigns(:quips)
  assert_response :success
  assert_template 'list_with_user_filter'
end
```

---

9. http://onestepback.org/software/flexmock/

On line 2, the flexmock method creates a mock object. The argument is a name that will be used in error messages. In the Java version, the mock had to have a specific interface so jMock could know what methods the mock should simulate. Since Ruby is dynamically typed, we do not specify any specific module or class for the mock.

On line 3, we set the expectations for the mock. FlexMock takes advantage of Ruby's blocks to set expectations through a recorder object. On line 4, the block parameter m is a recorder. Instead of saying m.should_expect.filter, we can simply say m.filter; the should_expect is implicit. Flex-Mock's matching of parameters takes advantage of Ruby's case equality operator (===). So, the first argument to filter must be an instance of Array. This array will be the result of Quip.find(:all), and we could have chosen to match it exactly by instantiating the entire collection in the test. The second argument nil matches the user's filtering preferences, which are initially nil.

On line 6, we set the controller's @filter_serviceto our mock filter. By calling instance_variable_set, we avoid the requirement that the controller provide a setter for @filter_service. There is no call to verify at the end of the method; FlexMock mocks verify automatically at the end of the test.

Ruby's blocks and case equality make it easy to define flexible argument matching. Imagine that we wanted to verify that none of the quips passed to the @filter_service has non-nil text. FlexMock would handle this with FlexMock.on:

```
code/rails_xt/test/functional/quips_controller_test.rb
matcher = FlexMock.on {|args| Array === args && args.all? {|a| a.text}}
filter.should_expect do |m|
  m.filter(matcher,nil).returns([quips(:quip_1)])
end
```

The previous tests demonstrates another advantage of mock objects. Mock objects allow you to test interactions with code that does not exist yet. In testing the QuipsController, we never create a real filter service. At the time of this writing, there *is no real filter service*. This decoupling lets teams of developers work on related subsystems without having to wait for completed implementations of every object.

The mock objects in this section replace objects not under test and verify that those objects are called in an appropriate fashion. Sometimes you want to replace objects not under test, but you don't care how they are called. This subset of mock object capability is provided by stub objects.

7.8 Reducing Dependencies with Stub Objects

It is all too easy to write fragile tests that depend on other classes. Think about how you might test this simple controller method:

code/people/app/controllers/people_controller.rb

```
def create
  @person = Person.new(params[:person])
  if @person.save
    flash[:notice] = 'Person was successfully created.'
    redirect_to :action => 'list'
  else
    render :action => 'new'
  end
end
```

To test both branches of the code, you will need a valid Person and an invalid Person. The problem is that you are supposed to be testing PersonController, not Person. If you pick valid and invalid arguments for the real Person class, you introduce a dependency on Person. This is a maintenance headache. When you change Person, you will break the PersonTest (OK), but you will also break the PersonControllerTest (aargh).

stub To avoid this problem, we can test a *stub* version of Person. The stub replaces Person with behavior that we define locally, breaking the external dependency. This probably sounds similar to the mock objects from the previous section, and it is. In fact, we will use the same library for stubs, FlexMock. Here is a stub-based test for creating a Person:

code/people/test/functional/people_controller_test.rb

```
def test_create_succeeds
  flexstub(Person).should_receive(:new).and_return {
    flexmock('person') do |m|
      m.should_receive(:save).and_return(true)
    end
  }
  post :create
  assert_response :redirect
  assert_redirected_to :action => 'list'
end
```

On line 2, flexstub temporarily modifies the behavior of Person. For the remainder of this test, calls to Person.new will invoke this block of code instead. On line 3 we mock an instance of Person, and on line 4 we cause save to always succeed. This test method will test how the controller handles a successful Person create, *regardless of how the real Person class works.*

Testing the failure case is a little more complex, because the failure case hands the Person instance off to new.rhtml. The template expects a Person to implement various accessors and to return a working errors property. This requires another mock for the errors collection, plus the should_ignore_missing call to make the mocks more forgiving:

code/people/test/functional/people_controller_test.rb

```
def test_create_fails
  flexstub(Person).should_receive(:new).and_return {
    errs = flexmock('errs') do |m|
      m.should_ignore_missing
    end
    inst = flexmock('person') do |m|
      m.should_ignore_missing
      m.should_receive(:errors).and_return(errs)
      m.should_receive(:save).and_return(false)
    end
  }
  post :create
  assert_response :success
  assert_template 'new'
end
```

Setting up stubs may seem like overkill for small projects, but it can be lifesaver as projects grow. The first time a refactoring sets off a chain of dependencies and breaks 500 tests, you will be wishing for those stubs.

7.9 Advanced Considerations

Now that you have seen the basics of unit testing in Rails, the following are some more advanced issues to think about:

Naming Conventions Considered Harmful?

The use of naming conventions—such as prefixing all unit tests with "test"—is troubling to some. The more recent versions of JUnit allows the use of Java 5 annotations for marking a test. For example, this is allowed:

```
@Test public void tag()
```

instead of the following:

```
public void testTag()
```

By comparison, Ruby doesn't have annotations. Since the object model is so flexible, results similar to annotations can usually be achieved with class methods. But nobody in the Ruby community cares. As far as we know, nobody has yet felt the need to provide an automated testing solution that avoids the use of naming conventions.

One Size Does Not Fit All

Not everyone on in the Java world uses JUnit. TestNG[10] is also popular. TestNG addresses a set of limitations in JUnit's approach to test setup, teardown, and integration with automation. Similar limitations in Test::Unit would not/do not drive anyone to write a new library. Ruby is flexible enough that issues with Test::Unit are likely to be handled in an ad hoc way.

Behavior-Driven Development

One possible competitor to Test::Unit in the Ruby world is RSpec.[11] RSpec is framework for writing executable specifications of program behavior. In terms of implementation, executable specifications may not be much different from unit tests. But the associated mind-set is different, and the terminology used in RSpec may lead to better project automation. Java got there first; RSpec is inspired by JBehave.[12]

The automated testing features discussed in this chapter provide a dynamic and active way to verify that your application code works correctly. Dynamic languages like Ruby are particularly well suited to writing automated tests, because it is easy to create a variety of different test-bed environments. This is fortuitous, since Rails applications need good tests—there is no compiler to catch simple mistakes.

Once you have written good tests, the next obvious step is to automate their invocation on a regular cycle. The next chapter, Chapter 8, *Automating the Development Process*, on page 217, explains how to use Rake to automate not just your tests but all the other repetitive tasks associated with software development and deployment.

7.10 Resources

A Guide to Testing the Rails http://manuals.rubyonrails.com/read/book/5
The Ruby on Rails manual for writing tests is fairly comprehensive and includes some pieces not covered here such as tests for ActionMailer.

---

10. http://testng.org
11. http://rspec.rubyforge.org/
12. http://jbehave.codehaus.org/

Annotation Hammer . . . . http://www.infoq.com/articles/Annotation-Hammer
Venkat Subramaniam explains Java annotations. In particular, he looks at the decision to use annotation to mark test methods in Java 1.4 and considers the trade-offs between naming conventions and annotation metadata.

In Pursuit of Code Quality: Don't Be Fooled by the Coverage Report. . .
. . . http://www-128.ibm.com/developerworks/java/library/j-cq01316/index.html?ca=drs
Andrew Glover analyzes ways the coverage reports can be misused and advises how to use coverage history to guide (but not dictate!) development efforts.

Ruby/Rails Unit Testing in Less Than 1 Second. . .
. . . http://jayfields.blogspot.com/2006/09/rubyrails-unit-testing-in-less-than-1.html
Jay Fields shows how to reduce test dependencies, particularly dependencies on the database, and explains how his team uses Stubba and Mocha (http://rubyforge.org/projects/mocha/) for mock and stub objects.

ZenTest . . . . http://rubyforge.org/forum/forum.php?forum_id=8885
ZenTest is a set of tools for doing Extreme Programming (XP) faster with Test::Unit. ZenTest includes tools to generate missing methods, interpret assertion diffs, run tests continuously, and automatically test on multiple version of Ruby.

Chapter 8

Automating the Development Process

The process of software development begs for a lot of automation. Given the source code and other files that make up a project, you may want to trigger processes to do the following:

- Compile the code
- Deploy from one environment to another
- Vary settings for development, testing, and production
- Run automated tests
- Start and stop server processes
- Collect profiling data
- Manage log files
- Handle dependencies on other libraries
- Configure databases and data
- And on and on and on...

You can bet that decent-sized projects will have lots of tasks like this. Most of these tasks, in their purest, raw form, can be individually triggered via some command-line tool (with appropriate settings). *Remembering* all the right settings, and what order to invoke the tools, is tedious and error-prone. Most programming environments include a basic tool for this kind of automation. In classic Unix development, the basic tool is make.[1] In Java, the tool is ant. In Ruby, the tool is rake. This chapter explains rake by comparison to ant and then demonstrates some of the ways we use rake to manage Rails applications.

---

1. We find it wildly amusing that we build this chapter by typing make Rake.pdf instead of rake Rake.pdf. Wonder whether this note will make it through the review process....

8.1 Rake Basics

In the Java world, rake is called ant. Let's start with a simple Ant build script that manages the compilation of a Java program:

code/Rake/simple_ant/build.xml

```xml
<project name="simple-ant" default="compile">
  <target name="clean">
    <delete dir="classes"/>
  </target>
  <target name="prepare">
    <mkdir dir="classes"/>
  </target>
  <target name="compile" depends="prepare">
    <javac srcdir="src" destdir="classes"/>
  </target>
</project>
```

target

Ant build scripts are written in XML. In this example, the top-level project element declares a name, which is the name of the project, and declares the name of the default *target* to invoke when the ant command-line tool is run. Our default target is compile, so you would expect that this script's default behavior is to compile Java source code. Here's the output from ant:

```
$ ant
Buildfile: build.xml

prepare:
    [mkdir] Created dir: /Book/code/Rake/simple_ant/classes

compile:
    [javac] Compiling 1 source file to /Book/code/Rake/simple_ant/classes

BUILD SUCCESSFUL
Total time: 3 seconds
```

Three good things just happened. First, notice that ant does not need to be told to use build.xml; it just assumes that unless told otherwise. This is an example of "convention over configuration." Second, even though the default target for this script is compile, ant knows to execute the prepare target first. If you refer to the XML configuration file, you can see that compile depends on prepare:

```xml
<target name="compile" depends="prepare">
  <javac srcdir="src" destdir="classes"/>
</target>
```

This depends declaration is an example of dependency-based programming. You do not have to explicitly call functions in some order. Instead, you just state the dependencies, and the tool figures out the right order. When you have only a few tasks, this may seem like nothing special; however, when you have tens or hundreds of tasks, dependency-based programming can enable cleaner, more readable code.

To see the third good thing that happened, you need to run ant again:

```
$ ant
Buildfile: build.xml

prepare:

compile:

BUILD SUCCESSFUL
Total time: 2 seconds
```

This time, Ant looked at the prepare and compile tasks but did not actually *do* anything. ant evaluates the dependencies and sees that prepare and compile are already up-to-date. The body of the prepare target calls the mkdir *task* to create a directory:

```
<target name="prepare">
  <mkdir dir="classes"/>
</target>
```

A task is simply a piece of code to be executed. Many of Ant's built-in tasks, such as mkdir, are smart enough to do nothing if their work has already been done. This becomes important for time-intensive tasks such as the javac task in the body of compile:

```
<target name="compile" depends="prepare">
  <javac srcdir="src" destdir="classes"/>
</target>
```

Now let's build a simple rake file. Since Ruby programs are not compiled, we will use a slightly different example. The following rakefile uses Rails' built-in CodeStatistics object to calculate lines of code and a few other statistics for some Ruby code:

code/Rake/simple_rake/rakefile
```
require 'rake/rdoctask'
require '../code_statistics.rb'
task :default => :stats
task :clean do
  rm_rf 'stats'
end
```

```
task :prepare do
  mkdir_p 'stats'
end
task :stats => [:prepare] do
  require 'code_statistics'
  File.open("stats/main.stat", "w") do |f|
    f << CodeStatistics.new(['App Main', 'src']).to_s
  end
end
```

Although this looks quite a bit different from Ant's build.xml file, they actually have quite a bit in common. Rake, like Ant, defines a set of tasks. Also, tasks can be related by dependencies. The => should be read "depends on." When you run rake, more similarities appear:

```
$ rake
(in /Users/stuart/FR_RAILS4JAVA/Book/code/Rake/simple_rake)
mkdir -p stats
+--------------------+-------+-------+---------+---------+-----+-------+
| Name               | Lines |  LOC  | Classes | Methods | M/C | LOC/M |
+--------------------+-------+-------+---------+---------+-----+-------+
| App Main           |    1  |   1   |    0    |    0    |  0  |    0  |
+--------------------+-------+-------+---------+---------+-----+-------+
   Code LOC: 1     Test LOC: 0      Code to Test Ratio: 1:0.0
```

Rake automatically knows what file to use—rakefile is the default, just as build.xml is the default for ant.

Although ant has a top-level project element specifying the default task, rake has no equivalent. Instead, rake assumes a task named default. To make other tasks run by default, simply make default depend on the other tasks you want to run:

code/Rake/simple_rake/rakefile

```
task :default => :stats
```

By far the biggest difference is the language syntax. Where Ant uses XML, Rake uses Ruby. All the syntax in a rakefile is "just" Ruby. The task names are symbols, the dependencies are Ruby hashes, and the task bodies are Ruby blocks. If you know Ruby, you know quite a bit of Rake already.

8.2 Setting Rake Options: It's Just Ruby

The ramifications of choosing a programming language (Ruby) instead of a text markup language (XML) are profound, and they become more significant as build files become more complex. To see this, let's refactor

both examples to deal better with input and output directories. The Ant
file specifies the output directory classes three times. If we make that
value a *build property*, it will be easy to change it if we ever want to   *build property*
output to a different directory.

```
code/Rake/better_ant/build.xml
<project name="simple-ant" default="compile">
  <property name="srcdir" value="src"/>
  <property name="destdir" value="classes"/>
  <target name="clean">
    <delete dir="${destdir}"/>
  </target>
  <target name="prepare">
    <mkdir dir="${destdir}"/>
  </target>
  <target name="compile" depends="prepare">
    <javac srcdir="${srcdir}" destdir="${destdir}"/>
  </target>
</project>
```

The property element lets us specify a value once and easily replace or
override it later. Once a property is established, scripts can refer to it
via the syntax ${propertyname}. Here is a similar improvement to the
rakefile:

```
code/Rake/better_rake/rakefile
Line 1   STATS_DIR = "stats"
    -    require 'rake/rdoctask'
    -    require '../code_statistics.rb'
    -    task :default => :stats
    5    task :clean do
    -      rm_rf STATS_DIR
    -    end
    -    task :prepare do
    -      mkdir_p STATS_DIR
   10    end
    -    task :stats => [:prepare] do
    -      require 'code_statistics'
    -      File.open("#{STATS_DIR}/main.stat", "w") do |f|
    -        f << CodeStatistics.count(['App Main', 'src'])
   15      end
    -    end
```

Since Rake is just Ruby, there is no specialized notion of "build properties." On line 1, STATS_DIR is a Ruby constant, and it can be passed to
methods (line 6) or interpolated into a String (line 13), just like any other
Ruby object.

8.3 Custom Rake Tasks: It's Just Ruby

Ant has more than 100 built-in tasks, if you include both core and optional tasks. Nevertheless, you may find that you want more. Never fear, Ant provides many extension points: You can define your own custom tasks in Java, you can define macros, or you can call out to a variety of scripting languages. For example, here is a fragment from Apache Commons Lang's build file:

```
code/commons-lang-2.1/build.xml
```
```xml
<target name="test.lang" depends="compile.tests">
  <runTestCase classname="org.apache.commons.lang.LangTestSuite"/>
</target>
<target name="test.builder" depends="compile.tests">
  <runTestCase classname="org.apache.commons.lang.builder.BuilderTestSuite"/>
</target>
```

You might guess that runTestCase is an Ant task that runs JUnit tests. You would be right about the JUnit part, but runTestCase is *not* an Ant task. It is a macro defined previously in the build file:

```xml
<macrodef name="runTestCase">
  <attribute name="classname"/>
  <sequential>
    <junit printsummary="true" showoutput="true"
           fork="${junit.fork}" haltonerror="${test.failonerror}">
      <classpath refid="test.classpath"/>
      <test name="@{classname}"/>
    </junit>
  </sequential>
</macrodef>
```

The macrodef defines a new task name, the attributes it allows, and how those attributes are used. To pass attributes through to other tasks, a new interpolation syntax @{varname} is introduced:

```xml
<test name="@{classname}"/>
```

We could show examples of the script task and custom tasks defined in Java, but suffice it to say that they provide alternative answers to the question, "How do I write functions in Ant?"

At this point, you have seen that Ant has variables/constants (properties), functions (custom tasks et. al.), and a standard library (the built-in tasks). *The more you look at Ant, the more it starts to look like a general-purpose programming language.* But it isn't. Ant is an example of a Domain-Specific Language (DSL). Its domain is dependency-based project automation. Because it is written in its own custom vocabulary (an XML dialect), Ant is rightly called an *external* DSL. That is, XML is external to the language (Java) that Ant usually manages.

Rakefiles are also written in a DSL. But because they are written within a programming language (Ruby), the rakefile syntax is an *internal* DSL. In other words, the rakefile language lives "inside" the Ruby language. As a result, rakefile authors use Ruby to provide any extension points they need. To demonstrate this, here is a more complex example, taken from the test automation built into all Rails projects. The recent task tests code that you wrote in the last ten minutes. (The idea is to support agile style by making it easy to run a subset of tests.)

`code/rails/railties/lib/tasks/testing.rake`

```
desc 'Test recent changes'
Rake::TestTask.new(:recent => "db:test:prepare") do |t|
  since = TEST_CHANGES_SINCE
  touched = FileList['test/**/*_test.rb'].select \
            { |path| File.mtime(path) > since } +
    recent_tests('app/models/**/*.rb', 'test/unit', since) +
    recent_tests('app/controllers/**/*.rb', 'test/functional', since)

  t.libs << 'test'
  t.verbose = true
  t.test_files = touched.uniq
end
```

This little bit of code does quite a bit. Rake::TestTask is a task built into Rake. It is configured by calling Ruby methods:

```
t.libs << 'test'
t.verbose = true
t.test_files = touched.uniq
```

The code to calculate which tests to run must perform two tasks: find tests that changed recently and find tests whose models or controllers changed recently. The first part (recently changed tests) is straightforward and takes place inline with a Ruby select:

```
FileList['test/**/*_test.rb'].select { |path| File.mtime(path) > since }
```

FileList and File are Ruby classes. In English, this line says "Find all files ending with _test.rb anywhere under the test directory, whose modified time is more recent than since (ten minutes ago)."

Finding changed models or controllers is a bit more complex. The goal is to find such classes and then apply a name transformation to predict their associated test class names. This code is complex enough to move into a separate method named recent_tests() (not shown here).

The key point here is that Rake is easy to extend. Instead of using a special-purpose extension mechanism, you have the entire Ruby standard library at your disposal. You can extend Rake tasks with Ruby code in situ or with any classes and methods that you define.

8.4 Using Rake in Rails Applications

And now for a bit of good news/bad news. Here is the bad news first: Build scripts tend to be ugly, unlovely parts of any software project. (Accuse us of prejudice if you want, but we have spent twenty years finding this to be true with shell scripts, Make, Ant, and Rake.) Now on to the good news: Rails applications begin life with a wonderful rakefile already in place. Here it is, sans comments:

```
require(File.join(File.dirname(__FILE__), 'config', 'boot'))
require 'rake'
require 'rake/testtask'
require 'rake/rdoctask'
require 'tasks/rails'
```

Surprised at how little is here? All the good stuff is required in. Since rakefiles are built atop a general-purpose language, they accrue the associated benefits—in this case reusable libraries of tasks. The paths that begin with 'rake' come from Rake itself, and the 'config' and 'task' bits come from Rails.

With a little luck, you can ship your first Rails app without ever writing a line of rakefile. All you need to know is how to use the tools that are already provided. Lesson one: The --tasks flag will tell you what tasks are available:

```
$ rake --tasks
(in /Users/stuart/website)
rake db:schema:load        # Load a schema.rb file into the database
rake db:sessions:clear     # Clear the sessions table
... 39 more omitted for brevity
```

Notice the colon-delimited names. Rake uses namespaces to organize tasks into groups. For example, the definition of db:migrate begins:

```
code/rails/railties/lib/tasks/databases.rake
```

```
namespace :db do
  desc "Migrate the database through scripts in db/migrate. Target..."
  task :migrate => :environment do
```

Notice that namespace does not introduce any new syntax. It is just a method that takes a Ruby block. The desc method before a task takes a description that will appear in the output of rake --tasks.

The --help option lists the various options for Rake. We have truncated the following output to show only a few of the most important options:

```
$ rake --help
rake [-f rakefile] {options} targets...

Options are ...

  --dry-run            (-n)
      Do a dry run without executing actions.
  --quiet              (-q)
      Do not log messages to standard output.
  --require=MODULE     (-r)
      Require MODULE before executing rakefile.
  --trace              (-t)
      Turn on invoke/execute tracing, enable full backtrace.
  --verbose            (-v)
      Log message to standard output (default).
```

The dry-run option is useful when you are exploring a rakefile and want to look before you leap. For continuous integration builds, it is nice to be quiet: "No news is good news." When things go wrong in rake, the symptom is usually a Ruby exception. Stack traces are not shown by default (a design decision we disagree with), but you can turn them on with verbose. The trace option is useful for developing and debugging rakefiles. Finally, the require option is one of many ways to change a rakefile's behavior. Since a rakefile is Ruby code, you can require in overrides for any constants, variables, classes, or methods you need to change.

Controlling Which Version of Rails You Use

Your Rails application depends on the Rails framework, but which version? Rails provides several Rake tasks to control which version of Rails your application will use. By default, your Rails application will use the latest gems on your machine. If you control when and how gems are installed on a machine and have only one Rails application, this may be fine. You can be more conservative in several ways and request a specific version of Rails. The tasks in the list that follows work by copying Rails into the vendor/rails directory of your project, which is early on the Ruby load path.

rake rails:freeze:gems
> Copies current gems into vendor/rails

rake rails:freeze:edge REVISION=nnn
> Copies svn revision nnn into vendor/rails

rake rails:freeze:edge TAG=rel_1-1-0
> Copies svn tag rel_1-1-0 into vendor/rails

On the other hand, you might want to take *less* control of which version of Rails you get. (This sounds unlikely but might be true during development, where you want to catch incompatibilities with newer versions of Rails.) These tasks work by associating your Rails application with a copy of Rails that is not directly managed by your project.

rake rails:freeze:edge
> Puts the svn edge (most recent revision) into vendor/rails

rake rails:unfreeze
> Undoes any freeze; back to depending on gems

If you are using Subversion as your version control system, you can use its svn:externals facility to link the vendor/rails directory to the official Rails repository. When you svn up the most recent changes to your own project, you will also get the latest, greatest, not-yet-released version of Rails. This is not recommended for production servers!

Rails also copies some files into your project that may need to be updated to take advantage of newer versions of Rails. The rake rails:update task, and its subtasks, copy the most recent versions of these files into your project.

File Cleanup Tasks

Of the file cleanup tasks, the most important is probably log:clear. Log files can grow without bound, so you will want to automate trimming them back on production servers.

rake log:clear
> Truncates the log files (log/*.log)

rake tmp:clear
> Clears various files in tmp

Figure 7.1, on page 195, covers test-related tasks.

8.5 Continuous Integration with Cerberus

Rake is an excellent tool for doing dependency-based tasks such as building and testing software projects. To complement Rake, we need tools for source control management and for continuous integration (CI).

Source control management tools allow you to track the history of a software project and to manage a code base across many different developers. Not much is language-specific about source control. Ruby programmers tend to use the same tools that Java programmers use: Subversion and CVS.

Continuous integration is a development practice where team members frequently integrate their work. Each integration is verified by an automatic build, so a developer will immediately know whether some part of the application code is moving in a bad direction.

In practical terms, a continuous integration builder is a tool that does the following:

- Monitors source control for new changes

- Automatically invokes builds with tools like rake

- Complains loudly when the build breaks, using email, chat, decorative lights, lava lamps, sirens, or anything else that will help to get a team member's attention

Java programmers often use CruiseControl[2] for CI. CruiseControl is an open source project with good basic CI abilities, plus lots of bells and whistles.

The Ruby world does not have anything as comprehensive as Cruise-Control. What we do have, however, is a few simple libraries that provide a good start for CI. Our current favorite is an open source project called Cerberus.[3] Cerberus provides a simple way to build one or multiple projects on a regular schedule and report build results to interested parties. Cerberus installs as a gem:

```
gem install -y cerberus-0.3.0
```

---

2. http://cruisecontrol.sourceforge.net/
3. http://cerberus.rubyforge.org/

The cerberus command-line tool lets you set up an automated build for a project. We used the following command to create a Cerberus build for the People application that accompanies this book:

```
cerberus add https://somewhere.pragprog.com/code/people\
APPLICATION_NAME=R4JD_People RECIPIENTS=contact@relevancellc.com
```

The https URL is the project repository URL. When a build fails, e-mails with the APPLICATION_NAME in their subject line will be sent to RECIPIENTS.

Since Cerberus sends e-mails, we will need to configure a valid e-mail account. Cerberus uses ActionMailer (a part of Rails) to send its e-mails, and the configuration lives at .cerberus/config.yml. Here is a simple example:

```
publisher:
  active: mail
  mail:
    address: www.relevancellc.com
    port: 25
    domain: relevancellc.com
    authentication: login
    user_name: some_real_user
    password: some_real_password
builder:
  rake:
    task: migrate test
```

Cerberus supports other publishers not shown here: Jabber, Internet Relay Chat (IRC), Campfire, and RSS. Adding "LavaLamp" is an exercise for the reader.

Now that we have configured the mail transport, we can build our project:

```
cerberus R4JD_People
```

Or all projects:

```
cerberus buildall
```

Cerberus reports nothing on the command line. However, a failed build of the People application leads to an e-mail like the one in Figure 8.1, on the next page. The e-mail includes the project name, the commit log from the last source control check-in, and the log from running the tests. Importantly, the commit log includes the identity of the person who broke the application, in this case the dastardly stuart.halloway.

From: Cerberus <cerberus@example.com>
Subject: **[R4JD_People] Build broken by stuart.halloway (#12940)**
Date: November 8, 2006 4:26:02 PM EST
To: Stuart Halloway

----

r12651 | stuart.halloway | 2006-11-01 18:08:23 -0500 (Wed, 01 Nov 2006) | 1 line
Changed paths:
 A /titles/FR_RAILS4JAVA/Book/code/people/snippets/person_soap_client.txt

oops

/opt/local/bin/ruby -Ilib:test "/opt/local/lib/ruby/gems/1.8/gems/rake-0.7.1/lib/rake/rake
(in /Users/stuart/.cerberus/work/R4JD_People/sources)
Loaded suite /opt/local/lib/ruby/gems/1.8/gems/rake-0.7.1/lib/rake/rake_test_loader
Started
...
Finished in 0.128789 seconds.

3 tests, 1 assertions, 0 failures, 0 errors
/opt/local/bin/ruby -Ilib:test "/opt/local/lib/ruby/gems/1.8/gems/rake-0.7.1/lib/rake/rake
Loaded suite /opt/local/lib/ruby/gems/1.8/gems/rake-0.7.1/lib/rake/rake_test_loader
Started
.........E..E
Finished in 0.577015 seconds.

Figure 8.1: CERBERUS REPORTS A FAILED BUILD

Once you have a Cerberus configuration you are happy with, you can use an operating system–level service such as cron or the Windows Task Scheduler to automatically run cerberus buildall on a regular schedule, perhaps every ten minutes. Builds will run only if the repository has changed.

Now that you are familiar with Rake and Cerberus, you are ready to use the entire Rails stack for website development. The chapters that follow expand from this base to web applications: web-based programs that deliver data and services beyond browser content.

8.6 Resources

Apache Maven Simplifies the Java Build Process. . .

. . . http://www.devx.com/java/Article/17204

Well-written introduction to Maven. Maven is a build tool for Java that relies far more on convention than on traditional Ant builds. This is useful for comparison with Rake.

Capistrano: Automating Application Deployment...

... http://manuals.rubyonrails.com/read/book/17

Capistrano is a Ruby-based deployment automation tool. Although developed for Ruby and Rails, it can deploy applications for other language platforms as well. Capistrano is beyond the scope of this book but well worth learning about.

The Onion Truck Strikes Again...Announcing Rake...

... http://blade.nagaokaut.ac.jp/cgi-bin/scat.rb/ruby/ruby-talk/66974

Jim Weirich describes the original development of Rake. Read this, and read the (linked) original Rake code. It is an incredibly powerful demonstration of the ease of iterative development in Ruby.

Using the Rake Build Language...

... http://www.martinfowler.com/articles/rake.html

Martin Fowler explains why Rake is so powerful and introduces DSLs.

## Chapter 9

Creating and Invoking Web Services

We don't have time for a "What are web services?" debate, so we will pick a simple definition: A web service provides a service over the Web in a form that can be easily consumed by other applications. This broad definition includes all the various candidates for the "right way to do web services":

- Services that use the "official" web service stack of XML, XSD, SOAP, WSDL, and the WS-* specifications

- Services that provide RESTful interfaces

- Services that deliver data in script-friendly formats such as YAML and JSON

Both Ruby and Java provide support for all of these approaches and various combinations thereof. (If they didn't, it would be a condemnation of web services, not the languages. Web services should make interop easy, regardless of programming language. It's just data.)

Although both Ruby and Java support web services, the level and style of support is much different. Java has some significant advantages:

- Far more investment has been made in the Java space. There are more parsers, better documentation, more tools, more commercial offerings, and better performance.

- Java interop with other platforms has been much more tested.

But Ruby has some latent advantages:

- Ruby is a more natural match with XML. XML is dynamically typed, like Ruby.
- Ruby is a particularly good match for JSON and YAML.

The upshot of all this is that at the time of this writing we prefer Java for problems that are performance-sensitive or require specialized libraries. We prefer Ruby for problems where developer productivity is the dominant factor or where we need to build new libraries.

In this chapter, we will demonstrate building and consuming web services in both SOAP and RESTful style. We will also talk about the XML parser options in case you need to roll your own solution. In both Java and Ruby, we could have taken dozens of possible approaches. We have tried to choose approaches that are simple and common.

9.1 RESTful Web Services

Representational State Transfer (REST) was coined by Roy Fielding in his doctoral dissertation.[1] It's worth reading the original paper, particularly if you plan to start a REST vs. SOAP brawl at your local pub. Here are a few key points:

- In REST, endpoints on the Web represent resources. The same resource may be exposed in different formats, and you can request the format you want with metadata (HTTP headers). For example, we might want to read the news in an HTML browser, and you might want the same news in an XML feed.
- The "interface" for modifying resources is limited to a small set of simple operations: Create, Read, Update, and Delete (CRUD). To make things confusing, these operations are traveling under the pseudonyms POST, GET, PUT, and DELETE.

REST advocates point out that REST scales well. The standardized CRUD interface is friendly to caches and layered systems. The most important reason for this is that read-only operations can be trivially identified by anyone and cached. On the other hand, naive SOAP-based web services bury their interfaces in application-specific XML message bodies. These bodies are then opaque to intermediate nodes on the Internet and cannot be cached.

---

1. http://www.ics.uci.edu/~fielding/pubs/dissertation/rest_arch_style.htm

The scalability argument implies that REST is something you ought to do, like eating your vegetables. In our opinion, REST's success depends more on a practicality: For simple tasks, REST interfaces are much easier to program than SOAP. So, REST is something you *want* to do, like eating chocolate cake.

SOAP is an XML protocol for accessing a web service. The "interface" to a SOAP service can be anything you want. The SOAP XML body can contain method names and parameters or simply be an arbitrary XML document. A key component of SOAP is the SOAP header, which can carry various kinds of metadata. SOAP headers are used to piggyback all kinds of additional services.

Many other specifications depend on SOAP. Taken together, the specs spell out standard ways to do error handling, transactions, end-to-end security, and more. REST has little to say about solving these problems.

This is all oversimplified, of course. We have deliberately drawn a sharp distinction between SOAP and REST. In practice, various in-between strategies take advantage of both styles. For the foreseeable future, you will need to know how to program against both SOAP and REST.

Reflecting REST's resource-oriented approach, Rails 1.2 includes a new generator, scaffold/resource. The easiest way to learn about REST on Rails is to run this generator and explore how the generated code differs from the Rails code we have seen throughout the rest of the book.

Creating RESTful Services with ActiveResource

For our REST example, we will create a RESTful interface for a database of authors and publications:[2]

```
script/generate scaffold_resource author canonical:string\
 legalname:string birthplace:string birthdate:date deathdate:date
```

The first argument, author, is the model name. As you have come to expect in Rails, this will create the Author model, plus the AuthorsController, plus associated tests. The remaining arguments are name/type pairs and are used to create the initial migration and the view code.

When you run the generator, it adds the following line to your routes.rb:

```
map.resources :authors
```

---

2. The example is a trimmed-down version of the Internet Speculative Fiction Database (http://www.isfdb.org).

The call to resource implements Rails' RESTful routing. We'll explain this line in detail after a few examples.

The scaffold generates a set of files whose names and locations are similar to the original Rails scaffold. The code in these files looks quite different. Here is the index method:

```
code/rails_xt/app/controllers/authors_controller.rb
def index
  @authors = Author.find(:all)
  respond_to do |format|
    format.html
    format.xml  { render :xml => @authors.to_xml }
  end
end
```

The respond_to method lets the same endpoint respond with different content, depending on the client. respond_to will execute different blocks, depending on the value of the HTTP Accept header specified by the client.

The format.html has no block, which means "respond as normal for HTML requests"—in this case render index.rhtml. The format.xml block renders an XML response, using a simple, Rails-provided to_xml conversion.

To see this in action, we can fire up the server with some sample data and then use Ruby from the console to request the /authors URL. First, start the Rails XT server:

```
rake db:fixtures:load
script/server
```

Then, from another console, run this simple Ruby script to GET the /authors URL:

```
code/rails_xt/samples/rest/get_authors_html.rb
require 'net/http'
r = Net::HTTP.get_response(URI.parse("http://localhost:3000/authors"))
puts r['content-type']
puts r.body
```

The server returns the default MIME type, text/html:

```
code/rails_xt/sample_output/get_authors_html.txt
$ ruby samples/rest/get_authors_accept_xml.rb
text/html; charset=utf-8
<h1>Listing authors</h1>
<table>
```

```
<tr>
  <th>Canonical</th>
  <th>Legalname</th>
  <th>Birthplace</th>
  <th>Birthdate</th>
  <th>Deathdate</th>
</tr>

<!-- many more lines omitted for brevity -->
```

To get the XML version of authors, specify an explicit Accept header of text/xml:

code/rails_xt/samples/rest/get_authors_accept_xml.rb

```
require 'net/http'
res = Net::HTTP.start('localhost', 3000) {|http|
  http.get '/authors', {"Accept"=>'text/xml'}
}
puts res['content-type']
puts res.body
```

Now the server returns an XML version of the data, with the MIME type text/xml:

code/rails_xt/sample_output/get_authors_accept_xml.txt

```
$ ruby samples/rest/get_authors_accept_xml.rb
application/xml; charset=utf-8
<?xml version="1.0" encoding="UTF-8"?>
<authors>
  <author>
    <birthdate type="date">2006-11-01</birthdate>
    <birthplace>MyString</birthplace>
    <canonical>MyString</canonical>
    <deathdate type="date">2006-11-01</deathdate>
    <id type="integer">1</id>
    <legalname>MyString</legalname>
  </author>
  <!-- remainder omitted for brevity -->
```

That is cool, but what about clients (including browsers) that will not generate an Accept header? These clients can get the XML version by requesting /authors.xml. When Rails sees the .xml extension, RESTful routing adds :format=>'xml' to the params hash. The following Ruby client will return XML exactly as if the request header had been set:

code/rails_xt/samples/rest/get_authors_xml.rb

```
require 'net/http'
Net::HTTP.get_print(URI.parse("http://localhost:3000/authors.xml"))
```

CRUD	HTTP	URL	MIME	Action
Read	GET	/authors	(Accept)	index
Read	GET	/authors.xml	text/xml	index
Read	GET	/authors/1	(Accept)	show
Read	GET	/authors/1.xml	text/xml	show
Read	GET	/authors/new	HTML	new
Read	GET	/authors/1;edit	HTML	edit
Create	POST	/authors	(Accept)	create
Create	POST	/authors.xml	text/xml	create
Update	PUT	/authors/1	(Accept)	update
Update	PUT	/authors/1.xml	text/xml	update
Delete	DELETE	/authors/1	(Accept)	destroy
Delete	DELETE	/authors/1.xml	text/xml	destroy

Figure 9.1: RESTful ROUTING EXAMPLES

The previous three examples illustrate the key concepts in Rails' approach to REST:

- Endpoints can return different MIME types based on the Accept header.

- As a fallback, endpoints can extract MIME type hints from the URL.

- The respond_to method creates a unified programming model that abstracts away the details of how the MIME type is discovered.

With these concepts in mind, examples of the various URLs generated by map.resources authors are shown in Figure 9.1.

Notice how the same URL, /authors/1, is used for read, update, and delete. The HTTP verb determines which action is invoked. This is consistent with the REST philosophy, but again, this has a catch. Just as browsers can't be trusted to set Accept headers, they cannot be trusted to use HTTP verbs other than GET and POST. Again, Rails is doing some trickery behind the scenes to make the world seem more RESTful than it is.

Take a look at form helper for the Authors edit view:

`code/rails_xt/app/views/authors/edit.rhtml`

```
<h1>Editing author</h1>

<% form_for(:author, :url => author_path(@author),
            :html => { :method => :put }) do |f| %>
  <p>
    <b>Canonical</b><br />
    <%= f.text_field :canonical %>
  </p>

  <p>
    <b>Legalname</b><br />
    <%= f.text_field :legalname %>
  </p>

  <p>
    <b>Birthplace</b><br />
    <%= f.text_field :birthplace %>
  </p>

  <p>
    <b>Birthdate</b><br />
    <%= f.date_select :birthdate %>
  </p>

  <p>
    <b>Deathdate</b><br />
    <%= f.date_select :deathdate %>
  </p>

  <p>
    <%= submit_tag "Update" %>
  </p>
<% end %>

<%= link_to 'Show', author_path(@author) %> |
<%= link_to 'Back', authors_path %>
```

It looks like Rails is asking the form to use the PUT verb, but the generated code tells a different story:

`code/rails_xt/samples/rest/simulated_put.html`

```
<form action="/authors/1" method="post">
  <input name="_method" type="hidden" value="put" />
  <!-- truncated for brevity -->
```

Rails stores the intended action in a hidden _method field. If the HTTP method is POST, Rails checks _method and use it instead, if available.

There is a good deal more to RESTful resources in Rails than we have covered here. See the references at the end of the chapter for additional information.

The RESTful approach taken in this chapter is a significant improvement over previous approaches to Rails routing. REST routes are simpler and more uniform, and the resulting routes.rb tends to be smaller and easier to read. Moreover, we have now exposed our application as a web application (HTML) and a web service (XML), with very little code duplication.

Of course, the web service is useful only if there a programmatic clients to take advantage of it. New to Rails 1.2, ActiveResource allows Rails applications to use other applications as resources.

Consuming RESTful Services with ActiveResource

ActiveResource is an API for accessing web services as model objects. Just as ActiveRecord hides the details of data access, ActiveResource hides the details of web service invocation.

ActiveResource is still fairly early in development, so some of what follows may change before ever appearing in a public release of Rails. At the time of this writing, you cannot get it by simply freezing to Edge Rails. Instead, you have to check out the most recent version of Rails into the vendor/rails directory of your application:

```
svn co http://dev.rubyonrails.org/svn/rails/trunk vendor/rails
```

Then, edit your environment.rb to include ActiveResource in the load path:

code/rails_xt/config/environment.rb

```
Rails::Initializer.run do |config|
  config.load_paths += %W( #{RAILS_ROOT}/vendor/rails/activeresource/lib )
```

Now you are ready to create an ActiveResource. Simply extend ActiveResource::Base, and tell your class the base URL of the service:

code/rails_xt/test/resource/author_resource_test.rb

```
class Author < ActiveResource::Base; end
Author.site = 'http://localhost:3000'
```

Just as with ActiveRecord, Rails uses naming conventions to maintain simplicity. For the Author.site shown, Rails will expect RESTful server endpoints localhost:3000/authors and localhost:3000/authors/1. You can override these naming conventions with element_name and collection_name class attributes, if necessary.

Finding an ActiveResource is similar to finding an ActiveRecord:

`code/rails_xt/test/resource/author_resource_test.rb`

```
a = Author.find(1)
```

Creating an instance also looks very like the ActiveRecord counterpart:

`code/rails_xt/test/resource/author_resource_test.rb`

```
a = Author.new :canonical=>'David Brin'
a.save
```

It is not worth delving much more deeply than this, because the current implementation is preliminary. However, the vision is clear: Active-Resource should make web services as simple as ActiveRecord made databases.

The RESTful approach works well when you care about simplicity and scalability and when your services imply a simple object model (or no object model at all). An alternative approach is to build "heavier" web services to support more complex XML, more complex object models, and interactions other than simply client/server. In the next section, we will look at Java and Rails SOAP servers.

9.2 SOAP Web Services

SOAP[3] is a W3C recommendation for exchanging structured and typed information between pairs. At its core, a SOAP message is simply a header+body expressed in XML. The SOAP header acts as an extensibility point, allowing applications to layer in features such as end-to-end security, transactions, and reliable messaging.

Creating SOAP Services with ActionWebService

For our Java SOAP implementation, we will use the most popular open source toolkit, Apache Axis (http://ws.apache.org/axis/), together with AppFuse (http://www.appfuse.org) to reduce the amount of drudge work.

---

3.   http://www.w3.org/TR/soap

We will begin by declaring the Java interface to a service we want to provide:

code/appfuse_people/src/service/com/relevancellc/people/service/PersonManager.java

```java
package com.relevancellc.people.service;

import com.relevancellc.people.model.Person;
import com.relevancellc.people.dao.PersonDao;

import java.util.List;

public interface PersonManager {
  public void setPersonDao(PersonDao dao);

  public Person getPerson(String id);

  public void savePerson(Person person);

  public void removePerson(String id);

  List getPeople(Person o);
}
```

In Rails we will use ActionWebService, a library for creating web services over SOAP or XML-RPC. We start by running a generator:

```
$ script/generate web_service PersonService get_person save_person \
                                        delete_person get_people
        create  app/apis/
        exists  app/controllers/
        exists  test/functional/
        create  app/apis/person_service_api.rb
        create  app/controllers/person_service_controller.rb
        create  test/functional/person_service_api_test.rb
```

The generator creates a directory we have not seen before: app/apis. The person_service_api.rb file contains the Ruby description of the web service interface. The generated version is just a stub, which we have edited to look like this:

code/people/app/apis/person_service_api.rb

```ruby
class PersonServiceApi < ActionWebService::API::Base
  api_method :get_person, :expects=>[:int], :returns=>[Person]
  api_method :save_person, :expects=>[Person], :returns=>[:int]
  api_method :delete_person, :expects=>[:int], :returns=>[:bool]
  api_method :get_people, :expects=>[], :returns => [[Person]]
end
```

Because Ruby does not have interfaces, ActionWebService defines api_method for describing web service methods. For each method, the expects array contains the parameter list, and the returns array contains the return value.

Primitive types are named with symbols such as :int. Complex types such as ActiveRecord models are specified by their class name, such as Person.

The Java implementation of PersonManager is named PersonManagerImpl. Our implementation is generated by AppFuse and simply delegates to the DAO layer:

```
code/appfuse_people/src/service/com/relevancellc/people/service/impl/PersonManagerImpl.java
package com.relevancellc.people.service.impl;

import com.relevancellc.people.dao.PersonDao;
import com.relevancellc.people.model.Person;
import com.relevancellc.people.service.PersonManager;

import java.util.List;

public class PersonManagerImpl extends BaseManager implements PersonManager {

  private PersonDao dao;

  public void setPersonDao(PersonDao dao) {
    this.dao = dao;
  }

  public Person getPerson(String id) {
    return dao.getPerson(Long.valueOf(id));
  }

  public void savePerson(Person person) {
    dao.savePerson(person);
  }

  public void removePerson(String id) {
    dao.removePerson(Long.valueOf(id));
  }

  public List getPeople(Person person) {
    return dao.getPeople(person);
  }

}
```

The Ruby implementation of PersonServiceApi is named PersonServiceController and simply delegates to ActiveRecord:

`code/people/app/controllers/person_service_controller.rb`

```ruby
class PersonServiceController < ApplicationController
  wsdl_service_name 'PersonService'
  web_service_scaffold :invoke

  def get_person(id)
    Person.find(id)
  end
  def save_person(p)
    p.save!
    p.id
  end
  def delete_person(id)
    Person.destroy(id)
    true
  end
  def get_people
    Person.find(:all)
  end
end
```

That is all the code you need. As you can see, both Axis and ActionWeb-Service take a similar approach to the code. You declare the interface in one file and the implementation in another.

Now that the implementation is in place, the job of the toolkits is to expose the service at a URL endpoint on the Web. For the Axis version, we follow the approach outlined in the Axis tutorial located at http://www.appfuse.org. This process includes the following steps:

1. Register the Axis servlet (thirteen lines of XML).
2. Register the MIME mappings (eight lines of XML).
3. Create an XDoclet task to build Axis's WSDD file (about 100 lines of XML).
4. Annotate any complex types for conversion to XML Schema (two lines of annotation for Person).
5. Create a PersonEndpoint class that delegates to PersonManagerImpl (thirty to forty lines of Java and annotations).

That sounds like a lot of code and XML, but it isn't that much work to put in place. Much of the code is boilerplate, so when you have done it once, you can reuse it on other projects. Tools like AppFuse automate the process so that you might not have to actually write any of this code.

The Rails equivalent is this line of code from PersonManagerImpl:

```
wsdl_service_name 'PersonService'
```

The call to wsdl_service_name tells ActionWebService that the Person-ServiceController implementation is associated with the PersonServiceApi. Everything else is discovered by convention. The servlet connection, the conversion to WSDL, and the mapping of Person to XML Schema are all derived automatically.

This example nicely demonstrates the difference in perspective between many Java frameworks and Rails. Java frameworks tend to have a great number of configuration options that are *explicitly* specified in XML, while Rails tries to have *implicit* defaults that will "just work" in the most common case.

Consuming SOAP Services with soap4r

In Ruby, you can create SOAP clients using soap4r, which is part of the standard library. To start, require the library:

code/people/samples/person_soap_client.rb

```
require 'soap/wsdlDriver'
```

Next, create a remote procedure call (RPC) driver to invoke your SOAP methods. To create the driver, you will need to have access to a Web Services Definition Language (WSDL) file that describes the service you plan to call. WSDL files describe services in a generic way, using a boatload of XML. For simple services, this XML is totally boilerplate, and toolkits generate it automatically. When you run the People sample application, the WSDL for the PersonService is at localhost:3000/person_service/wsdl. Here is the code to create the RPC driver:

code/people/samples/person_soap_client.rb

```
url = "http://localhost:3000/person_service/wsdl"
soap = SOAP::WSDLDriverFactory.new(url).create_rpc_driver
```

Now, you can use the soap object to invoke the methods described in the WSDL file. In our example, the original description of these methods is the PersonServiceAPI from the previous section. Invoking a SOAP message is as simple as this:

code/people/samples/person_soap_client.rb

```
puts soap.getPerson(1).inspect
```

Running the code returns a SOAP::Mapping::Object, which is a simple collection containing the values returned from the server:

`code/people/snippets/person_soap_client.txt`

```
$ ruby samples/person_soap_client.rb
#<SOAP::Mapping::Object:0x81c768 \
  {}id=1 {}first_name="Stuart" {}last_name="Halloway">
```

If you want to see the actual SOAP messages, you can set the wire-dump_file_base property:

`code/people/samples/person_soap_client.rb`

```
soap.wiredump_file_base = File.join(File.dirname(__FILE__), "../tmp")
```

soap4r will log SOAP calls to files in the directory specified by wire-dump_file_base. The log of the previous request to getPerson looks like this:

`code/people/snippets/tmp_getPerson_request.xml`

```xml
<?xml version="1.0" encoding="utf-8" ?>
<env:Envelope xmlns:xsd="http://www.w3.org/2001/XMLSchema"
    xmlns:env="http://schemas.xmlsoap.org/soap/envelope/"
    xmlns:xsi="http://www.w3.org/2001/XMLSchema-instance">
  <env:Body>
    <n1:GetPerson xmlns:n1="urn:ActionWebService"
        env:encodingStyle="http://schemas.xmlsoap.org/soap/encoding/">
      <param0 xsi:type="xsd:int">1</param0>
    </n1:GetPerson>
  </env:Body>
</env:Envelope>
```

And here is the response:

`code/people/snippets/tmp_getPerson_response.xml`

```xml
<?xml version="1.0" encoding="UTF-8" ?>
<env:Envelope xmlns:xsd="http://www.w3.org/2001/XMLSchema"
    xmlns:env="http://schemas.xmlsoap.org/soap/envelope/"
    xmlns:xsi="http://www.w3.org/2001/XMLSchema-instance">
  <env:Body>
    <n1:GetPersonResponse xmlns:n1="urn:ActionWebService"
        env:encodingStyle="http://schemas.xmlsoap.org/soap/encoding/">
      <return xsi:type="n1:Person">
        <id xsi:type="xsd:int">1</id>
        <first_name xsi:type="xsd:string">Stuart</first_name>
        <last_name xsi:type="xsd:string">Halloway</last_name>
      </return>
    </n1:GetPersonResponse>
  </env:Body>
</env:Envelope>
```

That's a lot of XML for a simple service invocation. When you compare REST and SOAP at the level of simple examples, as in this chapter, it is easy to conclude that REST is the way to go. Often that will be true; many service APIs start simple and never get more complex. In fairness to SOAP, though, we should point out the extensibility points that might become valuable in more complex applications:

- The namespace definitions on the env:Envelope element designate three different namespaces and the associated *schemas*. An XML Schema specifies the structure and data types that are legal for an XML document. By using multiple schemas and namespaces, you can build complex documents without needing a single, inflexible overarching schema.

  schemas

- The env:encodingStyle attribute specifies the serialization rules employed inside the SOAP message. In theory this allows SOAP to be used with a variety of different schema languages. In practice most developers end up using their development tool's defaults.

During the early days of web services, XML appeared to be the only game in town. This is less true over time. RESTful architectures focus more on HTTP verbs and content negotiation via HTTP headers, making XML one option among many. In the last few years, many developers have rediscovered dynamic languages such as JavaScript, PHP, Python, and Ruby as an alternative to the perceived complexity of Java and C# development. This search for simplicity has happened with data format as well, with the rise of YAML as an alternative to XML.

9.3 YAML and XML Compared

XML is the dominant data format for web service development. There are some good reasons for this. XML has a long lineage. XML evolved from Standard Generalized Markup Language (SGML), a metalanguage for defining document markup.

XML has become so popular that it is used for all things data. In the Java world, XML has become the standard mechanism for application configuration files. Many Java programmers have come to believe that XML is overkill for this purpose. To see why, imagine a hypothetical configuration file that stores user information:

```
<user>
  <username>stu</username>
  <homepage>http://blogs.relevancellc.com</homepage>
</user>
```

XML is intended to be human-readable and self-describing. XML is human-readable because it is a text format, and it is self-describing because data is described by *elements* such as <*user*>, <*username*>, and <*homepage*> in the preceding example. Another option for representing usernames and home pages would be XML attributes:

elements

```
<user username="stu" homepage="http://blogs.relevancellc.com"></user>
```

The attribute syntax is obviously more terse. It also implies semantic differences. Attributes are unordered, while elements are ordered. Attributes are also limited in the values they may contain: Some characters are illegal, and attributes cannot contain nested data (elements, on the other hand, can nest arbitrarily deep).

There is one last wrinkle to consider with this simple XML document. What happens when it travels in the wide world and encounters other elements named <*user*>? To prevent confusion, XML allows *namespaces*. These serve the same role as Java packages or Ruby modules, but the syntax is different:

namespaces

```
<rel:user xmlns:rel="http://www.relevancellc.com/sample"
          username="stu"
          homepage="http://blogs.relevancellc.com">
</rel:user>
```

The namespace is http://www.relevancellc.com/sample. That would be a lot to type in front of an element name, so xmlns:rel establishes rel as a prefix. Reading the previous document, an XML wonk would say that <*user*> is in the http://www.relevancellc.com/sample namespace.

YAML is a response to the complexity of XML (YAML stands for YAML Ain't Markup Language). YAML has many things in common with XML. Most important, both YAML and XML can be used to represent and serialize complex, nested data structures. What special advantages does YAML offer?

The YAML criticism of XML boils down to a single sentence. *XML has two concepts too many:*

- There is no need for two different forms of nested data. Elements are enough.
- There is no need for a distinct namespace concept; scoping is sufficient for namespacing.

To see why attributes and namespaces are superfluous in YAML, here are three YAML variants of the same configuration file:

```
code/rails_xt/samples/why_yaml.rb
```
```
user:
  username: stu
  homepage: http://blogs.relevancellc.com
```

As you can see, YAML uses indentation for nesting. This is more terse than XML's approach, which requires a closing tag.

The second XML example used attributes to shorten the document to a single line. Here's the one-line YAML version:

```
code/rails_xt/samples/why_yaml.rb
```
```
user: {username: stu, homepage: http://blogs.relevancellc.com}
```

The one-line syntax introduces {} as delimiters, but there is no semantic distinction in the actual data. Name/value data, called a *simple mapping* in YAML, is identical in the multiline and one-line documents.   *simple mapping*

Here's a YAML "namespace":

```
code/rails_xt/samples/why_yaml.rb
```
```
http://www.relevancellc.com/sample:
  user: {username: stu, homepage: http://blogs.relevancellc.com}
```

There is no special namespace construct in YAML, because scope provides a sufficient mechanism. In the previous document, user belongs to http://www.relevancellc.com/sample. Replacing the words "belongs to" with "is in the namespace" is a matter of taste.

It is easy to convert from YAML to a Ruby object:

```
irb(main):001:0> require 'yaml'
=> true
irb(main):002:0> YAML.load("{username: stu}")
=> {"username"=>"stu"}
```

Or from a Ruby object to YAML:

```
irb(main):003:0> YAML.dump 'username'=>'stu'
=> "--- \nusername: stu"
```

The leading -- \n: is a YAML document separator. This is optional, and we won't be using it in Rails configuration files. See the sidebar on the next page for pointers to YAML's constructs not covered here.

Items in a YAML sequence are prefixed with '- ':

```
- one
- two
- three
```

Data Formats: More Complexity

For Rails configuration, you may never need YAML knowledge beyond this chapter. But, if you delve into YAML as a general-purpose data language, you will discover quite a bit more complexity. Here are a few areas of complexity, with XML's approach to the same issues included for comparison:

Complexity	YAML Approach	XML Approach
whitespace	Annoying rules	Annoying rules
Repeated data	Aliases and anchors	Entities, SOAP sect. 5
Mapping to programming language types	Type families	XML Schema, various data bindings

If you are making architectural decisions about data formats, you will want to understand these issues. For YAML, a good place to start is the YAML Cookbook.*

* http://yaml4r.sourceforge.net/cookbook/

There is also a one-line syntax for sequences, which from a Ruby perspective could hardly be more convenient. A single-line YAML sequence is also a legal Ruby array:

```
irb(main):015:0> YAML.load("[1, 2, 3]")
=> [1, 2, 3]
irb(main):016:0> YAML.dump [1,2,3]
=> "--- \n- 1\n- 2\n- 3"
```

Beware the significant whitespace, though! If you leave it out, you will be in for a rude surprise:

```
irb(main):018:0> YAML.load("[1,2,3]")
=> [123]
```

Without the whitespace after each comma, the elements all got compacted together. YAML is persnickety about whitespace, out of deference to tradition that markup languages must have counterintuitive whitespace rules. With YAML there are two things to remember:

- Any time you see a single whitespace character that makes the format prettier, the whitespace is probably significant to YAML. That's YAML's way of encouraging beauty in the world.

- Tabs are illegal. Turn them off in your editor.

If you are running inside the Rails environment, YAML is even easier. The YAML library is automatically imported, and all objects get a to_yaml() method:

```
$ script/console
Loading development environment.
>> [1,2,3].to_yaml
=> "--- \n- 1\n- 2\n- 3"
>> {'hello'=>'world'}.to_yaml
=> "--- \nhello: world"
```

In many situations, YAML's syntax for serialization looks very much like the literal syntax for creating hashes or arrays in some (hypothetical) scripting language. This is no accident. YAML's similarity to script syntax makes YAML easier to read, write, and parse. Why not take this similarity to its logical limit and create a data format that is also valid source code in some language? JSON does exactly that.

9.4 JSON and Rails

The JavaScript Object Notation (JSON) is a lightweight data-interchange format developed by Douglas Crockford. JSON has several relevant advantages for a web programmer. JSON is a subset of legal JavaScript code, which means that JSON can be evaluated in any JavaScript-enabled web browser. Here are a few examples of JSON. First, an array:

```
authors = ['Stu', 'Justin']
```

And here is a collection of name/value pairs:

```
prices = {lemonade: 0.50, cookie: 0.75}
```

Unless you are severely sleep deprived, you are probably saying "This looks almost exactly like YAML." Right. JSON is a legal subset of JavaScript and also a legal subset of YAML (almost). JSON is much simpler than even YAML—don't expect to find anything like YAML's anchors and aliases. In fact, the entire JSON format is documented in one short web page at http://www.json.org.

JSON is useful as a data format for web services that will be consumed by a JavaScript-enabled client and is particularly popular for Ajax applications.

Rails extends Ruby's core classes to provide a to_json method:

```
code/rails_xt/sample_output/to_json.irb
```

```
$ script/console
Loading development environment.
>> "hello".to_json
=> "\"hello\""
>> [1,2,3].to_json
=> "[1, 2, 3]"
>> {:lemonade => 0.50}.to_json
=> "{\"lemonade\": 0.5}"
```

If you need to convert from JSON into Ruby objects, you can parse them as YAML, as described in Section 9.3, *YAML and XML Compared*, on page 245. There are some corner cases where you need to be careful that your YAML is legal JSON; see _why's blog post[4] for details.

JSON and YAML are great for green-field projects, but many developers are committed to an existing XML architecture. Since XML does *not* look like program source code, converting between XML and programming language structures is an interesting challenge.

It is to this challenge, XML parsing, that we turn next.

9.5 XML Parsing

XML parsing

To use XML from an application, you need to process an XML document, converting it into some kind of runtime object model. This process is called *XML parsing*. Both Java and Ruby provide several different parsing APIs.

Ruby's standard library includes REXML, an XML parser that was originally based on a Java implementation called Electric XML. REXML is feature-rich and includes XPath 1.0 support plus tree, stream, SAX2, pull, and lightweight APIs. This section presents several examples using REXML to read and write XML.

Rails programs also have another choice for writing XML. Builder is a special-purpose library for writing XML and is covered in Section 9.7, *Creating XML with Builder*, on page 260.

---

4. http://redhanded.hobix.com/inspect/jsonCloserToYamlButNoCigarThanksAlotWhitespace.html

The next several examples will parse this simple Ant build file:

```
code/Rake/simple_ant/build.xml
<project name="simple-ant" default="compile">
  <target name="clean">
    <delete dir="classes"/>
  </target>
  <target name="prepare">
    <mkdir dir="classes"/>
  </target>
  <target name="compile" depends="prepare">
    <javac srcdir="src" destdir="classes"/>
  </target>
</project>
```

Each example will demonstrate a different approach to a simple task: extracting a Target object with name and depends properties.

Push Parsing

First, we'll look at a Java SAX (Simple API for XML) implementation. SAX parsers are "push" parsers; you provide a callback object, and the parser pushes the data through various callback methods on that object:

```
code/java_xt/src/xml/SAXDemo.java
public Target[] getTargets(File file)
    throws ParserConfigurationException, SAXException, IOException {
  final ArrayList al = new ArrayList();
  SAXParserFactory f = SAXParserFactory.newInstance();
  SAXParser sp = f.newSAXParser();
  sp.parse(file, new DefaultHandler() {
    public void startElement(String uri, String lname,
                             String qname, Attributes attributes)
        throws SAXException {
      if (qname.equals("target")) {
        Target t = new Target();
        t.setDepends(attributes.getValue("depends"));
        t.setName(attributes.getValue("name"));
        al.add(t);
      }
    }
  });
  return (Target[]) al.toArray(new Target[al.size()]);
}
```

The Java example depends on a Target class, which is a trivial JavaBean (not shown).

An REXML SAX approach looks like this:

code/rails_xt/samples/xml/sax_demo.rb

```
def get_targets(file)
  targets = []
  parser = SAX2Parser.new(file)
  parser.listen(:start_element, %w{target}) do |u,l,q,atts|
    targets << {:name=>atts['name'], :depends=>atts['depends']}
  end
  parser.parse
  targets
end
```

Even though they are implementing the same API, the Ruby and Java approaches have two significant differences. Where the Java implementation uses a factory, the Ruby implementation instantiates the parser directly. And where the Java version uses an anonymous inner class, the Ruby version uses a block.

These language issues are discussed in the *Joe Asks...* on page 256 and in Section 3.9, *Functions*, on page 73, respectively. These differences will recur with the other XML parsers as well, but we won't bring them up again.

shortcut notations

There is also a smaller difference. The Ruby version takes advantage of one of Ruby's many *shortcut notations*. The %w shortcut provides a simple syntax for creating an array of words. For example:

```
irb(main):001:0&gt; %w{these are words}
=&gt; ["these", "are", "words"]
```

The %w syntax makes it convenient for Ruby's start_element to take a second argument, the elements in which we are interested. Instead of listening for all elements, the Ruby version looks only for the <*target*> element that we care about:

code/rails_xt/samples/xml/sax_demo.rb

```
parser.listen(:start_element, %w{target}) do |u,l,q,atts|
```

Pull Parsing

A pull parser is the opposite of a push parser. Instead of implementing a callback API, you explicitly walk forward through an XML document. As you visit each node, you can call accessor methods to get more information about that node.

In Java, the pull parser is called the Streaming API for XML (StAX). StAX is not part of the J2SE, but you can download it from the Java Community Process website.[5] Here is a StAX implementation of getTarget():

```
code/java_xt/src/xml/StAXDemo.java
```

```
Line 1  public Target[] getTargets(File f)
    -       throws XMLStreamException, FileNotFoundException {
    -     XMLInputFactory xif= XMLInputFactory.newInstance();
    -     XMLStreamReader xsr = xif.createXMLStreamReader(new FileInputStream(f));
    5     final ArrayList al = new ArrayList();
    -     for (int event = xsr.next();
    -          event != XMLStreamConstants.END_DOCUMENT;
    -          event=xsr.next()) {
    -       if (event == XMLStreamConstants.START_ELEMENT) {
   10        if (xsr.getLocalName().equals("target")) {
    -           Target t = new Target();
    -           t.setDepends(xsr.getAttributeValue("", "depends"));
    -           t.setName(xsr.getAttributeValue("", "name"));
    -           al.add(t);
   15        }
    -       }
    -     }
    -     return (Target[]) al.toArray(new Target[al.size()]);
    -   }
```

Unlike the SAX example, the StAX version explicitly iterates over the document by calling next() (line 6). Then, we detect whether we care about the parser event in question by comparing the event value to one or more well-known constants (line 9).

Here's the REXML pull version of get_targets():

```
code/rails_xt/samples/xml/pull_demo.rb
```

```
Line 1  def get_targets(file)
    -     targets = []
    -     parser = PullParser.new(file)
    -     parser.each do |event|
    5       if event.start_element? and event[0] == 'target'
    -         targets << {:name=>event[1]['name'], :depends=>event[1]['depends']}
    -       end
    -     end
    -     targets
   10  end
```

---

5. http://jcp.org/aboutJava/communityprocess/final/jsr173/index.html

As with the StAX example, the REXML version explicitly iterates over the document nodes. Of course, the REXML version takes advantage of Ruby's each() (line 4). Where StAX provided an event number and well-known constants to compare with, the REXML version provides an actual event object, with boolean accessors such as start_element? for the different event types (line 5).

Despite their API differences, push and pull parsers have a lot in common. They both move in one direction, forward through the document. This can be efficient if you can process nodes one at a time, without needing content or state from elsewhere in the document. If you need random access to document nodes, you will probably want to use a tree parser, discussed next.

Tree Parsing

Tree parsers represent an XML document as a tree in memory, typically loading in the entire document. Tree parsers allow more powerful navigation than push parsers, because you have random access to the entire document. On the other hand, tree parsers tend to be more expensive and may be overkill for simple operations.

Tree parser APIs come in two flavors: the DOM and everything else. The Document Object Model (DOM) is a W3C specification and aspires to be programming language neutral. Many programming languages also offer a tree parsing API that takes better advantage of specific language features. Here is the build.xml example implemented with Java's built-in DOM support:

`code/java_xt/src/xml/DOMDemo.java`

```
Line 1   public Target[] getTargets(File file) throws Exception {
  -        DocumentBuilderFactory dbf = DocumentBuilderFactory.newInstance();
  -        DocumentBuilder db = dbf.newDocumentBuilder();
  -        Document doc = db.parse(file);
  5        NodeList nl = doc.getElementsByTagName("target");
  -        Target[] targets = new Target[nl.getLength()];
  -        for (int n=0; n<nl.getLength(); n++) {
  -          Target t = new Target();
  -          Element e = (Element) nl.item(0);
  10         t.setDepends(e.getAttribute("depends"));
  -          t.setName(e.getAttribute("name"));
  -          targets[n] = t;
  -        }
  -        return targets;
  15     }
```

The Java version finds users with getElementsByTagName() in line 5. The value returned is a NodeList, which is a DOM-specific class. Since the DOM is language-neutral, it does not support Java's iterators, and looping over the nodes requires a **for** loop (line 7).

Next, using REXML's tree API, here is the code:

```
code/rails_xt/samples/xml/dom_demo.rb
```

```ruby
Line 1   def get_targets(file)
  -        targets = []
  -        Document.new(file).elements.each("//target") do |e|
  -          targets << {:name=>e.attributes["name"],
  5                        :depends=>e.attributes["depends"]}
  -        end
  -        targets
  -      end
```

REXML does not adhere to the DOM. Instead, the elements() method returns an object that supports XPath. In XPath, the expression //target matches all elements named target. Building atop XPath, iteration can then be performed in normal Ruby style with each() (line 3).

Of course, Java supports XPath too, as you will see in the following section.

XPath

XML documents have a hierarchical structure, much like the file system on a computer. File systems have a standard notation for addressing specific files. For example, path/to/foo refers to the file foo, in the to directory, in the path. Better yet, shell programs use wildcards to address multiple files at once: path/* refers to all files contained in the path directory.

The XML Path Language (XPath) brings path addressing to XML. XPath is a W3C Recommendation for addressing parts of an XML document (see http://www.w3.org/TR/xpath.html).

The previous section showed a trivial XPath example, using //target to select all <target> elements. Our purpose here is to show how to access the XPath API using Java and Ruby, not to learn the XPath language itself. Nevertheless we feel compelled to pick a slightly more interesting example.

Joe Asks...

Why Are the Java XML Examples So Verbose?

The Ruby XML examples are so tight that you have to expect there's a catch. Are the Ruby XML APIs missing something important?

What the Java versions have, and the Ruby versions lack utterly, is abstract factories. Many Java APIs expose their key objects via abstract factories. Instead of saying new Document, we say Document-BuilderFactory.someFactoryMethod(). The purpose of factory methods in this context is *keep our options open*. If we want to switch implementations later, to different parser, we can reconfigure the factory without changing a line of code. On the other hand, calling new limits your options. Saying new Foo() gives you a Foo, period. You can't change your mind and get subclass of Foo or a mock object for testing.

The Ruby language is designed so that abstract factories are generally unnecessary, for three reasons:

- In Ruby, the new method can return anything you want. Most important, new can return instances of a different class, so choosing new now does not limit your options.
- Ruby objects are duck-typed (see Section 3.7, *Duck Typing*, on page 70). Since objects are defined by what they can do, rather than what they are named, it is easier to change your mind and have one kind of object stand in for another.
- Ruby classes are open. Choosing Foo now doesn't limit your options later, because you can always reopen Foo and tweak its behavior.

In Java, having to choose between abstract factories and new undermines agility. A central agile theme is "Build what you need now, in a way that can easily evolve to what you discover you need next week." For every new class, we have to make a Big Up-Front Decision (BUFD, often also BFUD). "Will it need pluggable implementations later?" If yes, use factory. If no, call new. The more BUFDs a language avoids, the easier it is to be agile. In Java's defense, you can avoid the dilemma posed by abstract factories in several ways. You can skip factories and use delegation behind the scenes to select alternate implementations. A great example is the JDOM (http://www.jdom.org), which is much easier to use than the J2SE APIs. With Aspect-Oriented Programming (AOP), you can unmake past decisions by weaving in new decisions. With Dependency Injection (DI), you can pull configuration choices out of your code entirely. Pointers to more reading on all this are in the references section at the end of the chapter.

The following Java program finds the name of all *<target>* elements whose depends attribute is prepare:

`code/java_xt/src/xml/XPathDemo.java`

```
public String[] getTargetNamesDependingOnPrepare(File file)
    throws Exception
{
  DocumentBuilderFactory dbf = DocumentBuilderFactory.newInstance();
  DocumentBuilder db = dbf.newDocumentBuilder();
  Document doc = db.parse(file);
  XPathFactory xpf = XPathFactory.newInstance();
  XPath xp = xpf.newXPath();

  NodeList nl = (NodeList) xp.evaluate("//target[@depends='prepare']/@name",
      doc, XPathConstants.NODESET);

  String[] results = new String[nl.getLength()];
  for (int n=0; n<nl.getLength(); n++) {
    results[n] = nl.item(n).getNodeValue();
  }
  return results;
}
```

Java's XPath support builds on top of its DOM support, so most of this code should look familiar. Starting on line 4 you will see several lines of factory code to create the relevant DOM and XPath objects. The actual business of the method is conducted on line 10 when the XPath expression is evaluated. The results are in the form of a NodeList, so the iteration beginning on line 13 is nothing new either.

Ruby's XPath code also builds on top of the tree API you have already seen:

`code/rails_xt/samples/xml/xpath_demo.rb`

```
def get_target_names_depending_on_prepare(file)
  XPath.match(Document.new(file),
              "//target[@depends='prepare']/@name").map do |x|
    x.value
  end
end
```

That's it. Just one line of code. The XPath API in Ruby is all business, no boilerplate. In fact, the syntax can be made even tighter, as shown in the sidebar on the next page.

The Symbol#to_proc Trick

You may be thinking that this Ruby XPath example is a bit too verbose:

```
def get_target_names_depending_on_prepare(file)
  XPath.match(Document.new(file),
             "//target[@depends='prepare']/@name").map do |x|
    x.value
  end
end
```

The Rails team thought so and provided another syntax to be used when invoking blocks:

```
XPath.match(Document.new(file),
           "//target[@depends='prepare']/@name").map(&:value)
```

The new syntax &:value takes advantage of Ruby's alternate syntax for passing blocks, by passing an explicit Proc object. (A Proc is a block instantiated as a class so you can manipulate it in normal Ruby ways.) Of course, :value is not a Proc; it's a Symbol! Rails finesses this by defining an implicit conversion from a Symbol to a Proc:

```
class Symbol
  def to_proc
    Proc.new { |*args| args.shift.__send__(self, *args) }
  end
end
```

The Symbol#to_proc trick is interesting because it demonstrates an important facet of Ruby. The Ruby language encourages modifications to its syntax. Framework designers such as the Rails team do not have to accept Ruby "as is." They can bend the language to meet their needs.

9.6 Ruby XML Output

Configuration is often read-only, but if you use XML for user-editable data, you will need to modify XML documents and serialize them back to text. Both Java and Ruby build modification capability into their tree APIs. Here is a Java program that uses the DOM to build an XML document from scratch:

`code/java_xt/src/xml/DOMOutput.java`

```
Line 1  DocumentBuilderFactory dbf = DocumentBuilderFactory.newInstance();
   -    DocumentBuilder db = dbf.newDocumentBuilder();
   -    Document doc = db.newDocument();
   -    Element root = doc.createElement("project");
   5    root.setAttribute("name", "simple-ant");
   -    doc.appendChild(root);
   -    Element target = doc.createElement("target");
   -    target.setAttribute("name", "compile");
   -    root.appendChild(target);
   10   return doc;
```

After the boilerplate factory code, creating documents with the DOM boils down to three steps:

1. Create elements using methods such as createElement() in line 4.

2. Attach attributes using methods such as setAttribute() in line 5.

3. Attach created elements to a specific node in a document using methods such as appendChild() in line 6.

The REXML approach is similar:

`code/rails_xt/samples/xml/dom_output.rb`

```
Line 1  root = Element.new("project", Document.new)
   -    root.add_attribute("name", "simple-ant")
   -    Element.new("target", root).add_attribute("name", "compile")
```

The REXML API provides for the same three steps: create, add attributes, and attach to document. However, you can combine creation and attachment, as in line 1. If you are really bold, you can even combine all three steps, as in line 3.

XML documents in memory are often serialized into a textual form for storage or transmission. You might want to configure several aspects when serializing XML, such as using whitespace to make the document more readable to humans.

In Java, you can control XML output by setting Transformer properties:

`code/java_xt/src/xml/DOMOutput.java`

```
TransformerFactory tf = TransformerFactory.newInstance();
Transformer tform = tf.newTransformer();
tform.setOutputProperty(OutputKeys.INDENT, "yes");
tform.transform(new DOMSource(doc), new StreamResult(System.out));
```

Line 1

In line 2, the no-argument call to newTransformer() requests a "no-op" transformer. (We are using the transformer just for formatting, not to do anything more exciting such as an XSLT transformation.) The call to setOutputProperty() in line 3 specifies that we want human-readable indentation in the output.

The REXML version exposes output options directly on the document itself:

`code/rails_xt/samples/xml/dom_output.rb`

```
root.document.write STDOUT, 2
```

The call to write() takes an optional second argument that sets the indentation level.

Both the DOM and REXML are general-purpose, low-level APIs. For significant XML applications, such as calling or implementing web services, you are usually better off not using these APIs directly. Instead you should use the higher-level APIs for REST and SOAP discussed at the beginning of this chapter. For quick and easy emission of serialized XML data, Rails programmers also have another option that does not use the underlying tree APIs at all: Builder, which we turn to next.

9.7 Creating XML with Builder

Jim Weirich's Builder library is bundled with Rails or can be installed separately via this:

```
gem install builder
```

Builder takes advantage of two symmetries between Ruby and XML to make building XML documents a snap:

- Ruby classes can respond to arbitrary methods not known in advance, just as XML documents may have elements not known in advance.
- Both Ruby and XML have natural nesting: XML's element/child relationship and Ruby's block syntax.

To see the first symmetry, consider "Hello World," Builder-style. We'll use script/console since Rails preloads Builder, and irb does not:

In script/console output, we are omitting the return value lines (=> ...) for clarity, except where they are directly relevant.

```
$ script/console
Loading development environment.
>> b = Builder::XmlMarkup.new(:target=>STDOUT, :indent=>1)
<inspect/>
>> b.h1 "Hello, world"
<h1>Hello, world</h1>
```

As you can surmise from line 5, instances of XmlMarkup use method names as element names and convert string arguments into text content inside the elements. Of course, the set of all methods is finite:

```
>> Builder::XmlMarkup.instance_methods.size
=> 17
```

Obviously, one of those 17 methods must be h1(), and the others must correspond to other commonly used tag names. Let's test this hypothesis by finding a tag name that is *not* supported by Builder:

```
>> b.foo "Hello, World!"
<foo>Hello, World!</foo>
>> b.qwijibo "Hello, World!"
<qwijibo>Hello, World!</qwijibo>
>> b.surely_this_will_not_work "Hello, World"
<surely_this_will_not_work>Hello, World</surely_this_will_not_work>
```

What's going on here? XmlMarkup is using Ruby's method_missing() hook to dynamically respond to any legal Ruby method name. As a result, XmlMarkup can handle almost any XML element name you might want to create.

Let's create the build.xml example we have been using throughout this chapter. First, we'll need to add attributes to an element. Builder lets you do this by passing an optional hash argument:

```
>> b.project "", :name=>'simple-ant', :default=>'compile'
<project default="compile" name="simple-ant"></project>
```

Next, we'll need some way to nest one element inside another. Ruby's block syntax is perfect for the job. Instead of passing an initial string parameter for the element content, pass a block to generate element content:

```
>> b.project :name=>'simple-ant', :default=>'compile' do
?>   b.target :name=>'clean'
>> end
<project default="compile" name="simple-ant">
 <target name="clean"></target>
</project>
```

Ruby's blocks give the program a nested structure that mirrors the nesting of the (pretty-printed) XML output. This is even more visible when we put together a program to emit the entire build.xml sample:

```
code/rails_xt/samples/build_build_xml.rb
require 'rubygems'
require_gem 'builder'
b = Builder::XmlMarkup.new :target=>STDOUT, :indent=>1
b.project :name=>"simple-ant", :default=>"compile" do
  b.target :name=>"clean" do
    b.delete :dir=>"classes"
  end
  b.target :name=>"prepare" do
    b.mkdir :dir=>"classes"
  end
  b.target :name=>"compile", :depends=>"prepare" do
    b.javac :srcdir=>'src', :destdir=>'classes'
  end
end
```

That yields this:

```
code/Rake/simple_ant/build.xml
<project name="simple-ant" default="compile">
  <target name="clean">
    <delete dir="classes"/>
  </target>
  <target name="prepare">
    <mkdir dir="classes"/>
  </target>
  <target name="compile" depends="prepare">
    <javac srcdir="src" destdir="classes"/>
  </target>
</project>
```

Builder is fully integrated with Rails. To use Builder for a Rails view, simply name your template with the extension .rxml instead of .rhtml.

9.8 Curing Your Data Headache

In this chapter we have reviewed three alternative data formats: YAML, JSON, and XML. Choice feels nice, but sometimes having too many choices can be overwhelming. Combine the three alternative formats with two different language choices (Java and Ruby for readers of this book), add a few dozen open source and commercial projects, and you can get a big headache. We will now present five "aspirin"—specific pieces of advice to ease the pain.

Aspirin #1: Prefer Java for Big XML Problems

At the time of this writing, Java's XML support is far more comprehensive than Ruby's. We don't cover schema validation, XSLT, or XQuery in this book because Ruby support is minimal. (You can get them via open source projects that call to native libraries, but we had to draw the line somewhere).

It is also important to understand *why* Ruby's XML support is less than Java's. Two factors are at work here:

- Java and XML came of age together. Throughout XML's lifetime much of the innovation has been done in Java.

- Ruby programmers, on the other hand, have long preferred YAML (and more recently JSON).

Notice that neither of these factors have anything to do with language or runtime features. They are more about programmer culture. We believe that dynamic languages are a better natural fit to any extensible data formats and that in the future the best XML support will be in dynamic languages.

But that's all in the future. For now, prefer Java for Big XML Problems. How do you recognize a Big Problem? If you think you have a performance problem, write a benchmark that evaluates *your representative data*, and you'll know soon enough. If you need a specific API, google it. Maybe you will be lucky and turn up some choices that have evolved since these words were written.

Aspirin #2: Avoid the DOM

The DOM is ugly. We reference the DOM in this chapter because it is a common baseline that Java programmers are expected to know. Place the DOM on the list of things that were good to learn but never get used. If you must use a tree API in Java, at least use JDOM (www.jdom.org).

We don't really believe the DOM was good to learn but pretending it was makes us feel better about the lost hours.

Aspirin #3: Prefer YAML Over XML for Configuration

As we discussed in Section 9.3, *YAML and XML Compared*, on page 245, XML brings unnecessary document baggage to configuration files, such as the distinction between elements and attributes. Namespaces make things even worse.

Of course, we do not require that you drop your current project to write a YAML configuration parser when you already have an XML approach working. We tend to endure XML where it is already entrenched.

Aspirin #4: Be As RESTful As Possible

REST and SOAP are not wholly incompatible. REST deals with HTTP headers, verbs, and format negotiation. SOAP uses HTTP because it is there but keeps its semantics to itself, in SOAP-specific headers. This separation means that a carefully crafted service can use SOAP and still be RESTful. Unfortunately, given the state of today's tools, you will need a pretty detailed understanding of both SOAP and REST to do this well.

Another alternative is to provide two interfaces to your services: one over SOAP and one that is RESTful.

Aspirin #5: Work at the Highest Feasible Level of Abstraction

The XML APIs, whether tree-based, push, or pull, are the assembly language of XML programming. Most of the time, you should be able to work at a higher level. If the higher-level abstraction you want doesn't exist yet, create it. Even if you use it only once, the higher-level approach will probably be quicker and easier to implement than continuing to work directly with the data.

XML, JSON, and YAML share common goals: to standardize data formats so that application developers need not waste time reading and writing proprietary formats. Because the data formats are general-purpose, they do not impose any fixed types. (This is what people mean when they say that XML is a metaformat.) Developers can then develop domain-specific formats, such the XHTML dialect of XML for web pages.

Web services will greatly expand the amount of communication between computers. As a result, our mental model of the Web is changing. A website is no longer a monolithic entity, served from a single box (or rack of boxes) somewhere. Increasingly, web applications will delegate parts of their work to other web applications, invoking these subsidiary applications as web services. This is mostly a good thing, but it will put even more pressure on developers to make web applications secure. In the next chapter, we will look at securing Rails applications.

9.9   Resources

Builder Objects . . . . onestepback.org/index.cgi/Tech/Ruby/BuilderObjects.rdoc
Jim Weirich's original blog post explaining why and how he created Builder.
Explains how to use the instance_eval() trick to get builder methods to execute
in the correct context.

Creating XML with Ruby and Builder . . .
. . . http://www.xml.com/pub/a/2006/01/04/creating-xml-with-ruby-and-builder.html
A quick introduction to Builder by Michael Fitzgerald.

Design Patterns in AOP . . . . http://www.cs.ubc.ca/~jan/AODPs
Jan Hannemann argues that design patterns are language dependent. Using
AspectJ, many Java design patterns can be made into library calls: "For 12 of
[the GoF Patterns], we developed reusable implementations that can be integrated into software systems as library pattern aspects." Includes source code
for the aspects.

Introducing JSON . . . . http://www.json.org/
JSON's home on the Web. JSON is so simple there isn't much more to say,
but all of it is said here. Includes the JSON parser (www.json.org/js.html) and a
discussion about why you might prefer using it instead of relying on JavaScript
eval().

Inversion of Control and the Dependency Injection Pattern . . .
. . . http://www.martinfowler.com/articles/injection.html
Good introduction to IoC and DI from Martin Fowler.

JDOM: Mission . . . . http://www.jdom.org/mission/index.html
Motivates getting away from abstract factories and getting work done with
JDOM: "There is no compelling reason for a Java API to manipulate XML to
be complex, tricky, unintuitive, or a pain in the neck."

Rails, SOAP4R, and Java . . .
. . . http://ola-bini.blogspot.com/2006/08/rails-soap4r-and-java.html
Ola Bini describes getting SOAP4R to call Apache Axis web services. The hoops
he had to jump through are depressing, but he was able to get interop working
fairly quickly.

REXML . . . . http://www.germane-software.com/software/rexml/
REXML's home on the Web. Includes a tutorial where you can learn many of
REXML's capabilities by example.

YAML Ain't Markup Language . . . . http://www.yaml.org
YAML's home on the Web. YAML includes a good bit more complexity than
discussed in this chapter, and this site is your guide to all of it. We find the
Reference Card (http://www.yaml.org/refcard.html) to be particularly helpful.

Chapter 10

Security

Web applications manage huge amounts of important data. Securing that data is a complex, multifaceted problem. Web applications must ensure that private data remains private and that only authorized individuals can perform transactions.

When it comes to security, Java and Ruby on Rails web frameworks have one big aspect in common: *Everybody does it differently.* No other part of an application architecture is likely to vary as much as the approach to security. We cannot even begin to cover all the different approaches out there, so for this chapter we have picked what we believe to be representative, quality approaches. For the Java side, we will cover securing a Struts application with Acegi, a popular open source framework. To minimize the amount of hand-coding, we are again using AppFuse to generate boilerplate configuration. For Ruby and Rails, we will cover two plugins: acts_as_authenticated and Authorization.

We will begin with the traditional focus on authentication (authn) and authorization (authz). The authn step asks "Who are you?" and the authz step asks "What can you do?" With this basis in place, we will look at security from the attacker's perspective. For a list of possible flaws an attacker might exploit, we will use the Open Web Application Security Project (OWASP) Top 10 Project. For each of the ten web security flaws, we will present preventative measures that you might take in Ruby on Rails.

10.1 Authentication with the acts_as_authenticated Plugin

plugins

Ruby on Rails applications are typically secured with one or more open source *plugins*. Rails plugins are reusable code that is installed in the vendor/plugins directory of a Rails application. Probably the most popular security plugin is acts_as_authenticated, which provides the following:

- Form-based and HTTP BASIC authentication
- A session-scoped user object
- "Remember Me" across sessions with a hashed cookie
- Starter RHTML forms

The steps to configure authn are straightforward:

1. Install the authn library.
2. Specify which resources require authn.
3. Specify navigation flow for login, logout, and redirects.
4. Configure a database of usernames and passwords.

Installing Acegi is a matter of putting JAR files in the right places, which AppFuse does automatically. Installing acts_as_authenticated is described in the sidebar on the next page.

The most common form of Acegi security uses a servlet filter to protect any resources that require authn. To configure this filter, you need to add the filter to web.xml:

code/appfuse_people/web/WEB-INF/web.xml

```
<filter>
  <filter-name>securityFilter</filter-name>
  <filter-class>org.acegisecurity.util.FilterToBeanProxy</filter-class>
  <init-param>
    <param-name>targetClass</param-name>
    <param-value>org.acegisecurity.util.FilterChainProxy</param-value>
  </init-param>
</filter>
```

Next, make web.xml bring in the Spring context file security.xml so that the filterChainProxy bean is available at runtime:

code/appfuse_people/web/WEB-INF/web.xml

```
<context-param>
  <param-name>contextConfigLocation</param-name>
  <param-value>/WEB-INF/applicationContext-*.xml,/WEB-INF/security.xml</param-v
</context-param>
```

Installing the acts_as_authenticated Plugin

Rails plugins are installed into the vendor/plugins directory. Any way you get the files there is fine. You can download a plugin from its home page and unzip it into vendor/plugins. If the plugin has public subversion access, you can svn:external it and stay on the latest version at all times.

To make the process even simpler, many plugins are deployed to the Web so they can be installed via the script/plugin command. acts_as_authenticated is such a plugin, so all you have to do is enter the following two commands:

```
script/plugin source http://svn.techno-weenie.net/projects/plugins
script/plugin install acts_as_authenticated
```

Once you have installed the plugin, you need to create data tables for the username, password, and so on. The following two commands will create the necessary ActiveRecord classes and the migration to add them to the database:

```
script/generate authenticated user account
rake migrate
```

Inside security.xml, specify which resources should be filtered:

```
<bean id="filterChainProxy" class="org.acegisecurity.util.FilterChainProxy">
  <property name="filterInvocationDefinitionSource">
    <value>
    CONVERT_URL_TO_LOWERCASE_BEFORE_COMPARISON
    PATTERN_TYPE_APACHE_ANT
    /**=httpSessionContextIntegrationFilter, ... 7 more filter names
    </value>
  </property>
</bean>
```

The /** is a wildcard that filters all resources.

The database of usernames and passwords is configurable and involves a bit more XML not shown here.

When using Ruby's acts_as_authenticated, you could require authn by adding the following line to a controller class:

```
before_filter :login_required
```

If you want to require authn for some actions only, you can use the standard options to before_filter.

For example, maybe read operations do not require authn, but update operations do:

`code/rails_xt/app/controllers/people_controller.rb`

```
before_filter :login_required, :except=>['index', 'list', 'show']
```

The use of :except is a nice touch because you do not have to learn a security-specific filter vocabulary. You can use the common options you already know for before_filter.

Both Acegi and acts_as_authenticated support a "Remember Me" feature. When this feature is enabled, the application will generate a cookie that can be used to automatically log the user in. This creates the illusion of staying logged in, even across closing and reopening the browser application. Activating such support is trivial in both frameworks. In Acegi, the "Remember Me" filter is just another filter in the list of filters added to the filterChainProxy:

```
/**=...rememberMeProcessingFilter...
```

With acts_as_authenticated, you add a filter to the ApplicationController:

```
before_filter :login_from_cookie
```

That's it. Both AppFuse and acts_as_authenticated automatically install some minimal forms to create and manage logins. Depending on your policy for new account creation, you may want to modify or remove some of these forms. Now that we have authn in place, we can use attach user information to specific roles and use those roles for authz checks.

10.2 Authorization with the Authorization Plugin

To perform authorization, we need to do the following:

1. Associate the authorization with our authentication strategy.

2. Establish some named roles.

3. Map some users to roles.

4. Limit some actions or objects to roles.

For the Java side, we will continue to use Acegi for these tasks. For Ruby on Rails, we will use another plugin, the Authorization plugin. Both Acegi and Authorization allow pluggable authentication strategies. We will be using a database-backed approach for both the Java and Rails applications.

Joe Asks. . .
What about Single Sign-On?

Ruby and Rails have less support for SSO than the Java world provides. However, there are some bright spots. If you are accustomed to using Central Authentication Service (CAS)* in Java, you are in luck. The Ruby world sports a CAS filter for Rails[†] and the RubyCAS-Client.[‡]

If you are integrating with some other SSO provider, you can use the CAS implementations as a starting point.

∗. http://www.ja-sig.org/products/cas/
†. http://opensource.ki.se/casauth.html
‡. http://rubyforge.org/projects/rubycas-client/

Installing the Authorization Plugin

Follow the online instructions* to download the plugin, and then unzip the plugin to the vendor/plugins directory of a Rails application that you want to secure.

Since we are using a database for roles, you will need to generate and run a migration:

```
script/generate role_model Role
rake db:migrate
```

The complete installation instructions are worth reading online; they describe some other options that we will not be needing for this example.

∗. http://www.writertopia.com/developers/authorization

With Acegi, the authz and authn components are connected via Spring dependency injection:

```
<bean id="filterInvocationInterceptor"
    class="org.acegisecurity.intercept.web.FilterSecurityInterceptor">
  <property name="authenticationManager" ref="authenticationManager"/>
```

With the Authorization plugin, you annotate the authentication class to show that it is used for authorization:

```
class User < ActiveRecord::Base
  acts_as_authorized_user
```

Since we are storing users and roles in the database, the roles setup steps might seem like mere data entry. However, we will need sample data for our automated tests, so we'll cover how this data is populated. AppFuse will create an XML file with sample data:

```
<row>
  <value>1</value>
  <value>tomcat</value>
  <value>536c0b339345616c1b33caf454454d8b8a190d6c</value>
  <value>Tomcat</value>
  <value>User</value>
  <value></value>
  <value>Denver</value>
  <value>US</value>
```

This file continues to specify several users and roles. AppFuse then uses a dbunit Ant task to populate the database.

When you install Authorization in a project, it automatically creates a roles fixture file, which we can edit to create a few roles:

```
admin:
  id: 1
  name: admin
mortal:
  id: 2
  name: mortal
```

We already have sample users named Quentin and Aaron, installed by acts_as_authenticated.

Here is Quentin:

```
code/rails_xt/test/fixtures/users.yml
```

```
quentin:
  id: 1
  login: quentin
  email: quentin@example.com
  salt: 7e3041ebc2fc05a40c60028e2c4901a81035d3cd
  crypted_password: 00742970dc9e6319f8019fd54864d3ea740f04b1 # test
  created_at: <%= 5.days.ago.to_s :db %>
```

We have to create a roles_users.yml fixture by hand to populate the join table associating users with roles. We'll make Quentin an admin and Aaron a mortal:

```
code/rails_xt/test/fixtures/roles_users.yml
```

```
first:
  role_id: 1
  user_id: 1
second:
  role_id: 2
  user_id: 2
```

There is no need for a custom Rake task to load these security objects. They are simple ActiveRecord models, so they are automatically managed by the standard Rake tasks built into Rails.

Now we will get to the heart of the matter: protecting resources by role. With Acegi, this is done in an XML file. However, the syntax is not XML but is an embedded pattern language inspired by Apache Ant:

```
code/appfuse_people/web/WEB-INF/security.xml
```

```xml
<property name="objectDefinitionSource">
    <value>
        PATTERN_TYPE_APACHE_ANT
        /clickstreams.jsp*=admin
        /flushCache.*=admin
        /passwordHint.html*=ROLE_ANONYMOUS,admin,user
        /reload.*=admin
        /signup.html*=ROLE_ANONYMOUS,admin,user
        /users.html*=admin
        /**/*.html*=admin,user
    </value>
</property>
```

The patterns restrict URLs to certain roles. We believe that the language succeeds in its goal of being self-explanatory.

With the Authorization plugin, role permissions are assigned in the controller itself. Instead of using pure Ruby code, the permit code parses a mini-language that aspires to read like a human language. For example, the following lines in the controller will specify that only administrators can edit Quips, and mere mortals can only view them:

```
code/rails_xt/app/controllers/quips_controller.rb
READ_ACTIONS = %w(index list show)
permit 'admin or mortal', :only=>READ_ACTIONS
permit 'admin', :except=>READ_ACTIONS
```

As with the Acegi pattern language, we find the Authorization plugin's mini-language to be self-explanatory.

You can test that the authorization protections work by loading the test fixture data into the development database. Rails has a built-in task specifically for this purpose. From the rails_xt directory, rake db:fixtures: load will blow away the development database and replace its contents with the test fixtures. After loading the fixtures, you can run script/server and navigate to /quips. If you are Quentin, you will have read/write access, but as Aaron you will have read access only.

Both Acegi and the Authorization plugin are much more powerful than we have shown here. Both provide the ability to associate roles with particular objects. Acegi also has one incredible feature that we have not seen anywhere else. Because it integrates with the web tier, with simple method interception, and with AspectJ's pointcuts, Acegi can secure *just about anything*. Better yet, you can use the same configuration and roles from end-to-end in your application. You can use the same roles to secure web endpoints, methods, objects, and anything you can capture in an AspectJ pointcut. For the biggest, hairiest problems out there, we would not use anything else.

The acts_as_authenticated/Authorization plugin tandem also has its area of excellence: the tiny amount of configuration and code involved. The amount of configuration required is an order of magnitude less than Acegi, and it is not spread across multiple files and languages. This parsimony extends to the implementation as well. The entire runtime footprint of both plugins together is less than 1,000 lines of Ruby code. Security-related code is costly to develop and maintain, so getting a lot done in a little code is a big advantage.

10.3 Testing Authentication and Authorization

When you add authn and authz support to a Rails application, you will typically break any functional tests that are already in place. This is because functional tests exercise all controller code, including the filters that are used to implement security.

For example, when we added authn and authz to People and Quips in the previous two sections, we broke every test that invoked a secure action, for a total of fifteen broken tests.

We have two problems here. First, we would like to be able to test the logic of the controllers separately from the security constraints. So, we would like a set of functional tests that do not include any security filters. Second, we would like to be able to test the security constraints themselves. Moreover, both of these sets of tests must be easy to write. Otherwise, busy developers won't write them. It would be a shame to have an application where everything was testable except security.

The acts_as_authenticated plugin includes an AuthenticatedTestHelper module to simplify security testing. You can make AuthenticatedTes-tHelper available to all your tests by mixing the module into TestCase in test/test_helper.rb:

`code/rails_xt/test/test_helper.rb`

```
class Test::Unit::TestCase
  include AuthenticatedTestHelper
```

AuthenticatedTestHelper adds several new test methods. One of the most helpful is login_as. To get our tests to pass again, we can simply login_as some account that has every necessary role. A test case's setup method is a perfect place to do this, since it runs before every test:

`code/rails_xt/test/functional/people_controller_test.rb`

```
def setup
  @controller = PeopleController.new
  @request    = ActionController::TestRequest.new
  @response   = ActionController::TestResponse.new
  login_as(:quentin)
end
```

Since our authn and authz approach stores users and roles in the database, we also need to add the security-related tables to the test fixture.

For example, we have used role-based security for the QuipsController, so the functional test will need to have access to users, roles, and roles_users:

code/rails_xt/test/functional/quips_controller_test.rb

```
class QuipsControllerTest < Test::Unit::TestCase
  fixtures :quips, :users, :roles, :roles_users
```

We used the previous approach to fix the fifteen broken functional test for QuipsController and PeopleController. The fix required five total lines of changed code:

- Including AuthenticatedTestHelper (one line)

- Adding login_as(:quentin) to two test classes (two lines)

- Editing the fixture line for the same two test classes (two lines)

Now the functional tests are working again, so we can turn our attention to testing the security constraints themselves. The AuthenticatedTestHelper includes an assert_requires_login method that checks that a particular controller invocation gets redirected to login:

code/rails_xt/test/functional/quips_security_test.rb

```
assert_requires_login do |c|
  c.post :create, :quip => {}
end
```

Notice that this code lives in a different test class, QuipsSecurityTest instead of QuipsControllerTest. We are using a separate test class because the QuipsControllerTest always logs in as Quentin, and now we are testing what happens when there is no login. You can also use assert_requires_login to test that Aaron (a mortal) lacks a role that would be allowed to create a quip:

code/rails_xt/test/functional/quips_security_test.rb

```
assert_requires_login(:aaron) do |c|
  c.post :create, :quip => {}
end
```

The syntax is a bit twisted here, in that assert_requires_login(:aaron) actually means "Assert that logging in as Aaron isn't enough and that you get redirected back to login."

Rather than testing the redirect, you might want to test that failed logins do not change the database. AuthenticatedTestHelper provides a nifty assert_difference method for this kind of test. assert_difference takes three arguments: an object, a method name, and a difference (which defaults to +1). It also expects a block of code. assert_difference calls the method on the object, runs the block, and then calls the method on the object again and checks the difference from the original value. You can write this:

```
code/rails_xt/test/functional/quips_security_test.rb
```

```ruby
assert_difference(Quip, :count, 0) do
  post :create, :quip => {}
end
```

In other words, the Quips.count remains unchanged (difference of 0) when you post a new quip. This is the expected behavior, because posting a new quip will fail if you do not log in first. Although packaged with acts_as_authenticated, the assert_difference method is really a general-purpose method that you might find useful elsewhere as well. For example, the Rails scaffold tests that the create action inserts a new row into a database:

```
code/rails_xt/test/functional/people_controller_test.rb
```

```ruby
def test_create
  num_people = Person.count
  post :create, :person => {}
  assert_response :redirect
  assert_redirected_to :action => 'list'
  assert_equal num_people + 1, Person.count
end
```

Using assert_difference, this can be refactored to the following:

```
code/rails_xt/test/functional/quips_controller_test.rb
```

```ruby
def test_create
  assert_difference(Quip, :count) do
    post :create, :quip => {:text=>'Test Quip'}
    assert_response :redirect
    assert_redirected_to :action => 'list'
  end
end
```

People sometimes equate security with the steps we have just described, that is, enabling authn and authz for an application. We want to go much further than this. Instead of just bolting security on at the edges of an application, we can make security a pervasive concern, through the entire life cycle of design, development, deployment, and maintenance. That's a tall order, and no application will ever be perfectly secure. One reasonable step in the right direction is to look at common web security flaws and ask where in our application we can most effectively prevent these flaws from occurring.

10.4 Preventing the Top-Ten Web Security Flaws

The Open Web Application Security Project (OWASP) is a nonprofit organization that provides free, open source resources for finding and fighting insecure software. One such resource is the Top Ten Project, which represents a group of security professionals' consensus about the most critical web application security flaws. We'll cover each of these in turn and show how to translate your knowledge of Java coding practices into successful Ruby defenses against these flaws. With apologies to David Letterman, we will ruin the suspense by starting with number one.

#1. Unvalidated Input

Attackers can tamper with any part of an HTTP request: the URL, query string, headers, body, cookies, and form data. All parts of the request are user input and cannot be simply trusted. Programs that do not validate input may be subject to injection attacks and may disclose (or corrupt) data that the user should not be allowed to access.

Java web frameworks and Rails both provide declarative validation mechanisms to guard against unvalidated input. For example, in our sample Struts application, validation.xml contains rules for form validation. In Rails, validations are declared directly on the model classes themselves. Either way, the validations do their job only if developers are methodical in making sure that they are correctly applied to every single piece of input.

One concern with validation in Rails applications is that much "magic" happens automatically. For example, code like this is often used to create an ActiveRecord instance directly from form data:

`code/rails_xt/app/controllers/quips_controller.rb`

```
@quip = Quip.new(params[:quip])
```

Some good magic is happening here. Because validations are done at the ActiveRecord level, calling save on this new object will fail (without ever touching the database!) if validations fail. Since quips validate the presence of the text field, there is no danger that this line of code will create an invalid quip with a NULL text.

But maybe there is a little too much magic. Imagine that your form for creating new quips offers only two fields: text and commit. What happens if a user submits the following POST body?

```
quip%5Btext%5D=Hello%2C+world&quip%5Bauthor_id%5D=15&commit=Create
```

Oops. What is that author_id parameter doing in there? Even though you didn't include that value in the form, nothing stops a curious (or malicious) user from adding it to the POST body. The quip will now appear to be authored by the person with ID 15. If your database includes columns that are not intended to be accessed directly by users, then Rails' default mass assignment will be a problem. One (very poor) solution to this problem would be to go back to assigning each value manually:

```
@quip = Quip.new
@quip.some_attr = params[:quip][:some_attr]
@quip.other_attr = params[:quip][:other_attr]
@quip.another_attr = params[:quip][:another_attr]
# etc.
```

ActiveRecord provides a better solution. We can use the attr_accessible method to declare the exact list of attributes that can be mass-assigned. Alternately, we can use the attr_protected method to declare the list of attributes that *cannot* be mass-assigned. Of the two choices, attr_accessible is considered more secure, so we will use attr_accessible to make sure that only expected values get assigned:

> code/rails_xt/app/models/quip.rb

```
attr_accessible :text
```

You can use validations to validate the fields you expect to see and use attr_accessible to make sure that only expected fields get assigned.

#2: Broken Access Control

We have already covered access control in some detail in Section 10.2, *Authorization with the Authorization Plugin*, on page 270. Even with an authz mechanism in place, you have to be careful to avoid tricks that bypass authz entirely. Some of the dangers are as follows:

- Path traversal attacks that craft relative paths (../../../etc.) to back into supposedly inaccessible places

- Readable configuration files that contain sensitive information (including passwords in some cases)

- Browsing directly to deep URLs that are protected only by the presumption that users will pass through some other protected URL first

- Caching that bypasses security

Most of these issues play out similarly in Java and Rails, but you should pay special attention to one. Java programmers are accustomed to caching at the data level. In Rails, caching is primarily done at the view level. When you cache pages in Rails, they are delivered directly from the web server to the user, without Rails being involved at all.

action caching

Page caching is fast, but be careful. Any cached page will bypass all of Rails' security mechanisms. Rails provides *action caching* to deal with this problem. When a user accesses a cached action, Rails performs your controller's before_filters before returning the cached results. Since security checks are usually performed in before_filters, cached actions can be secured. See Section 6.7, *Caching Pages, Actions, and Fragments*, on page 162 for details about both page and action caching.

Action caching is, of course, slower than page caching. You get what you pay for. Use page caching for public resources and action caching for secured resources.

#3. Broken Authentication and Session Management

Even when access control is implemented correctly, security can be compromised by mismanaging authentication or session. Here are a few examples:

- Authentication usually places some information in the session so that subsequent requests can be aware the user is authenticated. The cookie that is used to identify the session must be protected. It does little good to use the Secure Sockets Layer (SSL) to secure the login step and then continue to trust that same login based on a cookie that is submitted in plain text over HTTP.

- Passwords should be strong (not likely to be guessed). Passwords should not be stored as plain text anywhere. (This is why system administrators can reset your password, but they cannot tell you what it was.)

- In both Java and Rails web applications, turning on SSL is a web server setting, separate from the application code itself. However, application code can (and should) double-check that requests that should be encrypted actually were. In a Rails application, requests implement the ssl? method, which returns true if the request was made over SSL.

The Acts as Authenticated home page[1] includes tutorials and code for adding various password management features to a Rails application: user activation, initial password generation, password reset, and password change.

#4. Cross-Site Scripting (XSS)

Cross-site scripting occurs when a web application sends malicious code to users. This is surprisingly easy to do. When we fill out some user information for some site, we set the last name to this:

```
"Halloway <script type='text/javascript'>(malicious code)</script>"
```

If a web application accepts this input, then anyone who views the List Users screen in a JavaScript-enabled browser will execute the malicious code. The best way to prevent this attack is to have rigorous positive validation. Instead of guessing all the ways that somebody might sneak in bad code, just validate the positive set of legal values, using the techniques in Section 4.5, *Validating Data Values*, on page 94.

What about data fields, where the positive validation is too open-ended to eliminate all possible XSS tricks? Guessing all the bad values may be impossible. XSS exploits often use Unicode escapes and other kinds of character set trickery so that there is no obvious <script> tag to hunt for. Nevertheless, it is worth stripping out the most obvious XSS attacks. The ERb templating library includes the method html_escape to escape HTML tags in rendered output. This method is so common that it has the short alias h, as shown in this code fragment from a scaffold list view:

```
code/rails_xt/app/views/quips/list.rhtml
```
```
<% for column in Quip.content_columns %>
  <td><%=h quip.send(column.name) %></td>
<% end %>
```

#5. Buffer Overflow

Buffer overflow attacks take advantage of the fact that in some runtime environments, program variables and stack frames share the same memory address space. If an attacker can corrupt a program variable, they may corrupt far more than just that value. If the corruption extends into the stack frame, an attacker can execute arbitrary code, often taking complete control of the entire machine.

---

1. http://technoweenie.stikipad.com/plugins/show/Acts+as+Authenticated

Java and Ruby programs are immune to buffer overflow, because their memory model does not permit the necessary kind of stack corruption. Your programs cannot directly run afoul of this problem. However, the Java virtual machine or Ruby interpreter might itself be subject to buffer overflow, so keep up with your security patches.

#6. Injection Flaws

Injection flaws occur when attackers can inject malicious code into the web application, which is then executed by some back-end process. In the Java world, the best-known injection flaw is SQL injection. When poorly written programs build SQL commands dynamically by string concatenation, attackers can use delimiters and comments to sneak in statements or clauses that execute arbitrary commands on the database.

SQL injection can occur in any language that has support for strings and SQL, that is, pretty much every language used in web application development, including Ruby. Here is the classic SQL injection error, translated into ActiveRecord code:

`code/rails_xt/app/models/person.rb`

```
  # This method demonstrates a SQL injection attack
  # DO NOT WRITE CODE LIKE THIS
  def self.find_by_any_name_UNSAFE(search)
    find(:all, \
:conditions=>"first_name = '#{search}' OR last_name = '#{search}'")
  end
```

The problem here is the use of string interpolation to insert the search term. If the user enters the term Fred, things will be fine. But a search for foo\' OR true OR id=\' will return every row in the table. (You can see this in action by running test/unit/person_test.rb. Yes, we wrote unit tests that prove our broken example is really broken.)

Returning unexpected rows can easily violate security constraints, and there are worse possibilities. Attack strings can be crafted to, well, do anything a SQL database can do: create, read, update, delete, and even run stored procedures. The solution for this problem in Ruby is approximately the same as in Java's JDBC: Do not build SQL commands with raw string concatenation. Instead, use an API that automatically quotes user input. In ActiveRecord, the :conditions clause quotes arguments automatically, so the preceding example should be rewritten as follows:

```
code/rails_xt/app/models/person.rb
```

```ruby
  def self.find_by_any_name(search)
    find(:all, \
:conditions=>['first_name = :search or last_name = :search', {:search=>search}])
  end
```

#7. Improper Error Handling

Web application errors will occur, and handling them is a challenge. The problem is one of balancing disparate audiences. Users should get help, administrators should get detailed diagnostics, and attackers should get nothing. An example will illustrate the problem. Ned logs into a site and does something that causes an exception in some Ruby code on the server. The log file should contain detailed information about the problem so that developers and administrators can troubleshoot it later. We can't be sure Ned is not an attacker, so Ned will get a generic error message. In particular, we do not want to provide detailed and varying error messages that encourage an attacker to analyze our system by making it fail in different ways.

Rails' default handling of errors is good. In a development environment, detailed error information is automatically written to the browser window and to the log/development.log. To make this easy to see, we have added a deliberately broken method named fail to the AccountController:

```
code/rails_xt/app/controllers/account_controller.rb
```

```ruby
# Demonstrates some of the possible dangers in error handling code
def fail
  raise "Failed"
end
```

If you run the Quips application and navigate to /account/fail/1, you will see an error message similar to the one shown in Figure 10.1, on the next page. You can follow the links to view the entire stack trace. The message in log/development.log is similar.

In a production environment, you would not want to provide this level of internal detail in an error message. Instead, Rails routes error messages to a static HTML page at public/500.html, which you can then edit as you see fit.

The default behaviors are a pretty good start, but that is not quite the end of the story. By default, Rails dumps HTTP parameters to the log file. Some of these form parameters, such as passwords, are sensitive

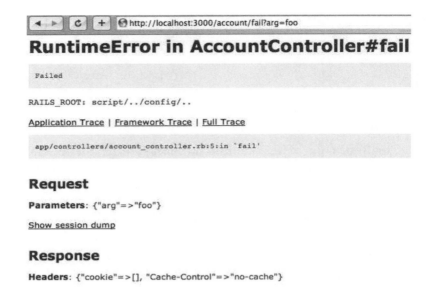

Figure 10.1: DEVELOPMENT ERROR MESSAGE

and should not be stored as plain text, in log files, or anywhere else. To deal with this, Rails controllers provide the filter_parameter_logging method. This class method can take regular expressions for parameter names that should not be included in log files. For example, the Quips application has the following line:

```
code/rails_xt/app/controllers/application.rb
```
```
filter_parameter_logging 'password'
```

As a result, any parameters that match /password/i will be filtered in the log file. For example, navigating to /account/fail?password=supersecret will leave the following in the log file:

```
Processing AccountController#fail (for 127.0.0.1 at 2006-09-25 14:07:41) [GET]
  Session ID: b2745e2f7ce5fb0201c030aa4a31986c
  Parameters: {"action"=>"fail", "controller"=>"account",
               "password"=>"[FILTERED]"}
```

That takes care of Rails' default logging. If you do your own logging of sensitive data, you will need to be careful to make sure the data is appropriately sanitized.

#8. Insecure Storage

Applications need to store sensitive information such as passwords and credit card numbers. Both Java and Ruby have libraries that provide the encryption and hashing functions that are needed to do this correctly. That said, storing secure data is difficult. Even if you use the best libraries, you have to think through how to use them in a secure fashion. Moreover, storing secure data often implies legal liability. So our strong recommendation is to take the following approach to secure data storage:

- Do not store secure data.

- If the design absolutely requires secure data, then use well-known existing systems instead of rolling your own.

- Kick and scream while continuing to insist on one of the previous approaches.

- Roll your own only as a last resort, and get a review from a security expert.

The acts_as_authenticated plugin demonstrates a reasonable use of hashing and salt to store passwords; look at user.rb for details.

#9. Application Denial of Service

Web applications are particularly prone to denial of service attacks, where an attacker consumes the processing resources of the application and legitimate users cannot get service. For the most part, these attacks do not target language-specific implementation details, so most preventive measures are the same for Java, Ruby, or any other language.

You should be aware of one Ruby-specific issue. Java applications use multiple threads to handle simultaneous requests and use database-level caching to improve performance. (Larger Java applications also use multiple processes and other kinds of caching, but many applications work fine from a single process.) Rails applications use multiple processes to handle simultaneous requests and use view-level caching to improve performance. This means that even a small number of expensive user requests can bog down a standard Rails configuration. The solution to this is to let the cache do as much as possible, ideally handling *all* unauthenticated requests. To handle the "real" work of authenticated users, you will need to add more processes and eventually more boxes.

#10. Insecure Configuration Management

To misquote Richard Dawkins: However many ways there are to correctly configure a server, it is certain that there are vastly more ways of misconfiguring it. The OWASP site lists several configuration problems that can weaken security, including the following:

- Default accounts and passwords
- Unnecessary services enabled (especially admin ones)
- Unpatched flaws
- Improper file permissions
- Misconfigured SSL

These issues are not language-specific, so for the most part there is not a distinct "Ruby" or "Java" approach. Rails does have one distinguishing characteristic. Because Rails is a full-stack framework with a standardized directory structure, most Rails applications look similar. This is mostly beneficial for securing application configuration, because good ideas are easily (sometimes automatically) available to all Rails applications. The downside is that a defect in Rails configuration security is likely to impact the entire Rails community.

This brings us to the most important Rails security flaw to date. On August 9, 2006, the Rails team announced a security flaw and an immediate mandatory patch. One day later, on August 10, 2006, they disclosed full details about the problem and provided more documentation about patching it. The flaw was in the Rails routing code, which would allow unexpected evaluation of Ruby code. For example, /script/* URLs would actually invoke the support scripts in Rails' script directory. This flaw is an example of several items in the OWASP Top Ten: denial of service, insecure configuration management, and broken access control at the very least. The solution is also on the Top Ten list: To prevent insecure configuration, you must always stay up-to-date with patches.

This chapter has provided only a brief overview of web application security. Since this book is about programming in Ruby and Rails, we have emphasized only some code-specific and language-specific concerns. Securing applications includes much more than just coding practices. In particular, code alone cannot resist a determined attacker. Attacks are dynamic, active, and guided by human intelligence. Defenses must include these elements as well. For a good, and not too technical, introduction to these issues, we recommend [Sch04].

10.5 Resources

Acts as Authenticated. . .

. . . http://technoweenie.stikipad.com/plugins/show/Acts+as+Authenticated
Acts as Authenticated used in Section 10.1, *Authentication with the acts_as_authenticated Plugin*, on page 268.

Authorization Plugin . . . . . . http://www.writertopia.com/developers/authorization
Authorization plugin used in Section 10.2, *Authorization with the Authorization Plugin*, on page 270.

Open Web Application Security Project. . . . . http://www.owasp.org
The Open Web Application Security Project (OWASP) is dedicated to finding and fighting the causes of insecure software. Everything on the side is free and open source.

Rails 1.1, backports, and full disclosure. . .

. . . http://weblog.rubyonrails.org/2006/8/10/rails-1-1-6-backports-and-full-disclosure
Explanation of a serious security flaw in Rails 1.1.0 through 1.1.5. Get off these versions, and read here to understand how the Rails team handled the problem.

Spring Acegi . . . . http://www.acegisecurity.org/
Acegi Security provides comprehensive authentication, authorization, instance-based access control, and channel security for Java applications. Because of its integration with Aspect-Oriented Programming and servlet filters, we prefer Acegi for Java projects.

Appendix A

Java to Ruby Dictionary

This dictionary maps Java concepts to Ruby and Rails concepts. The mapping is not always exact or one-to-one; for more details, follow the references.

AOP

> Aspect-Oriented Programming. AOP is a way to improve the modularity (and DRYness) of your code. Code that traditionally would be scattered across an application is gathered together in an aspect and then woven back into the application where needed. Because aspects can be used to circumvent language restrictions, aspects are essential in Java. Java has excellent AOP support through AspectJ.[1] Aspects are less important in Ruby, thanks to language features such as method_missing and the ability to rewrite methods at runtime. We use a simple Ruby aspect library called AspectR.[2]

block

> A block is a piece of code that can be passed to a method. Java has no equivalent. Where Ruby programs use blocks, Java programs use a combination of single-method interfaces and anonymous inner classes. Blocks are used throughout the book and are introduced in Section 2.4, *Collections and Iteration*, on page 28.

class

> Ruby has classes as well; see Section 2.6, *Defining Classes*, on page 38.

---

1. http://www.eclipse.org/aspectj/
2. http://aspectr.sourceforge.net/

cobertura

> Cobertura[3] is an open source tool measuring test coverage. The approximate equivalent in the Ruby world is rcov.[4] See Section 7.6, *Measuring Code Coverage with rcov*, on page 205.

constructor

> The Ruby equivalent of a constructor is a method named initialize(); see Section 2.6, *Defining Classes*, on page 38.

CruiseControl

> CruiseControl[5] is a popular, open source continuous integration framework for Java. *There is no comprehensive equivalent for Ruby yet.* We currently use Cerberus, covered in Section 8.5, *Continuous Integration with Cerberus*, on page 227. Other projects we have worked on chose to write adapters to integrate Ruby builds into CruiseControl. Stay away from DamageControl,[6] unless you want to be a hero and start maintaining it.

JavaServer Pages

> The approximate equivalent of JavaServer Pages (JSPs) are .rhtml files in ActionView. See Section 6.1, *Creating Basic .rhtml Files*, on page 150.

field

> Ruby has instance variables, which are named like @my_var. See Section 2.6, *Defining Classes*, on page 38.

hibernate.cfg.xml

> The Hibernate configuration file has database connection settings, plus configuration for model objects. In Rails, database connection settings live in database.yml (Section 4.1, *Getting Connected*, on page 78). Rails applications rely on convention for most model setting, but such configuration lives in the model classes themselves. See Section 4.6, *Lifecycle Callbacks*, on page 97 and Section 4.7, *Associations and Inheritance*, on page 100.

method

> Ruby also has methods, but they are named like my_method. See Section 2.3, *Objects and Methods*, on page 25.

---

3. http://cobertura.sourceforge.net/
4. http://eigenclass.org/hiki.rb?rcov
5. http://cruisecontrol.sourceforge.net/
6. http://damagecontrol.codehaus.org/

servlet filters

> The Rails equivalents to servlet filters are controller filters and verify. See Section 5.5, *Managing Cross-Cutting Concerns with Filters and Verify*, on page 129.

soap4r

> This is the Ruby API to call SOAP servers. It's like a lightweight, easy-to-use version of JAX-RPC. It is part of the Ruby Standard Library. Section 9.2, *Consuming SOAP Services with soap4r*, on page 243.

static method

> Ruby provides several ways to declare class-level methods. See Section 2.6, *Creating Static Methods*, on page 42.

tag libraries

> Rails has no direct equivalent to tag libraries. Instead, Rails applications use view helpers and collection partials. See Section 6.2, *Minimizing View Code with View Helpers*, on page 151.

Appendix B

Bibliography

[Goe06]   Brian Goetz. *Java Concurrency in Practice*. Addison-Wesley, Reading, MA, 2006.

[HT00]   Andrew Hunt and David Thomas. *The Pragmatic Programmer: From Journeyman to Master*. Addison-Wesley, Reading, MA, 2000.

[Pin06]   Chris Pine. *Learn to Program*. The Pragmatic Programmers, LLC, Raleigh, NC, and Dallas, TX, 2006.

[Sch04]   Bruce Schneier. *Secrets and Lies: Digital Security in a Networked World*. John Wiley & Sons, New York, NY, 2004.

[Tat06]   Bruce Tate. *From Java to Ruby: Things Every Manager Should Know*. The Pragmatic Programmers, LLC, Raleigh, NC, and Dallas, TX, 2006.

[TFH05]   David Thomas, Chad Fowler, and Andrew Hunt. *Programming Ruby: The Pragmatic Programmers' Guide*. The Pragmatic Programmers, LLC, Raleigh, NC, and Dallas, TX, second edition, 2005.

[TH06]   David Thomas and David Heinemeier Hansson. *Agile Web Development with Rails*. The Pragmatic Programmers, LLC, Raleigh, NC, and Dallas, TX, second edition, 2006.

Structure of a Rails Project

One factor that makes Rails easy to learn is the standardized directory layout of Rails projects. The following list highlights the directory structure of a Rails project, with references to sections in the book that cover each directory:

app/controllers

> MVC controllers live here. A file named people_controller.rb will contain a single Ruby class, PeopleController. See Chapter 5, *Coordinating Activities with ActionController*, on page 115.

app/helpers

> Every controller has an associated view helper, such as people_helper.rb, for example. View helpers typically contain utility methods for formatting output. See Section 6.2, *Minimizing View Code with View Helpers*, on page 151.

app/models

> Model classes are named in the singular; for example, person.rb contains the Person class. See Chapter 4, *Accessing Data with ActiveRecord*, on page 77.

app/views

> View code lives in a directory per controller. The naming convention is that the PeopleController will have a corresponding people directory here. See Chapter 6, *Rendering Output with ActionView*, on page 149.

components

> Rails components provide a way to modularize Rails code. Components are not widely used and are not covered in this book. See http://manuals.rubyonrails.com/read/book/14.

config

> The config directory contains database connection settings, web server settings, and settings for the different environments associated with a Rails project. See Section 1.7, *Rails Environments*, on page 13.

db

> This contains the data schema for your application, plus past versions of the schema in the form of migrations. See Section 4.2, *Managing Schema Versions with Migrations*, on page 81.

doc

> This contains generated documentation for your application, like javadoc creates.

lib

> This contains third-party library code.

log

> This contains log files for the different environments. See Section 1.7, *Rails Environments*, on page 13.

public

> This contains static web content that is rendered automatically, before consulting Rails routing.

Rakefile

> This is the project automation file. See Chapter 8, *Automating the Development Process*, on page 217.

script

> This contains various support scripts, including those for starting and stopping the application during development. See Section 1.9, *Rails Support Scripts*, on page 17.

test

> This contains automated tests: those in the unit directory test models and those in the functional directory test controllers. See Chapter 7, *Testing*, on page 181.

vendor

> This contains third-party code and plugins. Plugins are introduced briefly in the sidebar on page 269.

Index

D

A Pragmatic Career

Welcome to the Pragmatic Community. We hope you've enjoyed this title.

Interested in improving your career? Want to make yourself more valuable to your organization, and avoid being outsourced? Then read *My Job Went to India*, and find out great ways to keep yours. If you're interested in moving your career more towards a team lead or mangement position, then read what happens *Behind Closed Doors*.

My Job Went to India

The job market is shifting. Your current job may be outsourced, perhaps to India or eastern Europe. But you can save your job and improve your career by following these practical and timely tips. See how to: • treat your career as a business • build your own brand as a software developer • develop a structured plan for keeping your skills up to date • market yourself to your company and rest of the industry • keep your job!

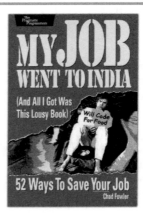

My Job Went to India: 52 Ways to Save Your Job
Chad Fowler
(185 pages) ISBN: 0-9766940-1-8. $19.95
http://pragmaticprogrammer.com/titles/mjwti

Behind Closed Doors

You can learn to be a better manager—even a great manager—with this guide. You'll find powerful tips covering:

• Delegating effectively • Using feedback and goal-setting • Developing influence • Handling one-on-one meetings • Coaching and mentoring
• Deciding what work to do-and what not to do
• . . . and more!

Behind Closed Doors Secrets of Great Management
Johanna Rothman and Esther Derby
(192 pages) ISBN: 0-9766940-2-6. $24.95
http://pragmaticprogrammer.com/titles/rdbcd

Pragmatic Methodology

Need to get software out the door? Then you want to see how to *Ship It!* with less fuss and more features. And every developer can benefit from the *Practices of an Agile Developer*.

Ship It!

Page after page of solid advice, all tried and tested in the real world. This book offers a collection of tips that show you what tools a successful team has to use, and how to use them well. You'll get quick, easy-to-follow advice on modern techniques and when they should be applied. **You need this book if:** • You're frustrated at lack of progress on your project. • You want to make yourself and your team more valuable. • You've looked at methodologies such as Extreme Programming (XP) and felt they were too, well, extreme. • You've looked at the Rational Unified Process (RUP) or CMM/I methods and cringed at the learning curve and costs. • **You need to get software out the door without excuses**

Ship It! A Practical Guide to Successful Software Projects
Jared Richardson and Will Gwaltney
(200 pages) ISBN: 0-9745140-4-7. $29.95
http://pragmaticprogrammer.com/titles/prj

Practices of an Agile Developer

Agility is all about using feedback to respond to change. Learn how to apply the principles of agility throughout the software development process • Establish and maintain an agile working environment • Deliver what users really want • Use personal agile techniques for better coding and debugging • Use effective collaborative techniques for better teamwork • Move to an agile approach

Practices of an Agile Developer: Working in the Real World
Venkat Subramaniam and Andy Hunt
(189 pages) ISBN: 0-9745140-8-X. $29.95
http://pragmaticprogrammer.com/titles/pad

Facets of Ruby Series

See how to integrate Ruby with all varieties of today's technology in *Enterprise Integration with Ruby*. And speaking of today's finest, you'll need a good text editor, too. On the Mac, we recommend TextMate.

Enterprise Integration with Ruby

See how to use the power of Ruby to integrate all the applications in your environment. Lean how to
• use relational databases directly, and via mapping layers such as ActiveRecord • Harness the power of directory services • Create, validate, and read XML documents for easy information interchange • Use both high- and low-level protocols to knit applications together

Enterprise Integration with Ruby
Maik Schmidt
(360 pages) ISBN: 0-9766940-6-9. $32.95
http://pragmaticprogrammer.com/titles/fr_eir

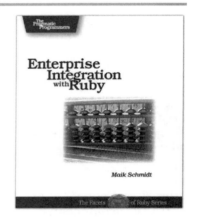

TextMate

If you're coding Ruby or Rails on a Mac, then you owe it to yourself to get the TextMate editor. And, once you're using TextMate, you owe it to yourself to pick up this book. It's packed with information which will help you automate all your editing tasks, saving you time to concentrate on the important stuff. Use snippets to insert boilerplate code and refactorings to move stuff around. Learn how to write your own extensions to customize it to the way you work.

TextMate: Power Editing for the Mac
James Edward Gray II
(200 pages) ISBN: 0-9787392-3-X. $29.95
http://pragmaticprogrammer.com/titles/textmate

Facets of Ruby Series

If you're serious about Ruby, you need the definitive reference to the language. The Pickaxe: *Programming Ruby: The Pragmatic Programmer's Guide, Second Edition*. This is *the* definitive guide for all Ruby programmers. For Rails, we have the definitive reference guide as well: the award-winning and best-selling *Agile Web Development with Rails*.

Programming Ruby (The Pickaxe)

The Pickaxe book, named for the tool on the cover, is the definitive reference to this highly-regarded language. • Up-to-date and expanded for Ruby version 1.8 • Complete documentation of all the built-in classes, modules, and methods • Complete descriptions of all ninety-eight standard libraries • 200+ pages of new content in this edition • Learn more about Ruby's web tools, unit testing, and programming philosophy

Programming Ruby: The Pragmatic Programmer's Guide, 2nd Edition
Dave Thomas with Chad Fowler and Andy Hunt
(864 pages) ISBN: 0-9745140-5-5. $44.95
http://pragmaticprogrammer.com/titles/ruby

Agile Web Development with Rails

Rails is a full-stack, open-source web framework, with integrated support for unit, functional, and integration testing. It enforces good design principles, consistency of code across your team (and across your organization), and proper release management. This is newly updated Second Edition, which goes beyond the Jolt-award winning first edition with new material on:

• Migrations • RJS templates • Respond_to
• Integration Tests • Additional ActiveRecord features • Another year's worth of Rails best practices

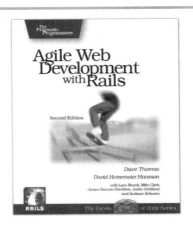

Agile Web Development with Rails: Second Edition
Dave Thomas, and David Heinemeier Hansson with Leon Breedt, Mike Clark, James Duncan Davidson, Justin Gehtland, and Andreas Schwarz
(750 pages) ISBN: 0-9776166-3-0. $39.95
http://pragmaticprogrammer.com/titles/rails2

The Pragmatic Bookshelf

The Pragmatic Bookshelf features books written by developers for developers. The titles continue the well-known Pragmatic Programmer style, and continue to garner awards and rave reviews. As development gets more and more difficult, the Pragmatic Programmers will be there with more titles and products to help programmers stay on top of their game.

Visit Us Online

Rails for Java Developers Home Page
http://pragmaticprogrammer.com/titles/fr_r4j
Source code from this book, errata, and other resources. Come give us feedback, too!

Register for Updates
http://pragmaticprogrammer.com/updates
Be notified when updates and new books become available.

Join the Community
http://pragmaticprogrammer.com/community
Read our weblogs, join our online discussions, participate in our mailing list, interact with our wiki, and benefit from the experience of other Pragmatic Programmers.

New and Noteworthy
http://pragmaticprogrammer.com/news
Check out the latest pragmatic developments in the news.

Save on the PDF and other Ruby Books

Save more than 60% on the PDF version of this book. Owning the paper version of this book entitles you to purchase the PDF version for only $8.50 (regularly $21.50). That's a saving of more than 60%. The PDF is great for carrying around on your laptop. It's hyperlinked, has color, and is fully searchable. Buy it now at pragmaticprogrammer.com/coupon

Contact Us

Phone Orders:	1-800-699-PROG (+1 919 847 3884)
Online Orders:	www.pragmaticprogrammer.com/catalog
Customer Service:	orders@pragmaticprogrammer.com
Non-English Versions:	translations@pragmaticprogrammer.com
Pragmatic Teaching:	academic@pragmaticprogrammer.com
Author Proposals:	proposals@pragmaticprogrammer.com